The Great War Comes to Wisconsin

THE GREAT WAR COMES TO WISCONSIN

Sacrifice, Patriotism, and Free Speech in a Time of Crisis

RICHARD L. PIFER
WITH MARJORIE HANNON PIFER

WISCONSIN HISTORICAL SOCIETY PRESS

Published by the Wisconsin Historical Society Press
Publishers since 1855

The Wisconsin Historical Society helps people connect to the past by collecting,
preserving, and sharing stories. Founded in 1846, the Society is one of the nation's
finest historical institutions.
Join the Wisconsin Historical Society: wisconsinhistory.org/membership

Front cover: World War I poster for the Woman's Land Army, image from the Library of
Congress, World War I Posters Collection

Printed in the United States of America
Cover design by Tom Heffron
Typesetting by Wendy Holdman Design
21 20 19 18 17   1 2 3 4 5

Library of Congress Cataloging-in-Publication Data
Names: Pifer, Richard L., 1950– author.
Title: The Great War comes to Wisconsin : sacrifice, patriotism, and free speech in a
    time of crisis / Richard L. Pifer.
Description: Madison, WI : Wisconsin Historical Society Press, 2017. |
Identifiers: LCCN 2017019397 (print) | LCCN 2017020123 (e-book) |
    ISBN 9780870207839 (E-book) | ISBN 9780870207822 (paperback)
Subjects: LCSH: World War, 1914–1918—Wisconsin. | BISAC: HISTORY / Military /
    World War I. | HISTORY / Military / General.
Classification: LCC D570.85.W6 (e-book) | LCC D570.85.W6 P48 2017 (print) |
    DDC 940.3/775—dc23
LC record available at https://lccn.loc.gov/2017019397

♾ The paper used in this publication meets the minimum requirements of the American
National Standard for Information Sciences—Permanence of Paper for Printed Library
Materials, ANSI Z39.48-1992.

To Silas Wright Pifer,
Who survived the Great War,

And to his great-great-grandchildren,
Margaret, Amalia, and Silas,
May they never know war.

CONTENTS

INTRODUCTION

The Great War, the World War, the War to End All Wars, the War to Make the World Safe for Democracy. These are all names given to what Western observers at the time considered the most cataclysmic conflict in human history[1]—what we now call World War I. Whatever you called it, this war was like none before it.

World War I was the first of the "total wars" of the twentieth century, wars that were so large and demanded so many resources that, for all practical purposes, they engaged all of American society. Virtually everyone on the American home front, even children, participated in the war effort. They worked in war factories, volunteered for charities and on farms, conserved food and fuel, adhered to meatless and wheatless days, planted war gardens, bought Liberty Bonds, rolled bandages and knit sweaters for the Red Cross, and donated money to the YMCA. From all over the country, young men went to war. Wisconsin and Michigan National Guard regiments joined to form the 32nd Division and achieved a well-deserved reputation as an effective fighting force. Sacrifices were asked of and made by everyone in the name of winning the war.

This book endeavors to capture the essence of the home-front experience: the debates over the nation's entry into the war, the patriotic fervor felt by most people once the war began, the worry experienced when loved ones went to fight "over there," the political debates about war policy, and the impact of the wartime hysteria that drove most dissent underground. This is not a comprehensive history of the war or Wisconsin's experiences during the war; that is beyond the scope of what could be accomplished in a book of this size. Rather, it illuminates the daily lives of people in Wisconsin during the war and, through that process, helps us better understand American society. The war brought out the best and the worst of human behavior. Day after day, average people worked hard and sacrificed in the name of the war effort, but one suspects motivations beyond simple patriotism. For the average American, winning the war was less about national priorities than about ending the conflict and bringing loved ones home safely.

In 1914, Wisconsin's agricultural and industrial sectors were well positioned to support the war effort. Wisconsin led the nation in dairy production and had more cows than people. Not surprisingly, hay and forage dominated crop production, followed by oats, corn, barley, and potatoes, all of which became important substitutes for wheat during the war. Similarly, the skilled workers, machine shops, and heavy industry of Milwaukee were well equipped to produce the weapons of war.

This book focuses on the experiences of people in and from Wisconsin. That emphasis makes it possible to tell complex stories in context. The fabric woven out of these stories includes German Americans who loved the United States and their ancestral homeland; individuals who desperately wanted to avoid war and the small number who welcomed the defining challenge war presented; men who joined the Wisconsin National Guard and went to war to fulfill their patriotic duty; draftees who served faithfully because they had no choice; housewives whose careful management of household affairs became the linchpin of Herbert Hoover's Food Administration; people who bought Liberty Bonds and donated to the YMCA; farmers who grew crops to feed Europe; and industrialists who revamped entire factories so they could produce war supplies.

The final chapter includes the stories of six politicians, each one honorable in his own right, who interpreted duty and responsibility in different ways. Daniel Hoan, mayor of Milwaukee, and Emanuel Philipp, governor of Wisconsin, were practical politicians who believed they had a responsibility to govern for all the people. They were largely responsible for maintaining good order in the jurisdictions they governed. Robert La Follette, Wisconsin's senior senator, and Victor Berger, editor of the *Milwaukee Leader* and a leading socialist, spoke out against the suppression of free speech and in favor of progressive war policies. In a climate of patriotic fervor and intolerance they paid a heavy price for their actions. Wheeler Bloodgood, a Milwaukee industrialist and founder of the Wisconsin Defense League, and Roy Wilcox, state senator and candidate for governor of Wisconsin, defined acceptable wartime behavior very narrowly and found enemies in anyone who disagreed with their view of the war. They suspected the state's political leaders and many of its residents of being pro-German and unpatriotic.

Wisconsin's housewives, farmers, and factory workers; its cities and rural communities; its Native Americans, Yankees, Germans, Scandinavians, and African Americans met every obligation of the war effort, but they still fought the war under a cloud created by super patriots who called Wisconsin the "traitor state."[2] Although most people willingly supported the war, they did so with clear knowledge of the social and legal penalties imposed on those who failed to do so.

The war demonstrated the frightening fragility of civil liberties. This was a time when neighbor informed on neighbor, when a wisecrack at a bar could get one tarred and feathered, when casting the smallest aspersion on wartime activities or policies could result in being jailed or fired. The Bureau of Investigation (precursor to the FBI), the Secret Service, and the US Marshals Service were all active in Wisconsin hunting for draft dodgers, German spies, and unpatriotic Americans.

Wisconsin's reputation as the most German of states made it an easy target for super patriots. The state's German Americans were loyal to the United States but had no desire to go to war against friends, relatives, and cultural kin of the fatherland. Likewise, Wisconsin's large Scandinavian population had little desire to enter a conflict in which their homeland had no vested interests. The people of Wisconsin, indeed the nation, wanted to avoid the European carnage in 1914, but German submarine warfare eroded American neutrality and pushed the nation into the arms of the Allies. In Wisconsin, progressives, Germans, and Scandinavians remained steadfastly opposed to the war. When President Wilson called for a declaration of war, the Wisconsin congressional delegation voted the wishes of their constituents and overwhelmingly opposed entry into the war. Their opposition and the large German American population helped solidify the state's undeserved reputation for traitorous behavior.

Finally, the book includes the experiences of Wisconsin soldiers, not only to honor their sacrifice, but because their experiences, conveyed through letters and newspaper accounts, helped shape the home front. Chapter 3 shares the story of the 32nd Division, which included the greatest concentration of Wisconsin soldiers in the American Expeditionary Force. The focus on a single division allows the narrative to follow a group of men through one coherent story.

My interest in the soldiers' experiences developed out of a desire to better understand the experiences of my grandfather, Silas Wright Pifer. Silas, from Youngstown, Ohio, was an automatic rifleman in Company C of the 11th Infantry Regiment. At the battle of St. Mihiel, a jagged piece of shrapnel the size of a man's thumb tore through his upper arm, partly crippling his right arm. Like so many veterans, he seldom spoke about his experiences as a soldier, but he suffered from night terrors as a result of the war. In 1942, my father graduated from college and the army offered him a lieutenancy in the infantry. Silas told his son, my father, to refuse the offer because "lieutenants in the infantry are cannon fodder." His advice reflected neither cowardice nor heroism but was the paternal wisdom of an old soldier. He had seen too many brave lieutenants killed in the meat grinder of the Great War. My father turned down the officer's rank, was drafted, and fought the war as a sergeant in the Army Air Corps weather service.

At St. Mihiel, Silas Wright Pifer won the Purple Heart when shrapnel from an exploding German shell tore through his upper arm. PHOTOGRAPH BY JAMES W. PIFER, COURTESY OF THE AUTHOR

This book does not attempt to answer all questions about World War I. There are many stories yet to be told about specific communities, the experiences of individual soldiers, and specific events. In trying to share a history of World War I in Wisconsin, this narrative focuses attention on Milwaukee, Madison, Green Bay, Eau Claire, and La Crosse as a way to tell the stories of the war with breadth and depth. These stories illuminate a society under stress. During World War I American citizens and society became more regimented than ever before, as the government intruded into daily life to ensure victory. Many individuals exhibited great heroism and patriotism, as well as intolerance and coercion. Ultimately, victory on the battlefield ended the carnage. As Americans celebrated at home, the 32nd Division marched into Germany as part of the occupation force. They would come home in 1919.

The War to End All Wars secured the peace for a meager twenty years.

CHAPTER 1

WISCONSIN IN 1914

T he modern world began in 1900. Of course, this is not literally true, but for people at the time, it seemed they were entering a marvelous, sometimes disconcerting, new age. Electricity offered new ways to light homes and run factories; automobiles provided new means of travel; assembly lines improved manufacturing productivity; telephones revolutionized communications; and airplanes would soon be the marvel of the age. Progressive reforms also laid the groundwork for a world we would recognize today: income tax, primary elections, social safety net programs, and modern municipal services. The suffrage and temperance movements seemed to be gaining strength every day. The United States also had demonstrated a new willingness to play a larger role on the world stage. The nation had delivered a decisive rebuke to Spain in Cuba and the Philippines, acquired colonial control of the Philippines, completed the Panama Canal, brokered a peace deal between Russia and Japan, and joined an international force to quell the Boxer Rebellion in China.[1] All of these inventions, movements, and events served to highlight the fact that the old century was gone and the beginning of the twentieth century marked a new era.

AN EVOLVING ECONOMY

As the new century unfolded, Wisconsinites had every reason to believe in a bright future. Single-commodity industries had exhausted the natural resources upon which they depended, and were being replaced by new, more sustainable economies. Improvements in the state had been breathtaking over the past century.

In 1800, the region that would become Wisconsin formed the farther reaches of the Northwest Territory. Technically the property of the United States by treaty, the British Empire still controlled the region, and fur trading dominated the economy as it had for more than 150 years. A handful of Europeans, mostly French, lived in Green Bay and Prairie du Chien. Wisconsin had long been home to the Ojibwe, Ho-Chunk, and Menominee. After the War of 1812, the United States Army finally asserted control over the region with forts at Green Bay and Prairie du Chien.

Early settlers to Wisconsin built regional economies based on the fur trade and logging in the north and lead mining in the southwest. By the 1840s the fur trade and lead mining were on the decline, and wheat was the crop of choice, particularly in the region southeast of the line from Oshkosh to Prairie du Chien. Lightweight and durable, wheat or flour could withstand the rigors of transportation to eastern markets. By the late 1850s intensive wheat farming in southeastern Wisconsin had depleted the soil. Farmers moved to western Wisconsin, Minnesota, and the Dakotas from whence their grain was shipped by rail to Milwaukee, where it was milled and sent to markets in the East. Although wheat farming began a slow decline in Wisconsin in 1860, Milwaukee continued to thrive as a shipping center; by 1862, the city had become the largest primary wheat market in the world. Drawing from the new wheat lands west of the Mississippi, Milwaukee exported more than 16 million bushels of wheat and 1.2 million barrels of flour in 1870—compared to only 213,000 bushels of wheat and 15,756 barrels of flour in 1840.[2]

As wheat production declined, Wisconsin agricultural leaders advocated that dairy farming take its place because it offered stable incomes, regular markets, and sustainability. Developments during the last quarter of the nineteenth century established dairy farming as one of the long-term foundations of the Wisconsin economy. The silo, imported from Germany, made it practical to feed a herd of cows during the winter, which in turn made year-round milk production possible. Stephen M. Babcock's butterfat tester allowed creameries and dairies to set standards for milk quality, thereby forcing farmers to improve their practices to produce higher-quality milk. Through the pages of *Hoard's Dairyman*, William Dempster Hoard tirelessly promoted dairy farming, and the Wisconsin Dairymen's Association. In conjunction with the University of

For a brief period during the 1860s, Wisconsin was the nation's bread basket. Wheat quickly exhausted the land, however, and production moved west. Pictured here is the Lemonweir River flour mill, built in 1852. WHI IMAGE ID 36904

Wisconsin's School of Agriculture he advocated for dairy farming across the state.

By 1914, the dairy cow had rapidly become part of Wisconsin's cultural identity. Wisconsin could don the mantle of "America's Dairyland," producing more dairy products than any other state in the nation.[3]

In northern Wisconsin, particularly north of the line extending from Green Bay to La Crosse, the lumber industry dominated Wisconsin's economy during the years following the Civil War. Men such as Orrin Ingram of Eau Claire, James Stout of Menomonie, and Philetus Sawyer of Oshkosh made great fortunes extracting trees from northern forests and turning them into lumber for markets in Chicago and St. Louis. The great pine forests of northern Wisconsin, once thought to be inexhaustible, lasted a little more than fifty years.

As the century came to a close, just as wheat farming had declined, the pine forests of the north proved all too limited. Astute political and business leaders began to recognize the need to create a new economic foundation for much of the state economy.

Northern Wisconsin's sawmill cities faced the unenviable prospect of

Wisconsin gradually became America's dairyland during the last quarter of the nineteenth century through dogged promotion by the UW School of Agriculture and leaders such as William Dempster Hoard, editor of *Hoard's Dairyman*. Introduction of the silo from Europe made it possible for farmers to feed their cows and produce milk year-round. Professor Stephen M. Babcock's invention of a simple butterfat tester, pictured here, allowed creameries and dairies to set standards for the milk they would buy from farmers.
WHI IMAGE ID 117417

Wisconsin's pine forests provided an economic foundation for northern Wisconsin, supporting such enterprises as the Peshtigo Sawmill. The forests were thought by many people to be inexhaustible, but the boom lasted a mere forty years. The best pine forests were largely exhausted by the mid-1890s. WHI IMAGE ID 78879

finding a new economic framework for their communities. In Eau Claire, for example, at least twelve lumber-related companies operated within the city limits during the industry's heyday, including sawmills, planing mills, shingle- and barrel-making shops, warehouses, and sawdust piles, as well as a furniture factory and an ironworks. By 1914 all but two sawmills had closed.[4]

The lumber barons, politicians, and, most importantly, the professors of the University of Wisconsin School of Agriculture believed that the natural successor to the forest would be the farm. In 1896, after a tour of the north country, the School of Agriculture produced the well-illustrated *Northern Wisconsin; A Hand-Book for the Homeseeker*, clearly designed to promote settlement of the old "cutover" lands. Benjamin Faast was a staunch advocate of creating thriving farms on the old pine lands. In the years before the World War, Faast was one of the most prominent land dealers in the north, and one of the longest-tenured members of the University of Wisconsin Board of Regents. He developed a settlement philosophy based on the premise that agricultural success required hard work by the farmer and services by the land dealer. Following his own advice, Faast built the small village of Ojibwa in Sawyer County as a service center for the families to whom he was selling land in the surrounding area. In addition, he offered farmers a selection of "ready-made" packages that provided everything a farmer needed to get started, in particular house-building kits.

During the first decades of the twentieth century, farmers in the cutover areas enjoyed some success thanks to strong demand for farm products. Competition from farmers further west and the onset of the agricultural depression of 1919 forced farmers, politicians, and the School of Agriculture to recognize that the economic future of northern Wisconsin would be based on reforestation, sustainable timber harvesting, paper production, and tourism. Ben Faast's dream that Ojibwa would become a thriving rural service center evaporated as the agricultural economy of Sawyer County declined after the First World War.[5]

For old lumber towns like Eau Claire, a new economic foundation often rested on old companies that had served the lumber industry and were now diversifying, and on new companies that brought new technological and economic development to northern Wisconsin. During the lumber era, A. A. Cutter made shoes and boots for loggers, and Phoenix Manufacturing and McDonough Manufacturing made equipment for sawmills and logging operations. Most notably, Phoenix made an innovative steam locomotive designed to pull strings of sleds piled high with logs out of the forest. The steam engine was equipped with a tractor tread drive train in the rear and skis in the front. It was capable of traversing the forests without the need of laying narrow gauge track, making it one of the most versatile pieces of equipment in the woods and allowing loggers to harvest trees in more remote locations. As logging declined, A. A. Cutter began making shoes for the general market, and the Phoenix and McDonough companies began the transition to general manufacturing.

By the 1890s, community leaders, including lumbermen, recognized the finite nature of the forests and began preparing for the future. New technologies made it possible to produce vast quantities of paper using easily renewed pulp wood. With an ample supply of water, paper production became the economic lifeblood of Park Falls, Rhinelander, Merrill, Wausau, Green Bay, Appleton, Menasha, Port Edwards, Kimberly, and

The Phoenix Manufacturing Company of Eau Claire invented this tractor tread for use on a steam locomotive. When outfitted with a pair of skis and a driver to steer, the engine could pull logs on skids from deep in the woods. As the logging business became a smaller part of the state's economy, companies such as Phoenix gradually transitioned to general manufacturing. WHI IMAGE ID 5820

numerous other towns that once relied on gristmills or sawmills for their economic foundation.

By 1914, the old lumber and flour economies of the Chippewa, Wisconsin, and Fox River Valleys had been replaced by economies based on furniture, wood pulp, and paper production. More than 80 percent of the paper produced in Wisconsin in 1895 came from mills in Brown, Outagamie, and Winnebago Counties; by 1900, Wisconsin was the fifth largest producer of paper in the United States. Recognizing the need for economic development, businessmen in the Fox River Valley, Wausau, Eau Claire, and Oshkosh formed commercial associations to assist in economic development. For example, local business leaders, primarily lumbermen, formed the Wausau Group and established a series of pulp and paper companies in Marathon County. In Rothschild they built a 450-foot dam to supply power to the Marathon Paper Mills Company, an enterprise employing 350 workers. Investments in paper mills and the infrastructure to support manufacturing often promoted new investment in non-wood industries and a general improvement in the local economy.

Between 1880 and 1915 a diverse array of new companies established operations in communities across the state. The companies that did best tended to be based on readily available raw materials. Eau Claire was typical. A trunk factory, the Dumphy Boat Works, and the Linderman Box Company made use of the local wood supply. Local dairy farms supplied an ever-growing number of creameries and dairies, while the Lange Canning factory and other agricultural processing companies relied on the local agricultural harvest. In contrast, several major figures in the Chippewa Valley lumber industry, including H. C. Putnam[6] and Frederick Weyerhaeuser, underwrote development of a linen mill that went bankrupt in 1906. Its source of raw fiber was not local, but from Archangel in Russia. By 1914 Eau Claire was a regional service center with a diversified economy based on wood products, dairy production, and light manufacturing. The Gillette Safety Tire Company, founded in 1916, was one of the most notable successes as old lumber towns adjusted to the end of an era. The company survived for roughly eighty years as the largest employer in Eau Claire and was the principal salvation of the local economy after the death of the lumber industry.

Although they no longer relied on logging to fuel their economies, many northern cities remained tightly tied to the timber industry. Thanks to an abundant supply of hardwood, towns such as La Crosse, Eau Claire, Chippewa Falls, Green Bay, Appleton, Oshkosh, and Fond du Lac turned to furniture, door, and window production. Eau Claire, La Crosse, and Oshkosh, each nicknamed "Sawdust City," also diversified by manufacturing a variety of other products, such as paper, canned vegetables, meat, barrels, and rubber products. Oshkosh became known as the largest producer of matches in the United States.

Along the Lake Michigan corridor from Racine to Green Bay, hundreds of small machine shops were busy converting the economy from manufacturing sawmill and grist mill equipment to a much more diversified base. Wisconsin's heavy industry was concentrated south of a line from Green Bay to Madison to Beloit. Milwaukee was an integral part of the heavy industry belt running from Buffalo to Detroit, to Chicago, to Milwaukee, and on to Duluth-Superior.

Transformative changes were under way in Milwaukee, as elsewhere in the industrial belt. By 1914 Milwaukee had become, in the words of historian Bayrd Still, a "mature metropolis." It was perhaps a bit more accurate to say that the city had reached the early stages of a vigorous adulthood.

The confluence of the Milwaukee River and Lake Michigan created

By World War I, hardwood furniture, boxes, paper production, and other wood products had replaced lumber as the economic driver of northern Wisconsin. Filtz and Sons Box Factory in Cadott was one of the largest wood products companies in northern Wisconsin during the early twentieth century. WHI IMAGE ID 84783

ideal conditions for development of a city. Milwaukee's founders based the new city's economy on the export of products from the hinterland. Thanks to the efforts of early entrepreneurs, Milwaukee's economy soon evolved from one of simple commerce to manufacturing, producing finished products that used the same raw materials that were being exported to the East Coast. Wheat milling, meat packing, and leather tanning all reflected this adaptation. In similar fashion, Germans such as Jacob Best, August Krug, Joseph Schlitz, and Valentin Blatz began making beer for the local market and soon were producing for the national market as well.[7]

In the 1890s, the city's industrialists began to transform Milwaukee into one of the great manufacturing centers of the country. The introduction of electricity revolutionized who could produce what and where. No longer was one tied to water power or to huge steam-generating equipment. In 1889, three firms made electrical equipment in Milwaukee and employed fifteen people who produced $38,870 in product value. By 1914, two thousand employees worked for twenty-five electrical equipment manufacturers producing $5 million in value. The internal combustion engine played a much smaller role in the production process but had a revolutionary impact on what was produced. As wagon makers pondered how to adapt to this new technology or went out of business, a dizzying array of automobile manufacturers came and mostly went. In Milwaukee alone, fifty different companies made automobiles before World War I. Thomas Jeffery, a bicycle manufacturer in Kenosha, made the first Rambler in 1902, a name plate that survived most of the twentieth century.

Some of Milwaukee's most iconic companies were founded to adapt the internal combustion engine to some new application. Briggs and Stratton began making small engines, and Harley-Davidson began producing its storied motorcycles. Four Wheel Drive Auto Company made vehicles in Clintonville, Bucyrus-Erie manufactured some of the world's largest excavating machines, J. I. Case and Milwaukee Harvester turned out their first tractors, and by 1914 Allis-Chalmers had begun making giant turbines. Its facility in West Allis could employ ten thousand men.

The power elite—lumber barons, railroad tycoons, business leaders, and Republican politicians—worked together during the nineteenth century to create an environment conducive to industrial development and political power. In a symbiotic relationship they worked to create the

Pawling & Harnischfeger, makers of heavy cranes, represented Wisconsin's growing manufacturing capacity at the 1904 World's Fair in St. Louis, with their thirty-ton bridge crane and trolley. By 1914 companies like Pawling & Harnischfeger had made Milwaukee one of the great manufacturing centers of the nation. WHI IMAGE ID 60666

economic foundation for a modern economy and to build their personal wealth and power, often at the expense of farmers and workers. By 1914, the cozy relationships between economic and political elites had run aground on the shoals of progressive reform.

AN EVOLVING POLITICAL CLIMATE

During the last decades of the nineteenth century, several coalitions of agrarian and labor interests tried to defeat the old guard, made up of Republican politicians and industry leaders, who had controlled state politics since the Civil War. Although occasionally successful, these reform coalitions were never able to hold together beyond one or two election cycles before the old guard surged back into power. After losing his congressional seat in 1890, Robert M. La Follette was among those who were increasingly concerned about the influence of big business on the Republican Party and on government. La Follette set his sights on capturing the Republican Party from within and winning the governor's office. During the 1890s he built a coalition consisting of his inner circle (wife Belle, law partners, and political mentor George E. Bryant), University of Wisconsin alumni and faculty (alumni gave him statewide contacts; faculty gave him access to experts in many fields), and disaffected senior Republicans (William Dempster Hoard gave him credibility with the state's dairy farmers, and Isaac Stephenson added credibility, money, and a Milwaukee newspaper to the coalition). La Follette also assiduously cultivated support from the Norwegian community, building his rural base. With the aid of operatives in virtually every small town in Wisconsin, he developed a comprehensive poll list of voters to whom he regularly sent speeches and legislative information.

After losing bitter fights for the governor's nomination at the state Republican convention in 1896 and 1898, La Follette recognized that a power vacuum had developed in the state party leadership. Old opponents had died or shifted their attention to national politics. Into this vacuum stepped La Follette and his new ally, Emanuel Philipp, a rising star in the conservative wing of the party. In 1900, La Follette mended fences, soft-peddled progressive issues, and negotiated his way to the nomination for governor as the "harmony" candidate. He won handily in the general election, earning 60 percent of the vote to become Wisconsin's first governor of the twentieth century.

From the beginning of his inaugural address it was clear La Follette did not plan to be the kind of passive governor common in the nineteenth century. He created great anticipation when he announced he would deliver the address in person instead of sending the speech over to be delivered by a clerk as had been done in the past. La Follette mentioned two dozen issues he thought the state legislature should address, including better supervision of state inspectors, reorganization of several state departments, appointment of more women to state boards, and an end to free railroad passes for legislators. He devoted most of the speech to advocating for tax reform and for the adoption of a direct primary, which represented a radical departure from selecting candidates at party conventions controlled by political bosses.

Almost immediately, La Follette's "harmony" coalition disintegrated, as the legislature split into warring camps over tax reform and the direct primary. By the time the legislature convened, members of the conservative wing of the Republican Party had begun referring to themselves as "stalwarts." When the legislature passed a weak primary bill that applied only to local government officials, Governor La Follette vetoed the measure and delivered a blistering critique. The stalwarts also defeated reforms designed to tax railroad property at full value like that of homeowners, instead of at half value. The "progressive" Republicans, as members of the liberal wing of the party had begun to call themselves, continued to lose legislative battles; but each defeat became a rallying point, and the progressives gained strength with each new election. By 1904 they controlled the state government. La Follette's political machine helped bring and keep the progressives in power for the next decade.[8]

After only two terms as governor, La Follette shifted his attention to the national stage. In 1905, when one of Wisconsin's senate seats became available, La Follette maneuvered to secure his own appointment from the legislature (prior to 1913, US senators were appointed by their state legislatures and not elected by popular vote). La Follette delayed taking his seat in Congress until 1906 so he could shepherd several bills through the Wisconsin state legislature. Before leaving the governor's office, he oversaw a referendum in favor of using direct primaries for state elected offices as well as the passage of legislation providing for a railroad commission. Although this commission was weaker than La Follette had hoped, as it could not set rates, the legislation gave the commission authority to review rates and to conduct investigations.

Through all of these political battles, "Fighting Bob's" greatest adviser and ally was his wife, Belle Case La Follette. Belle was a political power in her own right. Although she never held public office, she was the first woman to receive a law degree from the University of Wisconsin, and she actively participated in the struggles over progressive legislation, declaration of war, conscription, free speech, and war finance. She helped manage *La Follette's Magazine*, authored numerous articles, and worked assiduously to make the magazine a voice for progressive causes. Belle La Follette advocated for legislation to protect working women and children and became a master strategist in the fight for woman's suffrage. When Congress finally passed the Nineteenth Amendment in 1919, giving

Bob La Follette wrenched control from the conservative wing of the Republican Party and was the focus of countless political cartoons, such as this one, which ran in the *Chicago Tribune* on December 29, 1911. Between 1901 and 1915, La Follette helped Wisconsin progressives pass a stunning array of landmark legislation—including direct primary and popular election of senators, railroad regulation, worker's compensation, and factory safety—and lay the groundwork for honest government and the modern social safety net. WHI IMAGE ID 5586

women the right to vote, Belle organized the ratification effort in Wisconsin, which became the first state to ratify the constitutional amendment. The La Follettes became Wisconsin's most important political dynasty. When Bob La Follette died in 1925, his son Robert M. La Follette Jr. took his father's seat in the Senate and served until 1947 when he was defeated by Joseph McCarthy. Belle and Bob's other son, Philip, served as governor of Wisconsin during most of the 1930s. In their letters to each other and the children, Bob and Belle inevitably nurtured the political sensibilities of the family.

Two progressive governors, James Davidson and Francis McGovern, followed La Follette's tenure, and their leadership helped create the most productive decade in Wisconsin legislative history. Davidson worked with progressive legislators to strengthen regulation of railroads and extend regulatory authority over a variety of public utilities. Led by McGovern during the 1911 legislative session, the legislature achieved a truly remarkable record when it created a substantial foundation for the social safety

Bob and Belle La Follette were a political power couple. "Fighting Bob" devoted his life to politics, beginning with his election as Dane County district attorney in 1880. He would go on to serve as congressman, governor, and senator. Bob died in 1925 while still a senator. Belle was the first woman to graduate from the University of Wisconsin law school and proved a forceful advocate for equal rights for women and African Americans. Their son Robert La Follette Jr. held his father's senate seat for twenty-two years until he was defeated by Joseph McCarthy in 1947. Their son Philip La Follette held the governor's office for most of the 1930s. Daughter Fola La Follette became an actress, suffrage leader, and her father's biographer. Daughter Mary La Follette worked for the federal Department of Agriculture and the US Air Force. The family was a political force for more than sixty years. Clockwise from top left: Fola, Bob, Belle, Robert Jr., Philip, and Mary. WHI IMAGE ID 82953

net. Legislators passed a worker's compensation law, adopted factory safety regulations, promoted the establishment of cooperative associations, imposed the state's first income tax, and limited the number of hours women and children could work. They also funded the state park system and began an investigation of conditions on the state's Indian reservations.

The Socialist Party was a force for progressive ideas independent of the progressive movement within the Republican Party. In Milwaukee, the Socialist Party's Wisconsin stronghold, Victor Berger rejected Marxist ideology. A journalist, politician, and founding member, Berger "Americanized" the party by emphasizing gradual reform instead of revolution. The Milwaukee socialists were more concerned with honest government, efficient city administration, and public utilities. They won the mayor's office in 1910 but lost two years later when the Republicans and Democrats formed a united coalition. Of the socialists elected in 1910, only the city attorney, Daniel Hoan, kept his office after the 1912 elections. Hoan used his record as city attorney as a springboard to the mayor's office in 1916. In keeping with Berger's practical socialism, Hoan was more concerned with administering the city and improving life in Milwaukee than with ideological purity. Socialism in Milwaukee came to be known as "sewer socialism" because of the practical approach of Berger and Hoan.

Some of the most important accomplishments of the progressive era were not found in legislation or ideology, but in the relationships among the university, the government, and the people of Wisconsin. The Wisconsin Idea, as it came to be known, not only shaped the government but also clearly established the principle that the knowledge and expertise contained within the university should advance the common good in service to government and the public. The essence of the Wisconsin Idea was captured in the phrase, "the boundaries of university are the boundaries of the state."[9] As it was applied in the early twentieth century, the concept provided the philosophical foundation for the expansion of the University of Wisconsin extension program, which took the knowledge of the university, especially its agricultural knowledge, to all corners of the state.

By 1914, progressives in Wisconsin had created a more equitable system of taxation, implemented regulatory controls on major public utilities, and laid the groundwork for protecting the health and welfare of workers. Likewise, the university had adopted a philosophical framework that would inform administrative decisions well into the twentieth century.

Temperance and suffrage were also important in 1914, although the movements had failed to achieve their goals. The suffrage movement came closest in 1912 when the state held a referendum on whether women in Wisconsin should have the right to vote. After a vigorous campaign, with staunch opposition by the German-American Alliance, the brewers' association, and other business associations, the measure was defeated by a margin of two to one. The defeat inspired Wisconsin's woman suffrage advocates, including Belle La Follette, to set their sights on a constitutional amendment at the national level rather than seek incremental change one state at a time.

The Women's Christian Temperance Union, with approximately 10,000 members in Wisconsin in 1911 and 245,000 nationwide, was a formidable force not just on behalf of prohibition, but for a variety of other social causes, including suffrage, women's rights, workplace protections for children and women, and food and drug legislation. Although prohibition in Wisconsin remained elusive, especially with the prominence of brewing in both the economy and culture of the state, the coming war would give both suffrage and temperance a boost neither could have imagined in 1914.[10]

Despite its many successes, by 1914 the progressive movement in Wisconsin had begun to fracture. Bob La Follette had gone to Washington and was actively courting a national audience. Never very tolerant of progressive rivals, La Follette engaged in self-destructive disputes with Governors Davidson and McGovern. La Follette's onetime ally, stalwart Republican Emanuel Philipp, stood ready to take advantage of the progressives' internecine warfare and demonstrated that he was just as much a political tactician as "Fighting Bob." Philipp ran for governor in 1914 on a platform to rein in out-of-control state spending, revise the primary law to give political parties more control over the nomination process, and abolish many of the state boards and commissions or reduce their authority. Philipp's platform was a direct attack on the progressive era. Onetime La Follette supporters such as Hoard, Davidson, and Senator Isaac Stephenson backed Philipp in the general election, as did the voters.

Philipp won the governor's office with 40 percent of the vote in a five-man race. Progressive Republicans won all the other statewide races and secured majorities in both houses of the legislature. Although a progressive victory, the Progressive Era was ending. Many of the younger Republicans no longer followed the La Follette drummer. They came to the legislature prepared to listen to a new voice, the stalwart voice of Emanuel Philipp.[11]

AN EVOLVING POPULATION

Almost everything about Wisconsin—its politics, its religion, its culture—was influenced by its ethnic populations, whether Finns in the Lake Superior region, Belgians in the Door Peninsula, Norwegians in Trempealeau County, or Germans in Milwaukee. In many places the churches were Lutheran or Catholic, English was a secondary language, and the food was more likely dominated by the flavors of Europe than by the flavors of the Yankee Northeast. In 1914, Wisconsin was the most German of states numerically, culturally, and in the popular imagination. The identification of beer with Milwaukee symbolized the connection between Germany, Milwaukee, and ultimately Wisconsin. Anyone visiting Milwaukee and some rural areas of Wisconsin in the early twentieth century might well hear two neighbors speaking German and freely switching to English to converse with a visitor.

A regular flow of German immigrants came to Wisconsin during the late 1840s and did not abate until about 1890. They came to avoid political upheaval or military service, to find better agricultural opportunities, to rise out of poverty, to find industrial employment, and to escape persecution because of their ideas or religious faith. They were farmers, day laborers, skilled industrial craftsmen, and professionals. They were not a homogeneous group who could be packaged as "German." After creation of the German Empire in 1871, they might have spoken glowingly of German accomplishments, but when asked from what country they came, would likely revert to the old principalities and tell the inquirer that they were from Bavaria or Prussia or Schleswig-Holstein. Some were Lutheran, others were Catholic; some were rural, some urban. Some liked sausage and sauerkraut, while others preferred the rich, paprika-laced gravy of goulash. Despite the distinctions among German groups, Americans often thought of these immigrants as one homogeneous group because they spoke the same language.

In 1890, just after the peak of immigration, 15 percent of Wisconsin's 1,693,330 residents had been born in Germany. By 1910, the population had grown to 2,333,860 and 38 percent of Wisconsinites were either born in or had parents from Germany, Austria, or Hungary. In other words, more than one-third of Wisconsin's residents likely had grandparents, aunts, uncles, and cousins who would soon be fighting for the German or Austro-Hungarian empires. In comparison, 9 percent of Wisconsin's population had comparable ties to countries with allegiance to the Allies. The great majority of Wisconsinites of all nationalities were loyal Americans who would have found it difficult to be neutral when their homeland and their families were at war.

During the nineteenth century, Scandinavians comprised the second largest immigrant group in Wisconsin, at 11 percent of the population. Coming from Norway, Sweden, Denmark, and Finland, the Scandinavians

The Benedict Goldenberger family, seen here enjoying a cookout in the country near Madison. Food practices, particularly on holidays and special occasions, helped maintain sentimental attachment to the ancestral homeland for immigrant families long after other ties such as language had ceased to be important. WHI IMAGE ID 1971

were no more monolithic than the Germans. Indeed, Norway had wrenched its independence from Sweden in 1905. Norwegian immigrants established their earliest settlements in Wisconsin during the late 1830s. In 1910 the state population included 157,700 people born in or with at least one parent from Norway. Although they comprised only 7 percent of Wisconsin's population, their numbers far outstripped those of immigrants from elsewhere in Scandinavia. The Norwegians first settled among Yankee neighbors in the southeastern part of the state. Settlement followed the frontier into western Wisconsin during the 1860s and 1870s, producing a distinctively Norwegian American culture in western Wisconsin, from Crawford County north to Barron County. The Scandinavian homelands were uninvolved as war clouds gathered over Europe, and immigrants from those countries readily accepted neutrality as the best American course.

Polish allegiances were much more complex. By 1914 Polish immigrants were becoming an important element in the Milwaukee metropolitan area, where most of them settled. Russia, Germany, and Austria-Hungary controlled different segments of what we think of today as Poland, making it difficult to calculate how many Poles had settled in Wisconsin, but Polish immigrants probably were the third-largest ethnic group in the state. By 1930, when the census finally recognized Polish as a nationality, Wisconsin had 135,953 residents of Polish extraction, almost double the number who identified themselves as Norwegian in that year.

Nineteenth-century immigration produced an ethnically diverse society in Wisconsin. From a racial standpoint, however, Wisconsin had virtually no diversity at all. The census counted 10,142 Native Americans living primarily on lands in the central and northern part of the state. The tribes included indigenous peoples—the Ho-Chunk, Menominee, Ojibwe, and Potawatomi—as well as tribes who had moved to Wisconsin from New York during the 1820s and 1830s—the Mohican, Oneida, and Stockbridge-Munsee. During the years before the Great War, Native people endured assaults on their lands and culture. The General Indian Allotment Act of 1887 allowed reservation land to be allotted to individuals, usually 160 acres. In often questionable land deals during the next twenty-seven years, large portions of tribal lands were acquired by non-Indians through individual purchases from Native owners. In particular, tribes lost control over lands valued for agriculture, timber, or resort development. Traditional economic activities—hunting, fishing, wild ricing, gardening—provided a subsistence for many tribal members. Even these activities became more difficult after 1908, when the Wisconsin Supreme Court ruled that tribal members could not exercise treaty rights that had been the basis for spear-fishing.

American Indian families adapted to local economic conditions and opportunities. Ojibwe tribal members worked in the forests and as hunting and fishing guides; Ho-Chunk tribal members worked in the developing tourist industry at the Wisconsin Dells and in the cranberry industry. The Menominee possessed excellent timber land and had the greatest economic success as they developed and implemented sustainable forestry practices. Even in this case, large sections of tribal forest were illegally clear-cut by the US Forest Service.

The era before World War I not only eroded economic conditions for Native people, but also included active government efforts to undermine Native culture. Indian boarding schools were perhaps the most powerful tool in the drive for cultural assimilation. Although some schools were on or near tribal lands, many Native American children were taken from their families and sent to schools as far away as South Dakota, Pennsylvania, and Virginia. Almost all of the schools had one thing in common: assimilation, as they prohibited children from learning their native language or participating in cultural practices.

Before the Great War, Wisconsin had a relatively small African American population. Although former slaves founded agricultural settlements in Vernon and Grant Counties, most African Americans gravitated to the industrial opportunities of Wisconsin's cities. By 1910 the census listed 2,900 African Americans living in Wisconsin, approximately 0.1 percent of the state's population. Although African Americans lived in almost every county in the state, more than half of the state's African American population was concentrated in the eight cities with a population of twenty-five thousand or more. Milwaukee alone accounted for one-third of the state's black population. Superior, Wisconsin, where black men could find work on the docks, had the second-largest African American population in Wisconsin—but at 182 individuals, it lagged far behind Milwaukee with 980 black residents. Madison trailed a distant third with only 143 African American residents.[12]

Evaluating sympathies and estimating popular attitudes about the war is difficult. Scientific opinion polls were a thing of the future. Ethnicity provides one measure of likely sympathies and helps explain the charitable aid sent from Wisconsin to Germany, as well as the propensity in some circles to question the loyalty of Wisconsin residents and politicians. In 1914, Americans generally wanted no part in the war, but it would be naïve to believe they did not form personal opinions or have sympathies for one side more than another. Likewise, an immigrant who came to Wisconsin to avoid military service, political repression, religious persecution, or famine might have little sympathy for the government of their ancestral homeland, but they cared about the plight of parents, siblings, aunts, uncles, and cousins still in Europe.

Ethnicity could have a powerful impact on politics. Because of their size, the German, Norwegian, and Polish communities influenced many aspects of life in the areas where they predominated. For example, Republicans lost control of state government on only two occasions between 1860 and 1914. On both occasions, the Republican-led government had passed legislation that alienated several ethnic communities. In 1872 the legislature passed liquor regulations that Germans interpreted as an attack on their cultural practice of relaxing with family and friends in beer gardens on Sunday afternoons. The following year, German voters defected in large numbers, electing a Democrat to the state house for the first time since 1856. In 1888, Hoard, promoter of the dairy industry and editor of *Hoard's Dairyman*, ran for governor, promising to promote legislation that would hold parochial schools more accountable and require instruction in English. During the following term, the legislature passed the Bennett Law, requiring schools to teach in English. In the 1890 election, German and Norwegian residents revolted. The Assembly, the state Senate, the governor's office, and all other statewide offices went to the Democrats. Voters took their ire out on Congress, too. Even though the irritant was state legislation, all but one member of the Wisconsin delegation lost his seat, including the young La Follette, who would return to elected office as governor ten years later.

An individual's ethnicity was made manifest by surname, accent, religion, clothing, food preferences, and a myriad of other small personal characteristics. In some localities, one could grow up and live a long life without ever learning English. During the summer of 1914, as battle lines were being drawn in Europe, Wisconsin's residents had diverse reactions to the prospect of war, based on a mixture of ethnicity, values, culture, and politics. Affection for the land of their birth, their cultural homeland, and for the safety of relatives still in Europe made it very difficult for Wisconsinites to be truly neutral, but even as they chose sides one thing was clearly true—they wanted no part of the disaster developing in Europe.

CHAPTER 2

WAR COMES TO WISCONSIN

War engulfed Europe with unimaginable speed during the summer of 1914.

The peoples of the continent ushered in the new year in relative peace and were shocked at how quickly diplomacy failed and armies began to mobilize. Although the Balkan nations seemed to fight each other on a regular basis, the major European powers had been at peace since the last Franco-Prussian war of 1870–1871 almost forty-five years earlier.

The major European powers may have been at peace, but all was not well. Competition for territorial dominance, economic preeminence, and colonial empire fueled nationalistic rivalries. By 1914, all the major powers were armed for war. An alliance between Russia and France, promises by Great Britain to defend Belgian neutrality, and agreements between Germany, Austria-Hungary, and the Ottoman Empire virtually guaranteed that a major conflagration would soon engulf the continent. Unfortunately, the governments of these European powers were controlled by a mixture of autocrats, fools, and vainglorious officers who were ill suited or disinclined to find peaceful solutions to international disputes. In each country the romantic notion of the glory of war still lingered, despite becoming obsolete when the rifle and machine gun replaced the saber and lance. German leaders in particular believed that war and the use of military power were necessary, even desirable, to achieve that nation's destiny to become the dominant power in Europe.

Serbian nationalism and the Austrian desire to regain imperial dominance in the region created a powder keg that required only a small spark to explode. Into this charged atmosphere stepped Archduke Franz Ferdinand of Austria and Serbian patriot Gavrilo Princip. The archduke came to Sarajevo to inspect Austrian troops stationed in Bosnia. As the sun rose over the city on June 28, Ferdinand and his wife, Sophie, celebrated their fourteenth wedding anniversary. It promised to be a lovely, warm summer day. After a brief military inspection, the royal couple's motorcade drove toward the Sarajevo city hall, where the mayor awaited his visitors. Flags and flowers decorated buildings along the route and cheering crowds welcomed the heir to the Austro-Hungarian throne.

Seven Serbian assassins waited for the archduke along the parade route. One conspirator threw a bomb, but the archduke deflected it with his arm. The bomb landed in the street and wounded approximately a dozen spectators. Five other conspirators failed to act as the motorcade passed. Ferdinand ignored the wishes of his advisers and insisted on visiting the wounded spectators in the hospital. In the course of correcting a wrong turn, the archduke's driver stopped the royal car just five feet from Princip, the seventh assassin, who quickly fired two shots, mortally wounding the royal couple.

Austria blamed Serbia for the archduke's death and issued an ultimatum containing fifteen humiliating demands. To many observers' surprise, Serbia agreed to all of the demands but one: that Austrian officials be allowed to participate in the Serbian inquiry into the assassination plot. Austria's goal was not the resolution of the crisis but the subjugation of Serbia; the Austrian government used the rejected demand as a pretext for war and promptly invaded its neighbor.

Russia, which possessed the largest army in the world, immediately began mobilizing 1.4 million soldiers in defense of Serbia, and war became almost inevitable. Facing the prospect of a two-front war with France and Russia, Germany began mobilizing its forces and declared war. On Germany's eastern front lay the awakening Russian bear. In the west, France was still chaffing from its loss of Alsace-Lorraine in the Franco-Prussian War of 1870, and German strategists assumed France would come to the aid of its Russian ally. This presented Germany with the very real prospect of being crushed under the weight of a Russian onslaught from the east and a French assault from the west. The German General Staff had long prepared for this scenario. The Schlieffen plan was Germany's master blueprint for fighting a two-front war against France and Russia. It required a lightning stroke through neutral Belgium to quash French forces before Russia could complete full mobilization. Freed of the French threat in the west, the German army could be redeployed in time to meet the Russian juggernaut in the east. Once diplomacy failed and armies mobilized, assumptions about the behavior of allies and enemies combined with military timetables and strategies, created years earlier, to quickly escalate the diplomatic crisis into a massive clash of arms. Russia protected Serbia; Germany pledged aid of Austria; France agreed to aid Russia; and Britain guaranteed Belgian neutrality. Although troop mobilizations should have triggered extensive diplomatic discussions, they did not. Each new measure designed to prepare for war heightened the threat perceived by a neighbor.[1]

News of War

At first, the archduke's assassination was treated like any other news story in the United States. On June 29 and 30, the death of the royal couple was front-page news in Wisconsin, as it was across the country and in Europe. The story quickly slipped from US headlines, and Wisconsin went about the business of milking cows and preparing for the fall election season. But three weeks later headlines on the front page of the *Milwaukee Journal* suggested a festering crisis:

> Austrian reservists were instructed to be in readiness to join their regiments in twenty-four hours.
> This follows the strong note sent by Austria to Servia, which virtually took the form of an ultimatum demanding the suppression of the Pan-Servian movement and the punishment of those concerned in the assassination of Archduke Francis [sic] Ferdinand and his wife.
> Russia May Intervene.

Three days later, on July 27, 1914, the story came screaming back with a headline spread across the front page: "WAR IS ALMOST INEVITABLE, DECLARES MINISTER OF RUSSIA." Every day thereafter, the situation grew worse:

July 28, 1914

"Austria Officially Declares War and Seizes Servian Steamers"

"Russian Army Reported on Frontier; Kaiser's Uhlans Advance to Striking Distance of Czar's Western Domain"

July 29, 1914

"Servian Capital Is Bombarded by the Austrians"

July 30, 1914

"Germany Gives Russia Twenty-Four Hours to Explain Mobilization Move"

July 31, 1914

"Martial Law in Germany—War Fever Spreads"

August 1, 1914

"Armies of Germany and France Ordered Mobilized"

August 2, 1914

"War Dogs of German Empire Are Loosed Against Russia; France Ready to Enter the Fray and England Gets Ready"

August 3, 1914

"Army of England Is Ordered to Mobilize Tomorrow"

August 4, 1914

"England Gives Germany Until Midnight to Answer Her Ultimatum"

August 5, 1914

"Anglo-German War Declared"[2]

The Game of Dominoes

The Specter of Death became a common metaphor for the war. The clear implication of this cartoon, "The Game of Dominoes," was that war would bring death and collapse to the nations of Europe. SUPERIOR TELEGRAM, AUGUST 5, 1914

CAN HE RESTRAIN HIM?

In 1914 many government and military leaders believed modern war was so expensive as to guarantee short duration. They believed the threat of financial collapse would bring everyone to their senses in short order. *EAU CLAIRE LEADER*, AUGUST 5, 1914

For anyone reading the news, it became clear that Europe was hurtling toward a major conflict, but it was hard to imagine that in the modern, enlightened twentieth century, the powers of Europe would again go to war. Victor Berger was a socialist leader in Milwaukee. In a manner not unlike Bob and Belle La Follette, Victor and his wife, Meta Berger, were close confidants and advisers. Their letters are filled with news and opinions about the world around them, politics of the day, and the inner workings of the Socialist Party. Victor Berger was one of the state's most astute politicians;

and yet, on the day Germany issued its ultimatum to Russia, Berger sent Meta a wildly optimistic analysis of why war was unlikely:

> Some way [or] another it seems to me that the great European conflagration will not come at this time. . . . I am satisfied that England will never fight—surely not for France. Almost funny looked the report from Japan that that country would go to war to defend its "ally" England—and incidentally also Russia—with which England has the "entente"—when Great Britain did nothing absolutely nothing during the Russian-Japanese war to help Japan.[3]

As the French, British, and German armies fought to a futile, bloody stalemate in the trenches of the western front during 1915, former president and political pundit Theodore Roosevelt wrote a polemic critiquing Wilsonian policies and advocating greater military preparedness. Roosevelt reflected on the surprise most people felt when the war began:

> In this country we are both shocked and stunned by the awful cataclysm which has engulfed civilized Europe. By only a few men was the possibility of such a wide-spread and hideous disaster even admitted. Most persons, even after it occurred, felt as if it was unbelievable. They felt that in what it pleased enthusiasts to speak of as "this age of enlightenment" it was impossible that primal passion, working hand in hand with the most modern scientific organization, should loose upon the world these forces of dread destruction.[4]

Many individuals sympathized with one side or the other, but few Americans wanted to be involved. Most continued their normal daily lives. The war was a topic to be discussed after church, at the store, or with a neighbor. In September 1914, the carnage of the first battle of the Marne, with five hundred thousand casualties, was shocking but not an American affair.

But the war was quite personal for Americans living, traveling, or studying in Europe. They scrambled to find passage out of the war zone. On August 17 the *Laconia* arrived in New York with 1,600 passengers. Some borrowed money to buy tickets. One man left Wiesbaden, Germany, with his luggage in a wheelbarrow and walked miles to cross the border at Liege, Belgium. Americans from Munich, Berlin, Dresden, and Frankfurt began streaming into Holland in the desperate hope of finding berth on a ship headed home.

Many of the passengers on the Red Star liner *Finland* arrived in New York without money or luggage, having traveled through battlefields to reach Antwerp. US newspapers reported the stories of some passengers, such as Chicago native James Patten and his wife, who had been in Carls-bad, Germany, when the war started. The Pattens drove to Nuremberg, where they were interrogated by German authorities before being allowed to proceed on a crowded train to Ostend, Belgium. But the train got no farther than Cologne, Germany, where passengers found themselves in a maelstrom of mobilizing soldiers and civilians clogging the streets as they prepared to defend their homeland. After more delays, another crowded train ride, and an escape to safety via horse and cart, the couple bought steamship tickets back to the United States for themselves and nine other stranded Americans.

US diplomats were swamped by requests for aid from US citizens in the war zone who needed help getting back to the United States. President Woodrow Wilson and Congress responded promptly to the plight of stranded Americans by passing a $250,000 appropriation for their assistance. In addition, Herbert Hoover, who was then a little-known wealthy mining engineer living in London, organized a large group of volunteers to help stranded Americans with clothing, food, and tickets home.[5]

As the German army swept into Belgium and seemed on the verge of capturing Paris, foreigners sought every means possible of returning home. The *Milwaukee Journal* carried notices of Wisconsinites who were safe in London, Québec, or New York. The newspaper also kept a list of Americans abroad whose locations were unknown, such as Francis Connors, who was studying music at a German conservatory, and a group of University of Wisconsin women who had been traveling in Germany. Ominously, the paper also reported the execution of four Russians in Württemberg, Germany, on the charges of spying. The German Consul General warned that anyone found in the Baden or Alsace-Lorraine area without a passport was liable to be charged with spying and executed.[6]

Amidst the chaotic news of Europe going to war, the *Milwaukee*

Journal reprinted an article by Herman Ridder, editor of the influential German-language newspaper the *New York Staats Zeitung,* in which he heralded the marshal spirit of the German army and chided those who claimed conditions were dire for tourists. Ridder scoffed at reports of harsh treatment of foreign nationals and chaos in Germany. "Reports that describe Germany [sic] lines as demoralized and disorganized can be dismissed as absurd," he wrote. "Victorious armies are not in the habit of yielding to panics." Stories of Americans receiving harsh treatment in Germany were "lies, all lies," attributed primarily to the need for sensationalism in the American press.[7]

Germany was not the only country that inconvenienced American tourists. All of the belligerents placed military necessity ahead of the convenience of noncombatants. Wisconsinites Julie Avery and her mother, Rachel Foster Avery, arrived in Europe outfitted with a Harley-Davidson motorcycle and a sidecar with the goal of "visiting the home of the Alderney and Guernsey cattle of the Channel Islands and the Holsteins and Dutch Belted in Brittany and Holland." Mother and daughter were students at the University of Wisconsin College of Agriculture. Their trip came to an abrupt end when the Belgian army confiscated their motorcycle and sidecar for use in the defense of Belgium.[8]

NATIONALISM AND THE ILLUSION OF NEUTRALITY

As Americans adjusted to the reality of the war engulfing Europe's major powers, President Wilson tried the impossible in an attempt to keep the nation out of the war. On August 19, 1914, Wilson called on his fellow citizens to be "neutral in fact as well as in name during these days that are to try men's souls. We must be impartial in thought as well as in action, must put a curb upon our sentiments as well as upon every transaction that might be construed as a preference of one party to the struggle before another."[9] This was a noble sentiment born of the desire to avoid involvement in the war. But it was a hopelessly unrealistic goal.

For most Wisconsin residents, the war was blessedly far away. It was easy to look at the belligerents and find little in common with American interests or values—in fact, little seemed to differentiate the two sides. The French, British, and Russian Empires stood against the rising German

Empire and the failing empires of Austria-Hungary and the Ottomans. Some observers were sympathetic toward the democratic governments of France and Britain, but the government of Imperial Russia could hardly be considered an improvement over the government of Imperial Germany.

Ethnic heritage and bonds of family often created powerful ties to the belligerents. Those of German heritage readily supported the fatherland. For others, ethnicity and representative government made it easy to support the French Republic or the British monarchy. Immigrants and their children often saw nothing incompatible about identifying with their German, Norwegian, or Polish heritage and being American. When Peter Ackerson, editor of the *Svenska Tribune* in Superior, visited Milwaukee in August 1914, he found the German community there in a state of frenzy. "Great crowds of Germans stood on the corners talking excitedly of the war troubles," Ackerson wrote. He believed that hundreds of Milwaukee's "intensely patriotic" Germans would enlist in the German army if it were possible to do so.

Fritz Hertlien, for example, had lived in the United States for forty-two years and was fully integrated into American society. Yet Hertlien was fiercely patriotic where Germany was concerned. He had fought in the Franco-Prussian War of 1870, immigrated to the United States in 1872, and by 1914 had become mayor of Allouez. Despite being sixty-five years old, Hertlien told a reporter, "If there was some way of getting back to Germany I would start at once."[10]

For some people the pull of nationalism was strong enough to draw them directly into the fight. Forty Austrians left their jobs in the "copper country," presumably in the Upper Peninsula of Michigan, to enlist in the Austrian army. Fifteen Germans from Appleton signed up for military service with the fatherland. Efforts to Americanize immigrants and separate them from their ethnic heritage generally had failed. Maintaining a dual identity was one of the quintessential characteristics of being an American.[11]

On August 4, 1914, King Albert of Belgium called on all his subjects to defend their homeland. Two days later the Belgian Consul in Green Bay distributed notices instructing Belgian reservists to report to their posts. Allouez was home to about six hundred Belgians. Approximately two hundred were reservists in the Belgian army. In addition, Wisconsin was home to the largest rural settlement of Belgians in the United States. The order to report for duty presented Belgian families in the United States with a conundrum: how does one rationalize overlapping and sometimes incompatible loyalties to native fatherland, American homeland, and family? As residents of the United States, they could not be compelled to return to Belgium. Most of the reservists in Wisconsin had families and showed little interest in leaving unless they had assurances that provision would be made for the care and well-being of the families left behind. A reporter for the *Superior Telegram* estimated that only twenty young, single men from Superior's Belgian community would heed the call. The number might have been higher, but a month earlier 150 Belgian men went to North Dakota to find work after being laid off at the Great Northern Railroad ore dock. The reporter ended his story on a poignant note:

> Although most of the men of the Belgian colony were in a gay, light-hearted mood, the women viewed the situation quite differently. The women, natural conservatives, spoke of parents and sisters and brothers in the old country, many of whom will suffer the horrors of the war. They spoke of the millions of people who would be crippled and killed in the mad struggle—how many, they had no comprehension of. And they would not be comforted.[12]

The sense of obligation felt by many immigrants whose homelands were at war also manifested itself in fund-raising for war relief. Almost as soon as the war began, the German community in Milwaukee began raising funds to assist the families of German soldiers. The charitable effort quickly spread to other German communities in Wisconsin. On September 28, 1914, Leo Stirn, a leader in the Milwaukee relief effort, took his humanitarian message to an enthusiastic crowd of 350 people gathered in Manitowoc, the first step in building a fund-raising organization there. In his speech, Stirn defended the German army against charges of atrocities committed in Belgium, claiming those stories had been "manufactured to discredit the Germans and place them in a wrong light." His defensive posture came after Germany's invasion of Belgium the month before, the execution of more than five thousand Belgian civilian hostages (men, women, and children), and the burning of the world-renowned university library at Louvain.[13]

Between 1914 and 1917, many residents of German birth or heritage made no attempt to hide their favoritism toward the fatherland. They were proud of their heritage and of the rise to power of the unified Germany. The German-American Alliance, with thirty-seven thousand members in Wisconsin, sent money to war sufferers in Germany. This money was often raised by selling pictures of Franz Josef and the Kaiser. German Americans raised funds for the German Red Cross, sold German bonds, and disseminated information favorable to the German cause. In a weeklong bazaar in Milwaukee, for example, 175,000 people contributed $150,000 to the Central Powers (Germany, Austria-Hungary, Ottoman Empire, and Bulgaria).[14]

Efforts in Wisconsin to raise relief funds for neutral Belgium offer a clear contrast to the ethnically focused German relief efforts. Belgium had been brutally subjugated by the German army. Charitable organizations all over the state solicited funds for Belgian war relief from anyone willing to give during the fall of 1914, regardless of ethnicity. In Janesville residents collected clothing. In honor of Thanksgiving, people in La Crosse collected money to buy flour to send to Belgium. Banks in Eau Claire volunteered to collect funds for flour, and the *Eau Claire Sunday Leader* published the names of major donors: Lumberman John S. Owen pledged to buy ten barrels; Cutter Company, Pioneer Furniture Company, Eau Claire Creamery, Ideal Land and Loan Company, Union Mortgage and Loan Company, Union Savings Bank, and Eau Claire Savings Bank each pledged donations for five barrels of flour. Local banks, Baker's Drug Store, and the *Daily Gazette* office in Janesville posted subscription lists for pledging aid. In addition, several local organizations planned to circulate their own subscription lists, and Earle Brown, the manager of the Majestic and Lyric Theatres, planned to donate proceeds from a performance.

Individual Americans began forming opinions almost immediately. Even in Wisconsin, with its large German population, many—perhaps a majority—of people felt an affinity for the cause of Europe's democracies of Great Britain and France. Germany's violation of Belgian neutrality and their brutal practice of responding to armed resistance by shooting hostages and leveling villages made it difficult to be "impartial in thought as well as action."

Why all this attention for little Belgium? As the *Janesville Daily Gazette* told its readers, "It is not a question of the rights or wrongs of the present

European struggle that should appeal to the persons donating for the relief of the needy inhabitants of Belgium, but the general cause of humanity."[15] Nationalistic pride drove many of the donations to German relief; humanitarian concern fueled relief for subjugated Belgium. By its nature, even the dichotomy created by relief work tended to focus "neutral" Americans on the interests of one side or another.

Lines of allegiance were drawn quickly, even among colleagues and friends. Just one week into the war, Victor Berger wrote to Meta, his wife, expressing his frustration:

> I have my trouble with my crowd up-stairs [the staff of the Social-
> ist newspaper the *Milwaukee Leader*] on this war. They are thor-
> oughly pro-English which in this case means also pro-Russian
> and pro-French and—anti-German. The news all comes by the way
> of London and is colored that way anyhow. Now, the majority of
> our readers are of German descent and are protesting. Moreover,
> it seems that the *insane* Kaiser has made a bad mess of it.
> In short, I wish, the cruel war was over.[16]

Berger tried to follow a neutral course in his newspaper's coverage of the war. In 1914 the *Leader* lost subscribers for being too pro-Allies. In 1916 it lost readers for being too pro-Germany. An editorial about the *Lusitania* tempered its denunciation of the sinking with recognition that because the ship was carrying war supplies, passengers should not have been on board. It concluded by stating, "The *Lusitania* incident was a hellish incident. But war is hell and we want no war with Germany." During 1915 and 1916 the *Leader*, Victor Berger, and other Milwaukee Socialists advocated an embargo on American shipments to belligerent nations and campaigned for a preparedness plan designed to create "a citizen army" to defend the United States in the event of invasion.[17]

WAR WORRIES AND DAILY LIFE

Although important in shaping reactions to the war, ethnicity was not the only factor influencing reactions to the war. Many Wisconsinites had no ties to the warring nations. Instead, they were concerned about the impact of the war on mundane aspects of daily life: Would the war result in a tax increase? Would they experience shortages or inflation? How would it affect jobs?

Congressman John Esch, a Republican who represented Wisconsin's Seventh District, was the only member of Wisconsin's wartime congressional delegation who left a surviving set of constituent correspondence complete enough to allow an assessment of public opinion. These private letters from Esch's constituents illuminate the concerns of everyday Wisconsinites and business owners during the early months of the war.

When Richard Capen of Merrillan asked Esch to support a cost-of-living increase for military pensions, Esch replied reluctantly, "There is no prospect of any general pension legislation. . . . The war situation in Europe has reduced our revenues from tariff duties over one half and Congress is about to pass bills providing for the collection of war taxes in time of peace."[18]

The overwhelming majority of war-related letters sent to Esch in this early period came from business owners protesting the pending "war tax"

Representative John Esch served the Seventh Congressional District covering most of western Wisconsin. Like most of the state's delegation, he voted his constituents' wishes and opposed the declaration of war. Esch supported the war effort, including the draft, once the declaration became official.
WHI IMAGE ID 61456

legislation. The federal government relied heavily on customs duties to balance the budget. Foreign trade dropped precipitously during the first weeks of the war, customs revenue declined, and Congress was looking for a source of funding to replace the lost revenue. Just weeks into the war, Congress was contemplating taxes on bank transactions, tobacco, beer, liquor, and gasoline. As early as August 11, government officials had estimated the war would cost the United States $100 million annually in lost customs revenue. The "war tax" measure quickly moved through Congress with Democratic and presidential support. Business owners whose enterprises would be affected by the tax protested. Breweries felt pinched by the new revenue measures and pleaded with Esch for relief. They were already suffering from the rising costs of raw materials and could not afford higher taxes on each barrel of beer. Complaints came from bankers upset by a proposal to tax banks on capital and surplus, and from individuals unhappy about a tax on personal checks and legal papers. The Cigarmakers Union protested the tax on tobacco.

Opponents of the tax argued that their particular product or industry should be exempted. O. D. Brandenburg, president of the Democrat Printing Company and publisher of the *Madison Democrat*, wrote bluntly to Congressman Esch:

> Can't you cut $60,000,000 or $80,000,000 out of the harbor bill,
> and enough more millions out of the postoffice [sic] and other bills
> to avoid special taxes at this time? . . . In this state, among the papers
> denouncing them [special taxes] are The Sentinel, The Free Press,
> The Evening Wisconsin, The Democrat, and I don't know how many
> others. . . . The country will back you, and especially Wisconsin, in
> putting your heel on this everlasting tax business. Our people here
> are sick to the heart with it; . . . Cut the expenditures!

On September 21, 1914, Esch reported to Brandenburg: "The Republicans held a conference last week and unanimously decided to vote against any war tax revenue measure."

For some constituents, the war presented an opportunity to advocate for business advantage. Lumberman John S. Owen of Eau Claire wrote to Esch, "We are, of course, interested in this war that is going on and we think it is prefectly [sic] horrible and it is going to affect business, but it occurs to me that the wise legislator will be the man who will introduce a bill into Congress and give the manufacturers of dye stuffs a protection from Germany. We can't afford to be at the mercy of foreign chemists for all these things."

Owen's reference to "foreign chemists" was aimed directly at the massive German chemical industry then widely considered the best in the world. Owen was concerned with the war's effect on business, but he also used the war as an opportunity to advocate for tariff protection of a fledgling Wisconsin industry.[19]

The horrific nature of twentieth century warfare, with its huge armies, massed artillery barrages, and lethal machine-gun nests, reinforced the common belief in Europe and the United States that no nation could sustain the destruction of modern warfare for very long. The US decision to remain uninvolved was reinforced by the assumption that the war would end quickly. Newspaper coverage throughout fall 1914 emphasized the catastrophe created by the war, strongly supported neutrality, and anticipated an early peace.

The *La Crosse Tribune*, for example, reprinted a *Saturday Evening Post* article under the headline PEACE BEFORE A YEAR PASSES: "No matter what the fortunes of the battlefield are, a cumulative load of disgust and abhorrence and a steadily increasing economic pressure will stop it." The article continued, "In the first days ... they all talk about dying in the last ditch, as everyone does when he begins to fight, but after half a dozen kicks in the stomach any belligerent begins to comprehend the beauties of peace."[20]

The *Superior Telegram* predicted that economic and logistical issues would likely bring a swift end to the war:

> But another condition will count even more strongly [than the decline in commerce] for an early termination of the war. Each country involved in the war has provided a "war chest" of several hundred million dollars for immediate use. . . . The accumulations are large, but the heavy cost of war will use them all up in a few months. . . . Their credit will be gone.
>
> But when the means of war are exhausted the struggle must cease. . . . Even the winners will be great losers in this gigantic

struggle. The most hopeful feature of the situation is that the end may come soon.[21]

The *Eau Claire Leader* offered a more specific and, seemingly, more scientific prediction made by officials from the E. I. Dupont de Namoura Powder Company that the "war couldn't last 6 months." The officials reasoned that the six-month shelf life of smokeless powder would prevent the belligerents from maintaining stockpiles of powder large enough to sustain a long conflict.[22]

Unfortunately, predictions of a short war were hopelessly optimistic. As the conflict settled into the stalemate of trench warfare, hope for an early peace evaporated. The First Battle of Ypres in October–November 1914 demonstrated the lethal effect of modern weapons. As each side tried to outflank the other, the battle produced little more than dead and wounded soldiers. The two sides suffered more than 238,000 casualties during a month and a half of fighting, and the world was shocked at the carnage. Neither side was able to break through the other's defenses, and the battle signaled the end of open, flexible warfare on the western front. By the end of 1914, the opposing armies were well entrenched. Their fortifications stretched nearly four hundred miles from the Swiss boarder to the English Channel.

As the stalemate began on the western front, US banks and industries became the financiers and arms merchants to the Allies. Although businesses in the United States were willing to sell munitions and supplies to both sides of the conflict, the British navy effectively controlled the Atlantic Ocean and the North Sea and prevented US shipments to Germany from reaching their destination. This British blockade sparked protests by the American government, but Wilson declined to take forceful action to defend American rights to free transit of the high seas. Although still officially "neutral," the United States quickly became a major supplier and financier to Great Britain, France, Russia, and Italy. In 1914, US foreign trade with Allied countries equaled more than $824 million. Two years later that figure rose to more than $3.2 billion—a 390 percent increase. In contrast, trade with Germany and Austria-Hungary fell by 99 percent in that same period, from a modest $169 million in 1914 to a meager $1.1 million in 1916. By April 1917, American banks provided an additional $2.3

billion in cash and credit to the Allied nations; Germany received only $27 million during the same period. Wilson may have charted a neutral course, but American business and banking interests were solidly aligned with the Allies.[23]

PROPOSALS TO PROMOTE PEACE

As tensions increased between Germany and the United States, most Wisconsin residents, regardless of sympathies, wanted nothing to do with naval blockades or the murderous stalemate of trench warfare, and 1915 became a year for peace proposals.

On February 8, La Follette introduced into the Senate what came to be known as the La Follette Peace Resolution. He feared a resurgence of corporate power would dominate American life and politics at the expense of earlier progressive reforms. La Follette's resolution called for a conference of neutral nations to promote an early end to hostilities through mediation. La Follette hoped the conference would make future wars less likely by creating a forum for consideration of arms limitations, nationalization of military manufacturing, and limits on the export of war supplies. The resolution also called for the ultimate establishment of a tribunal to adjudicate international disputes and a federation of neutral nations to safeguard world peace. The proposal suffered for lack of support in the Senate and died in committee.[24]

Newspaper columns, particularly editorials, continued to both shape and reflect public support for neutrality. In the spring of 1915, an editorial in the La Crosse Tribune praised Wilson for his policy of "too proud to fight." War could be rendered obsolete, the editorial argued, if all nations adopted a policy of fighting only when invaded.[25]

By the summer of 1915 the raw horror on the battlefields of the western front fueled a growing peace movement. In Wisconsin, the proliferation of peace organizations and peace proposals mirrored the pacifist sentiment that prevailed during the early years of the war. While Belle La Follette participated in founding the national Woman's Peace Party, prominent Wisconsin women founded the state Peace Party. Meta Berger helped found the Milwaukee Peace League, which later affiliated with the Peace Party. Rose Keefe organized a La Crosse chapter of the International Conference of Women Workers, which advocated for permanent world peace and received strong support from local women and business owners.[26]

A plan born in Wisconsin was in many ways the most successful amateur attempt to bring peace to Europe. It was the brainchild of Julia Grace Wales, an English instructor and Shakespeare scholar at the University of Wisconsin. Titled "Continuous Mediation Without Armistice," Grace Wales's plan generated sustained interest among members of the peace movement. Supporters soon began calling it the Wisconsin Peace Plan. Wales proposed an international conference of neutral experts who would develop proposals and bring them to the warring countries. This process could be repeated and refined as many times as necessary without the prerequisite of an armistice. The Wisconsin Plan only required that neutral parties agree to mediate and that warring parties agree to listen.

The Wisconsin Peace Plan was promoted by the Wisconsin Peace Society, unanimously approved by the National Peace Conference, and endorsed by the San Francisco International Peace Conference. The Wisconsin Legislature endorsed the plan and recommended it for consideration by the United States Congress. Wales and Jane Addams took the plan to the International Congress of Peace in May 1915 at The Hague. The Peace Congress unanimously endorsed it.

When the Wisconsin Federation of Women's Clubs met in La Crosse in October 1915, the club women adopted the Wisconsin Peace Plan in a resolution calling for "an International Commission drawn from neutral nations of Europe and U.S. to submit to the belligerent nations propositions in the hope that such effort will not only clear the ground for final Peace negotiations but also influence such terms of settlement as will make for a constructive and lasting Peace." Anna Hardwicke Pennybacker, national president of the General Federation of Women's Clubs, attended the Wisconsin convention, as she had done in more than twenty-five other states. "This country wants peace," she told a *La Crosse Tribune* reporter. "The great silent masses of this country want peace. I have observed everywhere I have spoken that nothing else brought forth the spontaneous, hearty applause that followed a reference to peace. The spirit of national unity on this issue is wonderful. It is not confined to the clubwomen. It is general in everyone."[27]

Although it was widely promoted across the United States and Europe, the Wisconsin Peace Plan ultimately failed for lack of official support. Two basic ingredients were needed for the plan to succeed. First, the United States government or another major neutral country had to put its weight and authority behind the plan and host a convention of experts; second, the belligerent nations needed to participate. But Wilson never offered the effort his cooperation, and the warring nations, believing in their own victory, lacked any incentive to participate.

Nationally, in December 1915, Henry Ford captured public attention when he chartered the *Oscar II* and embarked on a quixotic voyage to bring peace to Europe. The Ford peace expedition failed for lack of cooperation with national governments, an outbreak of the flu, and infighting among the activists onboard.

The peace movement would effectively disintegrate with American entry into the war in April 1917.[28]

The War Preparedness Movement

Great Britain, with the world's greatest navy, imposed a blockade on the Central Powers in 1914 with the clear goal of starving Germany into submission. On February 4, 1915, Germany responded by declaring the waters around the British Isles to be a war zone in which German submarines would attempt to destroy all Allied vessels and would not guarantee the safety of neutral ships. Germany also refused to guarantee the safety of crews and passengers. In the weeks that followed, submarines sank freighters on a regular basis. One American died in the sinking of the British passenger liner *Falaba*, and three more Americans lost their lives on May 1, when a U-boat torpedoed the *Gulflight*, an American tanker. The stage was set for a major naval disaster.

Worried about the repercussions that might result from the deaths of Americans at the hands of submarine captains, the German Embassy took out an advertisement in the New York newspapers warning Americans not to sail on Allied vessels. On May 1, 1915, the *Lusitania*, one of the largest, fastest, most luxurious passenger ships afloat, left port bound for England. Seven days later the grand ship lay on the bottom of the Atlantic off the coast of Ireland, victim of a German torpedo and the exploding munitions secretly stored in her hold. The ship sank in eighteen minutes and took with it the lives of 1,198 passengers, including 128 Americans.

Disasters such as the sinking of the *Lusitania* made it difficult for the average American to remain neutral. As relations with Germany deteriorated, Teddy Roosevelt, the National Security League, and other politicians and pundits began expressing concern that the meager US Army was ill-prepared to fight a modern war in Europe.

Traditionally, American political leaders had viewed the existence of a large standing army as a direct threat to democratic government and they saw little need for that kind of military establishment. What was known as the Regular Army consisted of only 51,446 men and 2,935 officers available for frontline duty. The "organized militia," also known as the National Guard, could augment the Regular Army with an additional 119,087 enlisted men and 8,323 officers. But none of these men were trained or equipped to fight the kind of modern war then developing in Europe.[29]

As early as August 1914, Roosevelt complained privately that the US Army was in no condition to defend the nation. Roosevelt believed the attack on Belgium warranted an American response and would have preferred righteous intervention on behalf of the weak. He fumed that Wilsonian policy options were constrained by a military weakness that emasculated the nation's foreign policy and limited the range of responses available in a crisis.[30]

Roosevelt was not alone in calling for strengthened defenses. The National Security League, founded in New York City in December 1914, soon became the largest and most influential group advocating for war preparedness and universal military training and service. By the end of 1915, the league boasted thirty thousand members with chapters across the country. Wisconsin's first chapter, organized in Milwaukee by the Merchants and Manufacturers Association, thrived to become the second largest in the Midwest, after Chicago.[31]

Initially Wilson questioned the need for a preparedness movement. In his annual message to Congress on December 8, 1914, Wilson said, "In Europe it [the war] is destroying men and resources wholesale and upon a scale unprecedented and appalling." He argued instead for legislation that would develop a strong merchant marine fleet to be used when the United States was called upon to help rebuild Europe after the war.

Near the end of his speech Wilson responded to Roosevelt and other critics calling for greater military preparedness. The president spoke plainly: "It is said in some quarters that we are not prepared for war. What is meant by being prepared? Is it meant that we are not ready upon brief notice to put a nation in the field, a nation of men trained to arms? Of course we are not ready to do that; and we shall never be in time of peace so long as we retain our present political principles and institutions."

In Wilson's early view of the war, the best preparation was a strong National Guard. He reminded his audience that "we must depend in every time of national peril, in the future as in the past, not upon a standing Army, nor yet upon a reserve army, but upon a citizenry trained and accustomed to arms." [32]

Wisconsin Governor Emanuel Philipp exercised ultimate authority over the Wisconsin National Guard. A businessman, Philipp was elected governor in 1914 as a stalwart Republican who pledged to curtail or eliminate state agencies, commissions, boards, and programs that reflected progressive reforms or had grown, in his opinion, bloated and out of control. Once in office, however, he repeatedly demonstrated a willingness to listen and evaluate without the blindness of an ideologue. He reversed course in several instances, most notably when he maintained funding for the Legislative Reference Library and University of Wisconsin–Extension, institutions he had originally planned to eliminate or reduce. He abandoned plans to merge the Railroad and Tax Commissions in order to maintain each agency's distinct and technical work, although he moved forward with combining the State Park Board, Fish and Game Commission, Forestry Board, and State Conservation Commission to create a unified department to manage Wisconsin's wildlife, forests, and parks. In short, Philipp was a governor who took the time to understand proposals and recommendations, and he was willing to change his preconceived opinions when they did not match reality. This was the man who would be Wisconsin's war governor. [33]

In August 1915, Philipp became an early proponent of war preparedness when he voiced concern over the woefully inadequate US Army. He advocated a stronger army capable of defending the nation should neutrality and peace efforts fail, augmented by a trained citizenry, like the National Guard but broader in scope. He appointed eighteen mayors to a committee that would cooperate with the National Security League and coordinate preparedness. [34]

Back in Washington, La Follette believed nothing in Europe could be of such grave importance to the United States as to warrant American participation in the carnage. He consistently advocated measures to bring an end to the war or prevent US entanglement. During the first year of the war, La Follette and Wilson shared similar perspectives on American involvement. But by 1916 the preparedness movement had driven a wedge between the two political leaders. Independent of whether the United States went to war, Wilson had determined that the United States could not isolate itself from events in Europe, but should prepare its own defense. When Wilson's preparedness program came before Congress in July 1916, La Follette spoke in opposition for seven hours. He staunchly believed most Americans did not want war or preparedness and that large corporate interests would use the war to increase their profits. It was a classic La Follette position—progressives and peace versus corporate interests and war.[35]

La Follette favored coastal fortifications and artillery and a mobile force of soldiers sufficient to defend our sea and land borders. He saw no need for a larger navy and argued the nation's existing military force offered "adequate" protection, thanks in part to the buffer provided by the large oceans to the east and west. If a real danger confronted the country, La Follette believed the people would rise up in defense of the nation. Ultimately, he and the preparedness advocates had two very different goals. La Follette believed in a defense capable of defending the continental United States. Preparedness advocates wanted a military capable of fighting in Europe.[36]

At home in Wisconsin, Congressman Esch took a moderate approach to national defense. He reassured constituents, "You can rest assured that I am not one who wishes this country to rush into war without full justification." He believed that "prudence dictates that there should be a reasonable increase in both Army and Navy comporting with our needs and our growing strength as a nation. I regret to say that the time has not yet come when 'Peace on earth, good will toward men' has become the rule of conduct, either of individuals or states."[37]

Esch believed that the best method of protecting American security was through a strengthened National Guard with a more unified national structure. The industrial and inventive resources of the nation should be mobilized, he argued, and, as an emergency precaution, the nation should stockpile war material.[38]

By the spring of 1916, many Wisconsinites favored some form of war preparedness but still wanted nothing to do with the war in Europe. Esch sent his constituents a questionnaire to gather public sentiment on the war. His constituents' responses were "practically unanimous in favor of preparation of some kind and to some extent, but there is great contrarity of view as to where increases should be made or what arm of the service should be most strengthened." H. H. Thomas from Baraboo emphasized that the question was not whether to prepare but how much preparation was enough. A young bank cashier at the La Crosse County Bank in West Salem polled his customers before returning the questionnaire; all of his customers favored a better army and navy. Clark County Judge Oscar Schoengarth wrote to Esch, "I am in favor of reasonable preparedness but am against getting into trouble with other countries on trifles."[39]

The national preparedness campaign gradually gained momentum and swept the nation by the summer of 1916, when patriotic parades and demonstrations were organized across the country, including massive parades in New York City and Chicago. Milwaukee hosted its own preparedness parade on Saturday, July 15, along a 3.2-mile route down Grand Avenue and Wisconsin Street, festooned with American flags. Although the parade started at 2 p.m., spectators began arriving early in the morning. Many in the crowd wore white with accents of red and blue and carried American flags. All along the route, every room with a view—hotel rooms, apartments, store display windows—were rented or reserved for spectators. July in Milwaukee was often temperate, with cool breezes blowing inland from Lake Michigan. Unfortunately, on parade day the temperature was eighty-three degrees; it was humid and sweltering.

The *Milwaukee Leader* described the weather: "But the best prepared were illy prepared for such an onslaught as that Humidity made. He showed no mercy. Heat oozed from the mushy asphalt. Heat oozed from sidewalks of cement. Heat crushed down from above, rebounded from below."

Half an hour before the parade was scheduled to start, rain offered some damp relief from the oppressive heat. The parade went forth, festive in spite of the soaking rain. The *Milwaukee Leader* reported, "Grand Avenue and Wisconsin Street were not black with people, but red, white, and blue with them. The national colors dominated everything, the buildings, gay with flags and bunting, the marching multitude which, as it moved down the avenue, resembled a great undulating wave of banners, and watchers, as many as the marchers and more, with white gowns, patriotic parasols and buttonieres [sic]."[40]

Parade organizers predicted between 150,000 and 200,000 spectators would watch 70,000 marchers. Although the parade fell far short of these levels, it was hailed as a great success and received heavy press coverage. As the *Milwaukee Journal* headline proclaimed: 28,253 MEN AND WOMEN BY COUNT IN GREAT PREPAREDNESS PARADE OFFER TESTIMONY TO THE LOYALTY AND PATRIOTISM OF MILWAUKEE.

A platoon of police led the march, followed by a band and then the parade committee and city and county officials. The consummate politician, Governor Philipp stood in his car for two and a half hours, waving and saluting as the marchers passed: bands, veterans, fraternal orders, wom-

The *Milwaukee Journal* actively promoted the city's preparedness march and wrapped the event in the flag, a symbol of patriotism. *MILWAUKEE JOURNAL*, JULY 15, 1916

REAL PREPAREDNESS.

8 HOUR DAY
SOCIAL DEMOCRACY
SOCIAL JUSTICE
BETTER LIVING
CONDITIONS
EMANCIPATION
OF LABOR

WORKER!

THE BALLOT

GOOD NATURE.

The Socialist Party was contemptuous of the preparedness movement and its emphasis on military strength, which would only line the pockets of arms makers and bring the nation closer to war. In the Socialist view, only a healthy working class exerting its power at the ballot box would secure the nation. *MILWAUKEE LEADER*, JULY 15, 1916

en's organizations, service groups, and employees of many of Milwaukee's insurance, banking, and industrial companies. A dog even got into the act. Shortly after the parade began its way through the heart of the city, a sable collie expropriated the lead position until Seventh Street. "He ran back and forth, barking at motorcycle officers and enjoying himself generally."[41]

Socialists and many progressives feared that a large army, as advo-cated by preparedness supporters, could bring repression at home and, when augmented by a large navy, imperialism abroad. But they were not pacifists; they supported the National Guard, the "organized militia" con-trolled by the governor and comprised of neighbors, brothers, fathers, and friends. Support for the Guard grew even stronger after the federal government mobilized almost the entire National Guard from across the country for duty in Texas during the 1916 Mexican border crisis. People hailed that mobilization as evidence of American military readiness. By the time the soldiers had returned home at the beginning of 1917, the war in Europe had drawn so close that opposition to preparedness never re-appeared in strength.

Military readiness was an illusion. Although the US military in 1917 was, in reality, woefully unprepared for modern warfare, the Mexican border crisis, the mobilization of the National Guard, and the prepared-ness debate helped Americans adjust to the concept of going to war. The preparedness campaigns implied a willingness to fight and a realization that US involvement was possible, if not imminent. Conflict on the Mexi-can border highlighted the need for a larger and more modern army and made it more difficult for the anti-preparedness movement to withstand the pressures pushing the nation toward war.

An Escalation of War

The British naval blockade was gradually starving the life out of the Central Powers. As the last of the Wisconsin Guard units returned home from the US-Mexico border, Germany announced it was resuming unrestricted submarine warfare. Its submarines would sink all ships in the war zone re-gardless of whether they were military, passenger, or merchant. The Ger-man government recognized this drastic measure might force the United States into the war, but they calculated their submarine fleet could neu-tralize Great Britain before US troops had the chance to enter the fray.

One month later, the United States broke diplomatic relations with Germany and began a downward spiral toward war. Unrestricted sub-marine warfare violated the rights of non-belligerents to ply the seas unmolested, and it violated American moral sensibilities. Because *unter-*

seeboots were fragile and easily sunk, German submarine captains attacked without giving the crew and passengers an opportunity to escape in life boats. Sinking ships without warning seemed to many observers to be barbaric.

On February 4, 1917, the *Wisconsin State Journal* predicted: ACTUAL WAR BUT STEP AWAY. An editorial that same day called the Kaiser "the big brutal bully of the world" and delivered an ominous message to German Americans: "The time to parley and apologize, to compromise and to cover is gone. Every American voter must be one-hundred per cent an American citizen. Anything less is TREASON. . . . Our greatest danger comes not from without our borders but from the half-made Americans within our borders. We can no longer compromise. The time has come when America expects every citizen to be every inch an AMERICAN."[42]

To defend against the renewed threat of submarine warfare, Wilson spoke to Congress on Monday, February 26, and requested authority and funds to arm merchant ships. This request ended whatever tenuous connections La Follette had with Wilson's administration. La Follette argued "it was unnecessary for [Wilson] to have taken that step & it puts us in a perilous position where it won't take much to push us clear over the line." La Follette was convinced that the estimated $100 million cost of arming the merchant marine fleet was too expensive, that it gave the president too much power, and that it was tantamount to a declaration of war. As this "perilous position" became more and more tenuous, La Follette all the more strongly opposed measures he felt would lead to war. His struggle against the administration culminated in his filibuster of the Armed Ship Bill.[43]

The bill easily passed in the House on a vote of 403 to 13. La Follette believed that a delay of even a few days could mean the difference between peace and war. So when the bill came to the Senate, La Follette successfully requested that it be taken up on March 2.

On February 29, Wilson released a secret German cable that had been intercepted by the British. It was a message from Germany's foreign secretary Arthur Zimmermann instructing the German minister in Mexico to negotiate an alliance with Mexico should the United States declare war. In return, Germany promised that Mexico could reclaim much of Texas, New Mexico, and Arizona. Release of the Zimmermann telegram heightened

As the preparedness movement swept the nation and public opinion turned against Germany, the loyalty of immigrant communities increasingly came into question by advocates of preparedness. A year before the declaration of war, the seeds of intolerant patriotism had already taken root. To be loyal was equated with assimilation. Sympathy for Germany, hostility toward England or France, speaking German instead of English, criticizing American foreign policy—all were signs of questionable loyalty. *EAU CLAIRE LEADER*, MARCH 9, 1916

US animosity toward Germany and, in some circles, was considered an act of war.

In this politically charged atmosphere Wisconsin's senior senator organized a filibuster of the Armed Ship Bill. Debate began at 4 p.m. on March 2. The end of the congressional term was fast approaching on March 4. If La Follette and other antiwar senators could control the debate until noon on the fourth, they could prevent a vote and the bill would need to be reintroduced in the next session. The tactic would buy time and perhaps prevent war. It was an emotional, sometimes Kafkaesque scene as senators screamed at one another as they put forth the case for a positive or negative vote. La Follette dominated the scene. Walking the floor, ridiculing his colleagues, nurturing his own excitement as the culminating speaker, La Follette was a commanding presence. Tempers ran high. There were rumors of violence against La Follette and plans by his friends to stand in his defense. Having heard that Ollie James of Kentucky was carrying a gun and might attack La Follette, Harry Lane from Oregon armed himself with a rat-tail file to use as a dagger. La Follette also anticipated trouble and asked his son Bobbie to bring his traveling bag to the Senate. The bag contained the revolver La Follette carried for protection when traveling; Bobbie surreptitiously removed the pistol from the bag before delivering the traveling case to the Senate. Each side of the debate defined their position as vitally important to the future of the nation. As their behavior suggested, they were playing for high stakes.[44]

As the debate stretched into the morning of March 4, La Follette's colleagues realized the bill would die without a vote. La Follette had reserved for himself the final two hours of the filibuster, during which he had planned to deliver a grand and eloquent speech. His opponents could not force a vote, but they could humiliate him. Quietly his opponents secured approval of a list of speakers to precede La Follette. The list of speakers was so long that the clock would run out on the congressional session before La Follette could deliver his cherished speech. As the clock ticked off the waning minutes of the session, La Follette was relegated to his chair, fuming as he listened to others speak.

For La Follette it was a great moral victory, but he had made himself one of the most detested members of the Senate and the target of editorial venom in newspapers across the country. Wilson described the filibustering senators: "A little group of willful men, representing no opinion but their own, have rendered the great government of the United States helpless and contemptible." Wilson concluded he did not need congressional authority to arm merchant vessels after all. Using his authority as commander-in-chief, he bypassed Congress and implemented the arming of merchant ships.[45]

When Bob La Follette led eleven other senators to filibuster a bill authorizing President Woodrow Wilson to arm merchant vessels so they could defend themselves if attacked by a submarine, the filibustering senators faced a firestorm of criticism. The iron cross, Germany's highest award for bravery, had already become a symbol of traitorous behavior in the American press. *DALLAS MORNING NEWS*, MARCH 6, 1917

"The Litmus Test of Patriotism"

There was no consensus in the congressional delegation, among Wisconsin's voters, or in the newspapers about the proper course regarding preparedness, arming merchant ships, diplomacy, or a declaration of war. The majority of Wisconsin's congressional delegation voted consistently against measures they thought might draw the nation closer to war.[46] But the delegation found itself at odds with the rising national tide of bellicose anti-German attitudes and rhetoric. In Wisconsin, Richard Lloyd Jones, the young progressive owner and editor of the *Wisconsin State Journal*, had little patience for La Follette and his allies. In two separate editorials on March 6, the *Journal* labeled La Follette's actions on armed neutrality "most unamerican" and stated that, "in obstructing [by filibuster] the right of the Senate to register its will and in his failure to stand behind the President, La Follette has misrepresented Wisconsin." The paper readily labeled La Follette pro-German and equated pacifism with "bought-and-paid-for German propaganda." Support for Wilson and for war were rapidly becoming the litmus test of patriotism.[47]

As relations with Germany deteriorated so did the Wisconsin antiwar consensus. That spring, faculty of the University of Wisconsin voiced their support of Wilson's Armed Ship Bill and denounced the twelve senators who had filibustered. On March 31, 1917, the *Monroe Evening Times* reported patriotic parades and meetings in Madison, Fond du Lac, Green Bay, Superior, Oshkosh, La Crosse, Racine, Appleton, Beloit, Janesville, Kenosha, Marinette, and Wausau.[48]

But the rise in patriotic rhetoric did not directly translate into pro-war sentiment. For example, the German American community in Wisconsin generally remained opposed to United States involvement in the war.[49] And in letters to Esch and his colleague Henry Cooper, from Wisconsin's first district, voters continued to voice a preference for peace, although a growing number of constituents had concluded that war might be undesirable but necessary.[50] In February and March of 1917, not a single letter sent to Esch's office conveyed a desire to go to war, but a few writers supported preparedness, the president, or universal military service. The shift in focus was small in real numbers but quite marked compared to the earlier antiwar mail.

The mood of the electorate was clearly changing. In Spring Green, the Grand Army of the Republic Post No. 24 applauded Esch's support for the Armed Ship Bill. The Black River Falls Commercial Club sent Esch a letter plainly stating that "all true and loyal American citizens . . . should unqualifiedly support the President."[51]

Esch also had the benefit of an independent informant. His brother, William, was a postal inspector who traveled extensively across the state and who reported that most people agreed with arming the merchant fleet. In William's opinion, support for La Follette was evaporating.[52]

What Will Esch experienced probably was not a meaningful decline in support for La Follette but the rise of a vocal patriotic opposition to the senator. Unlike most representatives and senators, La Follette possessed a national reputation and had become a symbol for war opposition. According to La Follette, 90 percent of the letters he received were from supporters across the country. Based on this correspondence and his overwhelming victory in the 1916 Wisconsin election, La Follette believed the people of Wisconsin and the nation still wanted to stay out of the war.[53]

In addition, Victor Berger and the Socialist Party maintained a consistent position against any participation in a capitalist war. Shortly after Germany renewed unrestricted submarine warfare, Berger reasserted the party's position in an editorial titled "Let's End This War":

> There is no question that Germany's proclamation of unrestricted undersea boat warfare may bring about a break between the United States and Germany. The new German policy undoubtedly will interfere with business—especially with our ammunition and war business—and our capitalist class cannot stand for that. Moreover, our capitalists have been in partnership with the English capitalists all the time—during this war more than ever—and unless the allies win these investments will be lost.

Berger criticized J. P. Morgan, Theodore Roosevelt, and Charles Edward Russell for supporting war with Germany to protect their investments in the Allied war effort and for labeling anyone who disagreed as a German propagandist or anarchist. Berger favored a truly neutral position supported by a complete embargo designed to end the war by starving the war machines.[54]

By the time Wilson was poised to call for a declaration of war, whatever consensus that had once existed in Wisconsin had been replaced by an increasingly rigid divide. On one side stood German loyalists who would never be comfortable with war against the fatherland. On the other side were super patriots for whom anything German would be anathema, Americanization of immigrants was a hallowed goal, and any criticism of the war or nation should be a punishable offense. In the great middle between these two poles stood most residents of Wisconsin. It was impossible for the state's congressional delegation, or anyone else, to know with any precision how the majority wanted them to vote. They had to rely on impressions based on conversations and correspondence with constituents, newspaper accounts, and their own consciences.[55]

A Declaration of War

As April drew near it would have been obvious to anyone reading the newspapers anywhere in the country that war was only days away. In Wisconsin, state and local officials began planning for the security of local utilities and bridges over the Mississippi. The Third Wisconsin Infantry Regiment mobilized to guard infrastructure in northern Wisconsin and Minnesota. The National Red Cross Bureau of Supplies asked all of its chapters to report on their work capacity. Some of the state normal schools responsible for training most of Wisconsin's teachers began planning a course of "military training for the students and faculty."[56]

By April 1917, German brutality in Belgium, accentuated by skillful British propaganda, made it increasingly easy to believe the image of the bestial Hun. Americans read the daily news of renewed submarine warfare and deteriorating diplomatic relations. They read the Zimmerman telegram, which reinforced the idea of Germany as enemy. Many Americans still opposed US entry, but these events helped make the transition to war feel justifiable.[57]

In a long letter to her children back in Wisconsin, Belle La Follette expressed what must have been a common sentiment: a hope that peace might still be possible and a resignation that war was likely around the corner. She concluded the letter: "No one seems to doubt that Congress will declare war and yet I hope. It seems to me as though the catastrophe *must* be averted. . . . But more likely the situation is gone past control and the only chance of escaping war is some change in the European situation that may avert it."[58]

Events had clearly "gone past control." The language of public discourse began to create a clear dichotomy between the righteous people of the United States and the bestial Hun. As Congress prepared to assemble for Wilson's war message, an article in the *Wisconsin State Journal* created the emotional foundation for going to war. Senator Furnifold Simmons from North Carolina outlined what was at stake: "The interests of America demand that tyranny be beaten." Texas Representative Joe Eagle made the struggle more basic and visceral: "The Kaiser is a cave man with murder in his heart. . . . He is bent on the unwavering course of brute force and pillage. He must be put down or the democracies of the world are doomed." The language of peace, neutrality, and forbearance had given way to the language of war: bellicose, dehumanizing, and designed to create a noble enterprise worthy of the sacrifice of thousands of lives. The language of the congressmen ("tyranny," "cave man," "put down," "doomed") made it clear the nation faced a subhuman rival determined to subjugate its enemies under a brutal and tyrannical regime. According to the newspaper, a war in defense of "humanity and democracy" was the only choice. Nothing less than the future of the nation was at stake.[59]

Wilson called the Congress into special joint session on April 2, 1917, for the purpose of declaring war on Germany. He began his address with a recitation of the history of the submarine war. Although the freedom to travel on the high seas had been the nation's major grievance against Germany, Wilson emphasized a much higher objective:

> The present German submarine warfare against commerce is a warfare against mankind. . . . It is a war against all nations. . . . We must put excited feeling away. Our motive will not be revenge or the victorious assertion of the physical might of the nation, but only the vindication of right, of which we are only a single champion.

The president concluded by reminding his audience of his goals:

> But the right is more precious than peace, and we shall fight for those things which we have always carried nearest our hearts—for democ-

racy, for the right of those who submit to authority to have a voice in their own governments, for the rights and liberties of small nations, for a universal dominion of right by such a concert of free peoples as shall bring peace and safety to all nations and make the world itself at last free.[60]

At the conclusion of Wilson's address, most members of the audience rose to their feet. But La Follette stayed rooted to his seat with arms tightly crossed over his chest. He saw little in Wilson's remarks or in the arguments of others to convince him that war was the proper course. La Follette was ready to do battle in defense of peace.

The congressional debate that ensued hinged on the definition of what constituted an act of war. But the outcome was never much in doubt. The vast majority of senators and representatives entered the debate ready to vote for war. When La Follette took the floor to speak, he faced an overwhelmingly hostile audience. Undeterred, he implied that his colleagues were blindly following the president instead of thinking for themselves—an approach typical for La Follette but not designed to endear him to his colleagues. To demonstrate that the will of his constituents was against the war, La Follette cited referenda in Monroe and Sheboygan that showed overwhelming support for peace. La Follette had received similar communications from around the country.

La Follette reminded his colleagues that Germany had begun its aggressive submarine warfare after the Royal Navy choked off commerce with Germany by mining the North Sea and blockading sea lanes. If Germany is engaged in "a war against all nations," he asked his colleagues, why are the other nations of the world not up in arms? Wilson had called the war a fight for democracy and against German autocracy. La Follette stretched the credulity of his colleagues and the modern reader by likening the German monarchy, which by 1917 was close to being a military dictatorship, to the British monarchy. Finally, he charged that the United States had never been neutral; had the nation been truly neutral instead of trading with the Allies, Congress would not now be asked to declare war. As he finished, La Follette stood silently with tears streaming down his face.

John Sharp Williams, Democratic senator from Mississippi, responded immediately:

Mr. President [president pro tem of the Senate], if immortality could be attained by verbal eternity, the Senator from Wisconsin would have approximated immortality. We have waited and have heard a speech from him which would have better become Herr Betmann-Hollweg, of the German Parliament, than an American Senator. . . . I fully expected before he took his seat to hear him defend the invasion of Belgium—the most absolutely barbarous act that ever took place in the history of any nation anywhere. I heard from him a speech which was pro-German, pretty nearly pro-Goth, and pro-Vandal, which was anti–American President and anti–American Congress, and anti–American people.

When Williams relinquished the floor, Wisconsin's junior senator, Paul Husting, also a Democrat, delivered a measured defense of Wisconsin and a rebuttal of La Follette's arguments. Husting suggested that in any war referendum, virtually everyone would vote for no war. "But that is not the question," Husting said. "The question is, shall the people of the United States suffer Germany to make war on us without defending ourselves?" The argument boiled down to a simple question: Did Germany's submarine warfare rise to the level of "making war" on the United States? La Follette would answer no; Husting would answer yes.

Husting defended the loyalty of Wisconsin's German Americans and then turned his attention to refuting La Follette's arguments. He acknowledged that Great Britain had confiscated American ships and cargo illegally and mined the North Sea. Nonetheless, he argued, a qualitative difference existed between the two sides. Grievances against the Allies were about confiscation of property. In stark contrast, Germany was actively engaged in killing Americans: "Again and again boats were sunk without warning, and again and again men, women, and children went down to their death [sic] defenseless and undefended. So, in all, 310 American lives have been ruthlessly and wantonly taken [by Germany]." To Husting the moral dichotomy was clear: Both Germany and Great Britain sowed mines in the North Sea. If a ship hit one of those mines, it might sink. In contrast, when a German submarine captain torpedoed an unsuspecting freighter or passenger ship, the captain committed a willful act, an act of war.

La Follette and Husting each played critical roles in the Senate debate.

They helped clarify and define the issues distinguishing the pro-war and antiwar factions. Husting voted in favor of the joint resolution declaring war and, as expected, La Follette voted against. The final tally was eighty-two votes in favor, six votes against, with eight Senators not voting.[61] As everyone had expected, the Senate voted overwhelmingly to go to war.

On April 5, the House of Representatives took up the debate. Representative Henry Flood of Virginia, chairman of the Foreign Affairs Committee, opened the debate with a recitation of the grievances against Germany. Henry Cooper, of Wisconsin's first congressional district, argued, as had La Follette, that England had violated American rights and sunk American ships by mining the North Sea. Cooper could see no good reason for war with England or Germany. He concluded with a clear sense of resignation: "My time has expired. I assume that the war is to come. . . . When it comes we will be united in support of the Government. I shall do all that I can to help achieve a victory for our country, but I shall not vote to send the Nation to war in accordance with this resolution."[62]

In response, Flood delivered the clearest, most succinct explanation of the pro-war perspective: "Germany has murdered over 250 of our people. We are going to war with Germany for murdering American citizens who were sailing the high seas under the American flag, and who have the right to expect the American Nation to protect them, for murdering American citizens in violation of the laws of God and man, in violation of Germany's treaties and its promises."

The debate went on for some eighteen hours, much of it repetitive. Congressmen debated the actions of the belligerents, the meaning of international law, and the costs of war. From the Wisconsin delegation, Cooper, William Stafford, and Edward Browne spoke against the war. Irvine Lenroot spoke in favor. In the end, the House voted 373 to 50 to go to war. The Midwest, with its large German and Scandinavian populations and its agrarian reformers and progressive politicians, became the heart of antiwar sentiment. Although it is difficult to judge the level of opposition with any certainty, a majority of Wisconsin residents probably still opposed taking sides as late as April 1917. Almost certainly voting the will of their constituents, nine of Wisconsin's eleven representatives voted against the declaration of war.[63]

War of any kind is a messy, nasty business. World War I was a "total war"—a war that required harnessing the total resources of the nation toward the goal of defeating the enemy. Ideally, the process of going to war should have produced a national consensus to fuel the patriotic pursuit of victory. The United States went to war without a consensus, especially in Wisconsin. Although most opponents of going to war quickly fell into line or fell silent, the lack of consensus placed Wisconsin society under stresses that were both unnecessary and counterproductive.

On April 6, 1917, the United States went to war. Wilson called the National Guard back to the colors, the nation began building a massive national army, and the Council of Defense began mobilizing the entire society. To fight the war would require great sacrifice on the battlefield and the home front. No one would escape playing a role in the fight against Germany. Americans would be called to give their sons and daughters to the cause, to conserve food and donate money, and to honor the flag with a loyal heart and patriotic spirit. Total war demanded total commitment to fight a war unlike anything Americans had seen before.

CHAPTER 3

The 32nd Division, "*Les Terribles*"

A people go to war as a nation. Soldiers fight for a cause or country; they fight as members of military units; they fight for their comrades. But war is experienced by individuals. The individual feels the anger, fear, joy, happiness, sorrow. The individual feels the pain, becomes disabled, dies. At home, the individual's family and friends care for the returning wounded soldier, mourn the soldier's passing, or celebrate his return.

The history of Wisconsin's military participation in the Great War is in many ways the history of individual experiences. Approximately 118,000 young men from Wisconsin, 5 percent of the state's population, served in the military during the war, and the vast majority saw duty in the army. Although many servicemen never saw combat, Wisconsin's National Guard was well represented on the western front. Of the Wisconsin servicemen, 18,000 were members of the National Guard. An additional 10,000 enlisted during the patriotic fervor of the first weeks of war. The final 90,000 soldiers were drafted into the armed forces during the fifteen months from June 1917 to November 1918. They were assigned to units wherever they were needed, filling the ranks of the rapidly expanding army.[1]

The single largest concentration of Wisconsin troops served in the 32nd Division. The letters, diaries, and reminiscences of Wisconsin soldiers in the 32nd Division provide a window through which we can explore what it meant to be a soldier in the Great War and the shared experience that developed between soldiers and friends and family on the home front.

In mid-July 1917, the army created the 32nd Division by merging fifteen thousand Wisconsin National Guardsmen with eight thousand National Guard troops from Michigan. This left the new division approximately four thousand troops short of war strength. The War Department made up the difference with three thousand draftees from Wisconsin and one thousand draftees from Michigan.

Americans on the home front participated in the war most directly by giving their sons, brothers, husbands, friends, and neighbors to national service in the armed forces. Wisconsinites, like their fellow Americans in other states, experienced the war through letters sent home by friends and loved ones, combined with newspaper coverage of the war. In their letters home, soldiers shared a version of their experiences that was often sanitized and sometimes censored, but that nonetheless allowed readers to understand a little about life at the front. Local newspaper coverage of the war provided context within which to understand personal communications from men at the front. Individual participation coalesced into community involvement when the National Guard mobilized and host communities saw their "boys" off with great fanfare. These public celebrations allowed local communities to honor the patriotic spirit of the departing troops and express heartfelt good-byes. Communities inevitably reflected some of their soldiers' patriotic glow.

TRAINING ON THE MEXICAN BORDER

The people of Wisconsin got their first taste of war when the Mexican Revolution turned into a civil war and different factions battled for supremacy. As the violence spilled across the border, communities throughout the United States received a firsthand introduction to preparedness and the meaning of going to war.

On March 9, 1916, Americans woke to the news that Francisco "Pancho" Villa, a Mexican revolutionary leader and guerrilla fighter, had sacked and burned the small town of Columbus, New Mexico, and engaged in a ferocious gun battle with American troops. Although Pancho Villa is often called a bandit, his raid was a by-product of the Mexican Revolution. Begun in 1910 as a political revolt following a rigged presidential election, the revolution quickly expanded into an agrarian insurrection against political elites. By 1915 Venustiano Carranza had emerged as the most powerful of the revolutionary leaders and was elected president in 1917. As he consolidated power, Carranza fought a civil war with several of the other revolutionary generals, most notably former ally Pancho Villa. The Wilson administration reluctantly recognized the Carranza government as the best route to promoting stability in Mexico. Hoping to ignite a nationalist backlash that he could use against Carranza, Villa began attacking Americans to provoke an invasion by the United States. On January 12, 1916, the nation's newspapers reported that Pancho Villa's men had massacred eighteen American and two Canadian mining engineers near Santa Ysabel, Mexico. The following day Wisconsinites read unconfirmed reports that Villa forces near Madera, Chihuahua, had executed a dozen Americans, including two women. Then Villa burned Columbus, New Mexico.[2]

In response, Wilson ordered Brigadier General John Pershing to lead an expedition into Mexico to capture Villa. Pershing had commanded troops during the last phase of the Indian Wars on the Great Plains, in Cuba during the Spanish-American War, and in the Philippines during the Filipino Insurrection, so he had considerable experience with this kind of small-unit, highly mobile warfare. His relative success in Mexico would make Pershing a leading candidate to command the American Expeditionary Force in France a year later.

Pershing crossed the border on March 15, 1916. He took virtually all available regular army units into Mexico and eventually commanded more than ten thousand men. By mid-April, Pershing's troops had dispersed Villa's forces and neutralized his military strength. But the American incursion sparked an international crisis when Carranza threatened to attack the expeditionary force. Wilson defused the crisis by ending the advance. The army pulled back and spent the next nine months patrolling northern

Columbus, New Mexico, after Pancho Villa's raid on March 9, 1916. In the foreground are the ruins of the Commercial Hotel. WHI IMAGE ID 131026

Mexico. Although Villa was still at large, this prudent move de-escalated the conflict. Pershing's troops remained on patrol in Mexico until February 1917.

To secure the southwest and to deter attacks on Pershing's men by Mexican government troops, Wilson ordered most of the nation's National Guard units to the border with Mexico. Soon the American people were experiencing on a small scale what it meant to go to war.

On June 19, in response to the president's order calling state militias into federal service, Governor Emanuel Philipp issued a proclamation mobilizing the First, Second, and Third Infantry Regiments, Troop "A" First Cavalry, Battery "A" First Field Artillery, and Field Hospital Company Number One of the Wisconsin National Guard. In turn, Wisconsin's adjutant general, Orlando Holway, instructed all Wisconsin Guard units to assemble at their armories and proceed to Camp Douglas to be mustered into federal service three days later. All across Wisconsin, in the more than thirty communities that hosted Guard units, people greeted this news with exuberance and reflection. Mustering the troops often included parades, patriotic music, flags, and speeches about God, country, sacrifice, and honor—community rituals that were both festive and somber. Troops were feasted and fêted before heading to the train depot for final farewells with anxious families, friends, and neighbors staying home. The ceremonial send-offs provided an opportunity for the community to be actively involved and validated the commitment and sacrifice reflected in the departures.

In a typical send-off, La Crosse civic leaders planned a large demonstration to honor departing troops, and relief organizations began arrangements for the care and comfort of soldiers' families while they were away. On June 21, a La Crosse crowd gathered for a "Good Luck Dinner" and patriotic program, followed by a demonstration at Riverside Park that included a concert by the North La Crosse Band and patriotic speeches. At 6 a.m., more than ten thousand people gathered at the train station as the soldiers departed for Camp Douglas. On June 22, the La Crosse Tribune filled almost the entire front page with news about the city's National Guard unit. The paper also included news of an ambush near Carrizal, Mexico, that had killed twelve African American soldiers from the 10th Cavalry; it looked as if war had finally arrived.[3]

Planners expected mobilization to take twelve to eighteen hours and require eleven trains. According to the schedule, the first train would leave West Superior at 5 a.m., and the final train would arrive at Camp Douglas by 2:30 p.m. on the same day. Mobilization proved more time consuming and complex than anticipated. It took three days for troops to put personal affairs in order, report to their armories, and travel to Camp Douglas, located near Tomah in Juneau County.

According to the *Oshkosh Daily Northwestern*, "The entraining of the National Guard boys throughout the country for the Mexican field of battle has spread a fever of patriotism and enthusiasm which recalls the days of the civil war."[4]

The trip to Camp Douglas often had a festive quality for the soldiers. William Bruce and Emory Rogers of Appleton rode together and enjoyed a lunch packed by Bruce's mother. In a thank-you note to Mrs. Bruce, Rogers wrote, "We got here about 4:00 and got all the tents set up before supper. Your lunch sure did taste good. The ride down was long but not lonesome."[5] As in thousands of other similar cases, friends, neighbors, and siblings rode together to Wisconsin's military reservation and shared the excitement of beginning a new adventure.

Several thousand well-wishers from the surrounding area greeted the troops as they detrained at Camp Douglas. By June 22, 4,500 men had arrived, including more than 1,000 raw recruits who had responded to a call for volunteers.[6]

Across the country National Guard units commonly maintained peacetime strength of approximately half the level of a wartime muster. Planners correctly assumed that patriotic fervor and energetic recruiting would bring units to their wartime strength. Most of the new recruits possessed an abundance of enthusiasm but little or no military experience. The Wisconsin Guard units needed this influx of men, but these recruits created significant training and supply problems.

Fortunately, the Wisconsin National Guard was better prepared than most militia units to deal with the logistics of rapid growth. Wisconsin appointed only qualified military personnel to its officer corps and, assuming acceptable performance, allowed them to serve until age sixty-four. Unlike many states, which treated officer appointments as political plums to be dispensed with each new administration, Wisconsin gradually increased the standards expected of officers, producing leaders who were trained, knowledgeable, and committed to maintaining the quality of the Wisconsin Guard. Major Glenn Garlock from West Salem, for example, possessed more than twenty years of experience and had previously been mobilized for duty during the Spanish-American War. In addition to his regular work as a publisher of *The Wisconsin Poultryman*, Garlock was committed to a military career as a citizen soldier.

Army regulations specified that the National Guard possess enough clothing, equipment, and arms sufficient to supply the peacetime unit strength. In 1916 the military supply system was incapable of outfitting the new recruits in a timely fashion. Federal supplies arrived at Camp Douglas well after most of the troops had already arrived in Texas. Fortunately, Major Charles Williams, chief quartermaster for the Wisconsin militia, had been stockpiling equipment, arms, and clothing to fully equip the state's regiments at their wartime level. Because of Williams's forethought, the Wisconsin militia arrived in Texas fully equipped. With obvious pride, the adjutant general reported "the completeness of the equipment of the Wisconsin troops on arrival at Texas stations was the cause of much favorable comment."

Being fully equipped did not mean fully prepared. Their adequate supply of small arms meant they received training in marksmanship, but nearly 1,100 men failed to qualify as second-class shots. Army doctrine considered expert marksmanship key to military success, but one-quarter of the men in the Wisconsin National Guard could not shoot.

The war still raging in Europe had demonstrated the pivotal importance of the machine gun as one of the dominant weapons on the battlefield. In 1915 the Wisconsin National Guard created three machine-gun companies, one for each of Wisconsin's regiments. Federal standards specified that each company be supplied with four Benet-Mercier machine guns, a meager number by European standards, but Wisconsin's three machine-gun companies possessed a total of only three guns instead of the twelve required. In addition, transporting three-hundred-pound machine guns required that each company maintain a stable of six horses and twenty mules. Neither the Wisconsin Guard nor the machine-gun companies had horses or mules. In short, Wisconsin's soldiers had the manpower they needed, but neither the livestock nor the equipment to be operational.

The Wisconsin field artillery battery faced a different but equally serious problem: Although it had the requisite four 3-inch guns, owned its own horses, and was praised for the handling of its equipment, ironically the battery had no qualified gunners. As Wisconsin prepared to send its troops to the border, soldiers could take pride in being better prepared than the militias from many other states, but their preparedness was undermined by training, equipment, and logistical deficiencies.[7]

Camp Douglas functioned as a depot for collecting Wisconsin's guardsmen, ushering them into federal service, and shipping them south. On July 9, the headquarters and hospital units of the Second Wisconsin Infantry Regiment boarded a train for San Antonio. As a member of the Hospital Corps, Sergeant Bill Bruce from Appleton was one of the first to go. The trip took five days, with stops in Milwaukee, Chicago, East St. Louis, and Little Rock. A crash near Texarkana delayed their travels, as did two broken drawbars on their own train near San Antonio.

With the exception of the disruption from a noisy bunch of guys from Oshkosh, Bruce seemed to enjoy the trip. At almost every stop the regimental band performed an impromptu concert, the food was "pretty good . . . considering that we are on a train," and they slept somewhat comfortably after dismantling their seats to make beds. Local crowds greeted them at every stop, and strangers often performed small kindnesses that eased the monotony of the trip. In a letter sent from Little Rock, Arkansas, Bruce wrote to his mother:

> We are stalled because of a breakdown; we were delayed in Texarkana by a wreck ahead of us about 20 miles. Dick and I were lucky; a man and his wife took us out for a spin around the town. Our band gave a concert and when they played "Dixie" the crowd went foolish.
>
> Everybody is well and kicking. The band plays on the train once a day; we have lots of fun listening to the Southerners talk. All kinds of Negroes now. The people here are pretty good—they can not do enough for us. The couple we were with last night wanted to take us to their home and give us a feed but we did not have time.[8]

Bruce joked in one letter, "When we get back we'll all talk like Southerners."[9] The trip gave Bruce and many other Wisconsin boys their first introduction to new landscapes, language patterns, sharecropper's shacks, oil wells, African Americans, and Mexicans.

On July 14, Major Garlock wrote home to report that his regiment had arrived at Fort Sam Houston and that everything was "running smoothly." The fort was the largest military base in the army's Southern Department and the supply depot for Pershing's expedition into Mexico. Despite being a major installation, the logistics of housing and supplying thousands of temporary troops was not as smooth as anyone would have preferred. The Wisconsin National Guard arrived wearing wool uniforms in the midsummer heat of Texas. "It is hotter than the dickens here but we are getting used to it," Bruce wrote home. Optimistically, he looked forward to receiving a cotton uniform within the week. A week later the cotton uniforms had not arrived, and rain made walking across camp difficult as the dusty streets of the military base turned into a sea of mud six inches deep: "Friday it rained and talk about black sticky mud—this has Wisconsin's clay stuck a mile. Everything is dry and hard now. . . . We are still wearing our woolens but are going to have our cottons this week. Last night I used a wash board for about the first time in my life. I got most of the mud out."[10] Major Garlock considered the Texas gumbo so problematic that he suspended drill until the mud dried.[11]

The need for border security was so short-lived that they arrived just when the conflict was almost over. They spent the next six months marching, pitching tents, breaking broncos for mounts, fighting insects, trying to stay cool in August and warm in December, and doing anything to relieve the boredom. They suffered thick mud when it rained and dust when it did not. Arriving in mid-summer 1916, Wisconsin guardsmen found they had little meaningful to do. The training regimen helped make the troops physically fit, but it failed as an antidote for boredom. On Monday, August 7, the Wisconsin National Guard left Fort Sam Houston for a twenty-two-mile march to Leon Springs to participate in a week of maneuvers and target practice. In the heat of a Texas August this was uncomfortable work, but it broke the monotony.[12]

Soon, soldiers and civilians grew frustrated over the Guard's seemingly unnecessary mobilization. Soldiers wrote numerous letters home, questioning their purpose on the border and wondering why they were not permitted to leave. This sentiment was particularly acute in the Wis-

The First Wisconsin Infantry encampment at Leon Springs, Texas, a maneuver and training base, in 1916. This small community was a twenty-two-mile hike from the National Guard's regular base near San Antonio. WHI IMAGE ID 131028

consin Guard, as their deployment stretched into six months and they were among the last units to be sent home. Governor Philipp's attempts to secure their return were of no avail. All that could be done was to wait and surmise, as did one newspaper, that the Wisconsin Guard was being kept at the front because it was "the best" of the nation's National Guard units.[13]

The reasons for keeping the National Guard near the border were never very clear to the enlisted men, officers, or politicians from Wisconsin, but the answer probably lay in the fear that the expedition to capture Villa would escalate into a full-scale war between Mexico and the United States.

In the meantime, a few officers brought their wives to San Antonio, but most officers and enlisted men had to settle for the mail, an imperfect mechanism of correspondence through which they conveyed news; solved family problems, often financial; and participated in parenting. Letters from home played a major role in maintaining morale. Soldiers regularly chided their friends and family for not writing more often. On one weekend Garlock ended his day with a letter and gentle reminder: "Almost 9 oclock [*sic*] Sunday night and I have spent all the day in camp reading most of the time & will relax by writing another letter to you just to please myself and jog you along into answering my last."[14]

The lack of meaningful activity made the homesickness of the Wisconsin troops all the more poignant. They could get passes to go to San Antonio for diversion, but that provided only temporary relief from the reality of being away from friends and family for little reason. Garlock's home-sickness was palpable, and his letters home clearly convey his loneliness. One October night he ended his letter to "Sweetheart" with a poetic twist:

> When nightfall comes you will likely find the "little dipper" almost overhead and it then shines before my tent door in the east about 45° up in the sky and the "big dipper" swings around across the north just as at home. Look at them some night and if they twinkle think that I am thinking of you and wirelessing through the stars. I too will look at them and if I find two that are near together and bright I will think of the eyes that shall shine with love when we come back again.[15]

By mid October the weather had turned beautiful, fifty degrees in the morning with afternoon highs of seventy-five degrees under clear skies. Everyone took heart when Governor Philipp began calling for the return of Wisconsin's militia. His motivation was both straightforward and nuanced. He had become increasingly concerned for the well-being of service families back in Wisconsin. The men had gone south four months earlier, and constituents were beginning to express concern. He was also in the middle of a re-election campaign, and doing the right thing was good politics. Unfortunately, his plea went unanswered. Although Wisconsin's Third Infantry Regiment went home in November, most of the state's National Guard remained in Texas for Thanksgiving and then Christmas.[16]

The weather in November turned biting cold, and football became a welcome diversion. "This afternoon," Garlock wrote to "Dear Sweetheart" on November 12, "a group of officers attended a football game between the 1st Wisconsin team and the 7th U.S. Field Artillery. We won by a score of 23 to 0 much to the delight of Wisconsin rooters." During the next two and a half weeks Garlock attended four more games played by Wisconsin National Guard teams. Although his teams lost three out of the four games, his letters make it clear that these weekend games provided a welcome opportunity to focus on something other than the normal military routine.[17]

As for the cold, it became an unwelcome distraction.

> Monday and Tuesday were the two worst days I have ever put in in a military camp. The wind blew a gale and the temperature went down

to 28°. It rained Monday and during the night the water froze on the tents so that the canvas crackled all night long. I slept by fits and woke up often because I was cold. This in spite of the fact that I had my horse blanket, quilt, heavy blanket and a new woolen blanket I purchased Monday afternoon.

His tent was equipped with an oil stove, which does not seem to have been adequate. He sought comfort in his adjutant's tent warmed by a woodstove.[18]

The Wisconsin Third Infantry arrived home in December 1916. Communities welcomed their troops as heroes. In La Crosse, thousands came to greet the train, despite a temperature of minus four degrees. The Municipal and North Street Bands could manage only squeaks and squawks on their frozen instruments, but no one seemed to mind, for the troops were finally home.[19]

In Sparta the fire whistle blew at 8 p.m. on December 14 to signal the arrival of the troop train an hour later. Despite the bitter cold, a large crowd gathered to welcome "the boys" home. Residents greeted the train "with cheers and Sparta yells," reminiscent of scenes repeated across the state. The next evening, the Spanish-American Auxiliary hosted a sumptuous homecoming feast of "escalloped potatoes, escalloped corn, roast pork, salmon, white bread, brown bread, cheese, olives, pickles, fruit salad, Jello, ice cream, assorted cakes, wafers and coffee." It was a grand affair with music by the West Salem orchestra, a speech by Mayor F. P. Stiles, and dancing late into the evening. In Monroe, residents greeted the return of Company H with similar enthusiasm. Hundreds of people met the troops at the railroad station and escorted them to the armory. The next evening, the Company H Relief Committee hosted an elaborate dinner and dance. It was a time to be happy and grateful for the safe return of the young guardsmen.[20]

With Pancho Villa still at large and Pershing's troops still patrolling northern Mexico, the First and Second Regiments had to wait until February to return home. When at last they arrived, they were greeted warmly as military heroes by hometown crowds. The mobilization for border defense was considered a major advancement in preparedness. A *La Crosse Tribune* article titled "Border Situation Brings U.S. Defense

Nearer Perfection" boasted that "the border is now a gigantic eighteen hundred-mile-long training station." Soon there would be 150,000 trained and equipped "citizen soldiers" from all over the nation added to the defense network.[21]

The men who returned from Texas were more soldier than when they had left. They had lived under military regimen for six months. They took orders, drilled, marched, ate army food, lived in tents with fellow soldiers, suffered the heat of summer, the cold of winter, the mud, and the boredom of army life. They had become more physically fit. They had learned to live and work together; they became a more cohesive military unit. But Mexico was not France. Their sojourn on the border did not train them to fight in Europe.

MOBILIZED FOR WAR

The Wisconsin National Guard returned home with their nation hurtling toward war. By the time they left Texas, diplomatic relations between the United States and Germany were getting worse by the day. By any reasonable measure the US Army was unprepared to fight a major European country. British, French, and German military leaders dismissed the United States as a third-rate military power. Germany could mobilize roughly four million men, and France could put three million soldiers in the field. Although Great Britain had a small, well-trained army designed for colonial service, it relied on the world's greatest navy to keep its homeland safe. The regular army of the United States consisted of 4,701 officers and 87,781 enlisted men. After subtracting the troops stationed in the Philippines, the US coastal defenses, and administrative staff, recruiters, and other noncombatant staff, the "mobile army" consisted of a paltry 2,935 officers and 51,446 men. In some areas of military science American practice remained mired in the prewar era. Despite two and a half years of air combat in Europe, Wisconsin's Billy Mitchell still had to defend use of the airplane as a military weapon and not just a new tool for observing the enemy. The United States went to war in 1917 with an army led by officers who had fought Native Americans, Spanish imperialists, Philippine insurrectionists, and Mexican revolutionaries—all quite unlike the war they faced in Europe.

During the first decade of the twentieth century, US Secretary of War Elihu Root initiated a series of reforms designed to modernize the nation's army. Better military education for officers lay at the heart of these reforms. Root established the Army War College to provide advanced education for senior officers and revitalized the School of the Line and Staff College at Fort Leavenworth to provide tactical training. A few officers also had the opportunity to serve as observers in foreign armies, but the vast majority had little experience with modern warfare.

The National Guard offered a more substantial reserve force numbering 9,818 officers and 148,492 enlisted personnel, but the Guard often had a tenuous relationship with the regular army. Root tried to improve relations between the army and the militia and improve local performance by implementing joint maneuvers, tighter standards for the National Guard, and federal inspections. The combined strength of the regular army and the National Guard gave the United States a practical fighting force of about two hundred thousand men, 75 percent of whom were state militia of inconsistent training and leadership. Although the army had a stockpile of small arms and ammunition sufficient for twice its number, it possessed little in the way of artillery and specified only four machine guns per regiment. A battalion in the German army carried at least thirty-six machine guns. By any measure, the United States was ill-equipped to fight a modern land war.[22]

The navy was better prepared. Early in 1916 President Wilson and Congress embarked on a major modernization program calculated to build what the president called, "unquestionably the greatest navy in the world." By 1917 the US navy ranked third in the world behind Great Britain and Germany. The "Great White Fleet" of Teddy Roosevelt's day, the fleet of Admiral Dewey and the Spanish-American War, had been replaced by modern heavy cruisers and dreadnaughts, the newest class of heavy battleship.[23]

Newly home from Mexico, any guardsman paying attention to the news must have wondered how long he would enjoy the comfort of his own bed, the pleasure of home cooking, and the joy of being with family and friends. Submarines were once again wreaking havoc in the Atlantic, and Wilson had decided to arm merchant ships. The cloud of war darkened further when Wilson released the Zimmermann telegram, making clear Germany's plan to foment war between the United States and Mexico should the American government join the Allies in Europe.

As relations with Germany continued to deteriorate during February and March and the possibility of war loomed ever more likely, Wilson took the precaution of calling the Third Wisconsin back into federal service to provide security for bridges, railroads, munitions, factories, and other facilities important to national defense. The men of the Third Wisconsin hailed primarily from the cities and small towns of northwestern Wisconsin: Viroqua, Portage, Mauston, La Crosse, Sparta, Tomah, Neillsville, Hudson, Menominee, Eau Claire, Wausau, Rice Lake, and Superior. For these men and their loved ones, the war had suddenly taken on a new reality. On March 27, the *Eau Claire Leader* virtually shouted the news of their deployment with a headline across the top of the entire front page: NORTH WISCONSIN TROOPS ORDERED TO ARM[S]. With a healthy dose of hyperbole, the paper announced:

> The dread spectre of war cast its black shadow over many homes in
> Eau Claire yesterday morning when the news came that Company E
> had been called on to mobilize and recruit up to war strength as rap-
> idly as possible along with other companies of the Third Regiment,
> Wisconsin National Guard, and many a wife, mother, father, child
> bewailed the fact that their loved one was to be torn from their home
> and fireside for what they felt certain would be war and all its atten-
> dant sorrow, misery and pain.[24]

As the guardsmen put their personal affairs in order and prepared for federal service, they greeted mobilization as a sober duty, an obligation, and the beginning of a great adventure.

When Congress declared war on April 6, the United States faced a monumental problem: it could marshal the regular army and the national guard relatively quickly, but that would result in a fighting force only a fraction of the size that would be needed. The problem could be solved by recruiting volunteer regiments, as had been done during the Civil War, or through a draft system. Wilson rejected volunteer recruitment for fear it might disrupt the economy by pulling key individuals or occupations out of the workforce. The War Department feared that celebrity volunteer units, such as proposed by Teddy Roosevelt, would attract able and ambitious officers away from the commands where they were needed. In addition, military leaders worried that someone like Roosevelt, who desperately wanted a command, would be uncontrollable within the chain of command.

Roosevelt was not alone in his desire to create a special division. Remembering the Civil War, leaders in many communities immediately thought in terms of the local volunteer units that formed to fight for the Union. The declaration of war in 1917 produced a surge of patriotic fervor in the Native American community. Jonas Wheelock and Jonas Metoxen, both Oneida football heroes, immediately began promoting the idea of recruiting a Native American regiment. Frank Antoine, a seventeen-year-old Ojibwe orphan, took two patriotic actions: he withdrew almost half of his savings from the bank and bought $7,500 in Liberty Bonds, and he promptly enlisted in the army. A mass meeting of Menominee held in the assembly hall of the Keshena Indian School passed a resolution promising President Wilson that the tribe would supply recruits and tribal resources to the war effort. Ultimately, twenty-six Ho-Chunk also volunteered to fight.[25]

Politicians and army officials had already decided to abandon the raising of volunteer regiments in favor of a draft. Now they needed to answer a fundamental question as they began building the new, massive army for the war in Europe: should Native American troops be placed in segregated units or integrated into regular units? Preconceived ideas, prejudices, and political objectives shaped the answer. Advocates for preservation of Native cultures often sought to keep Native American troops together in segregated units that would foster greater cultural identity. However, cultural preservation had never been a goal for most policy makers. For more than a hundred years, the government had been trying to assimilate Native Americans, Christianize them, turn them into sedentary farmers, and replace Native cultures with European values. Now, these goals coincided with the larger agenda of assimilating European immigrants into American society. Integration of Native Americans into existing military units became army policy.[26]

African Americans, however, joined the national army in segregated units. The question of assimilation into existing units was never considered seriously. Recruiters acted on stereotypes. White soldiers, and most importantly white officers, were likely to view Native American soldiers as natural and instinctive warriors. In contrast, politicians, government officials, and military personnel acted on the racist assumptions that African Americans could not or would not fight and were best suited to manual labor. These assumptions were reinforced by Wilson administration policies that re-segregated many federal offices. General Pershing, who commanded the African American 10th Cavalry during the Spanish-American War, clearly knew better, but he chose to do little to counteract federal policies. The African American community responded to the call for military service with the same devotion to the nation as was common throughout the country. In Wisconsin, the Native American and African American communities sent their young men to war with great pride and no small amount of trepidation, just as was true in every community across the state.

As African American communities encouraged, welcomed, and heralded the record of their young men in service, they did so within the context of racial prejudice and violence. No other group of recruits lived with the reality of segregation, race riots, and lynch mobs. Almost one hundred African Americans across the nation died at the hands of lynch mobs in 1917 and 1918. African Americans who confronted white authority, or who seemed to do so, risked a gruesome death. In July 1917 a white mob ransacked a black neighborhood in East St. Louis. On August 23, 1917, enraged by treatment at the hands of the local police and a rumor that police had shot one of their comrades, 75 to 100 African American soldiers from the 24th Infantry took arms and marched on Houston. The 24th Infantry had fought in the Indian wars of the late nineteenth century, the Spanish-American War, and against Filipino insurgents. They were proud of their service to the nation and had little patience for the ill-treatment they received at the hands of the police. In the confrontation that ensued, four policemen, nine civilian Houstonians, two white national guardsmen, and four soldiers from the 24th Infantry died. Although the black community did not condone the violent actions of the soldiers, African Americans were outraged when the army responded by court-martialing more than one hundred soldiers and executing thirteen, without appeal to the War Department.[27]

During the fall of 1917, fifty-four young African American men from Wisconsin went to training camps in places such as Fort Custer in Battle Creek, Michigan, and Camp Grant in Rockford, Illinois. Wherever they trained, African American soldiers were segregated from white soldiers, but they were led by white officers. If they were lucky, their officers were men of intelligence and goodwill. If unlucky they were commanded by men who looked upon the job as a second-class assignment and the end of their military careers. In spite of segregation, poor officers, and relegation to work details, African American troops committed their lives to the nation out of patriotism and the fervent hope that national service would bring respect and a claim to equality.[28]

Regardless of race, a draft could supply the necessary men in a predictable fashion, but politicians worried a draft might bring a repeat of the Civil War experience when the army administered the program autocratically and riots ensued. Secretary of War Newton Baker solved the dilemma by placing control in the hands of local civilian boards. Although still a federal program, local control integrated the draft into the life of the community. Baker created a system that could effectively apply deferments to protect the economy, while the War Department maintained control over the distribution of draftees to military units where they were most needed. Baker successfully created a Selective Service system capable of supplying millions of men for what was commonly called the "national army" to distinguish it from the existing National Guard and regular army. Baker's system of local control became the model for draft administration during World War II, the Korean War, and the Vietnam War.

In the regular army, noncommissioned officers, or NCOs, and lieutenants provided leadership for the average soldier. NCOs came up through the ranks and had years of experience as they learned on the job. Lieutenants in the prewar army often served a long apprenticeship before being promoted to captain. This slow, deliberate process for training leaders through experience was quite effective but could not be duplicated in an army soon to grow twentyfold.

The Selective Service proved itself admirably suited to supplying privates. These were the riflemen the army wanted. The army could turn them into skilled marksmen in a matter of months. Neither the Selective Service nor the army could supply leaders for these men, however. The

Wisconsin National Guard had the relative luxury of being composed of men who had served together in Mexico and, in many cases, for years before that. They were commanded by men of substantial experience. After Wilson ordered the National Guard into federal service, draftees from the Selective Service replenished the ranks of these older units, but they primarily supplied the manpower for the new National Army. If time and experience created the leaders needed as NCOs and lieutenants, the only answer for an army ballooning to four million men was to throw units into the maelstrom and hope they survived long enough to mature. Because of the limits to their training, even the older units of the regular army and National Guard faced this shock.

In May 1917, the *Wisconsin State Journal* reported an estimate from the War Department's militia division "that from six weeks to two months of intensive training will suffice to put these units into war condition." This wildly optimistic timetable failed to account for the complexities of equipping and transporting hundreds of thousands of men across the country and then on to Europe. Ultimately, the men of the 32nd Division trained in Texas for five to six months during the Mexican border crisis, then trained in Texas after war was declared for almost six months before shipping to France, where they underwent more training for two months before being assigned to a quiet zone in Alsace for two more months.

Because the training in Texas was inadequate for the realities of fighting on the western front, the soldiers of the 32nd Division received their real education from British and French veterans and from the German troops they faced across no-man's-land. The Allies and their German adversaries occupied opposing trench fortifications built in 1914 and 1915. Between the fortifications lay territory neither side controlled, a wasteland of tangled barbed wire, shell craters, and mud where each side delivered death to the enemy charging into their guns. The war itself would be the Americans' schoolhouse.

The army that would go to Europe would be far larger than any military force ever fielded by the United States, even during the Civil War. Wilson picked Pershing over more senior generals to organize and command the American Expeditionary Force in France. Pershing was the only officer since the Spanish-American War to command a major military force in the field, and despite disagreeing with the order to withdraw in

Mexico, he had the discretion to follow orders without public complaint. Discretion and loyalty to the president distinguished him from his closest competitor, Leonard Wood. In 1917, Wood and Pershing both held the rank of major general (two stars), but Wood had greater seniority and believed he deserved command of the American army in Europe. Wilson had little confidence in Wood, who was a close friend of Roosevelt and a vocal critic of Wilsonian foreign policy. On May 2, 1917, Pershing was instructed to select the first units to go to France. Shortly thereafter he received command of the Expeditionary Force, which as yet did not exist, and by the end of the month was on his way to build an army in France.

The declaration of war made it obvious that Wilson might mobilize the full state militia at any time. The order came all too soon. On May 18 the War Department announced mobilization of all Wisconsin National Guard units not already on security duty and instructed Adjutant General Orlando Holway to have his men ready for induction into federal service on July 15. Mobilization created the need for an infusion of new recruits to bring the militia up to war strength. Holway immediately announced the Guard would need ten thousand volunteers; the state would need to enlist another seven thousand for the regular army and the navy. The National Guard was a community-based organization of citizen soldiers. With the cooperation of the newly formed state and county councils of defense, seventy-five recruiting stations opened across Wisconsin. In each community hosting Guard units, the first weeks of the war brought a flurry of patriotic enlistments. Articles in the local newspaper, notices in post offices, and sermons from the pulpit all encouraged young men to do their patriotic duty.[29]

The National Guard had benefited from a steady flow of recruits since the beginning of February. Because of a dramatic increase in enlistments since March 25, when war seemed inevitable, the number of new recruits soon topped two thousand. Holway anticipated having enough men to create the Fourth Infantry Regiment of the Wisconsin National Guard. Recruiting went far better than Holway anticipated. Three Wisconsin infantry regiments, one troop of cavalry, one artillery battery, and a field hospital existed at the time of the Mexican border crisis. By the middle of July 1917, the Wisconsin National Guard mustered 15,256 enlisted men and officers, all volunteers, organized in six infantry regiments, individual regiments of cavalry and artillery, one battalion each of engineers and signalmen, two field hospitals, and two ambulance companies. Volunteer recruiting had gone well indeed.[30]

Once Holway issued the mobilization order, guardsmen met at their local armories. Reminiscent of the Mexican border mobilization in 1916, communities marked the departure of their National Guard units with parades, patriotic music, and flags. Dignitaries heralded the sacred duty and heroic spirit of the troops, soldiers hugged loved ones, friends and family shed tears and bid the men farewell. The train whistles blew. Young men—soon to be soldiers—leaned out of windows to wave good-bye, and then they were gone. In the hearts of well-wishers resided pride for the men who had volunteered to serve their nation and perhaps also a sense of foreboding born of the certain knowledge that some of these young men would not come home.[31]

The well-wishers and soldiers alike could imagine the potential cost of going to war. The daily newspapers regularly ran articles describing battlefront conditions. The *Milwaukee Journal* published an article in March 1917 describing the "underground city of trenches." Journalist Henri Bazin

The men of Company D, Fifth Infantry Regiment of the Wisconsin National Guard received a heartfelt send-off when they left Hartford to be mustered into federal service. Similar events were repeated in towns large and small across Wisconsin.
WHI IMAGE ID 99997

toured a segment of the trench system with a French lieutenant and wrote an account of what he saw: "It was bitterly cold, the coldest night in northern France for twenty-five years. . . . There was little or no wind. The moon was shining full, a polar-like moon, shedding a mystic light upon the floor of the trench—a floor of ice and snow. Beyond the observation post, the tangled mass of barbed wire supported upon its spiral-ended metal posts seemed to take vague, fantastic form, something menacing and at the same time grotesque."

The lieutenant led Bazin through a hole in the side of the trench, down twenty-seven steps, and into a long, well-lit corridor braced like a mine shaft but lined with doors. Passing through one of the doors, Bazin met two French officers sitting at a table, smoking. One of the officers told of collecting stories of the superstitions of trench life and remarked, "If I am alive at the end of the war [I] shall put them in some sort of form as a legacy for my son." In that underground bunker deep in the earth, the officer was both fatalistic and focused on the future.

Bazin next observed,

In a great cavern-like space, through the dim light of a burning briquet [sic], I could see a confused mass of men completely dressed and booted, each wrapped in a brown blanket, each huddled against the other. There were perhaps 100 — some on the earthen floor, some in double bunks of three tiers that suggest the steerage section upon ancient steamers. The atmosphere was heavy and warm. All was silent safe for heavy breathing. These [brave men] had not undressed for a long time. They had almost forgotten the luxury of a sheeted bed. They were waiting, ready at the instant to go forth to death if need be.

It was a solemn thing to see, these sleeping men of France, men of all ages and conditions in life together in their soiled gray uniforms, together in purpose, ready to give, as had thousands and thousands before them, all they held dear for the cause of right and liberty. Some were doomed to die, and very shortly.

Bazin and the lieutenant returned to the trenches above. At an observation post overlooking no-man's-land, they talked with a French soldier muffled against the cold, then returned to the warmth of the underground for a cup of hot chocolate, and a cigarette. "Wonderful, our *poilu* [infantrymen]," said the lieutenant as they relaxed in relative safety. "They are all like that. Always ready and never afraid. That is what is so remarkable to me—among 3,000,000 men, none is afraid." The French lieutenant confidently told Bazin that these soldiers "are thrust into the vortex of the most frightful catastrophe that ever came to the world, entering it and meeting the death it contains without a 'particle of fear.'"[32]

The newspaper account was romantic and starkly realistic at the same time. To readers on the home front, the picture was all too clear. Death was stalking the earth and reaping a windfall of heroes.

FROM WISCONSIN TO WAR ZONE

The troops of the Wisconsin National Guard arrived at Camp Douglas by August 2. A few days later units began leaving the familiar Wisconsin military camp for the dusty plains of Camp MacArthur near Waco, Texas. Once again, Wisconsin fully equipped its troops. This time there were no stockpiles from which to draw. Anticipating the sluggish army supply system and expecting federal compensation, Governor Philipp authorized Holway to spend up to $780,000 to properly outfit their guardsmen.

During the next two months Michigan and Wisconsin National Guard units poured into Waco and began the work of creating the 32nd Division out of whole cloth. The new division consisted of the two brigades divided into two infantry regiments each. The Michigan National Guard units became the 125th and 126th Infantry Regiments, comprising the 63rd Brigade. The Wisconsin First, Second, and Third Infantry Regiments became the 64th Brigade's 127th and 128th Infantry Regiments, and the Wisconsin artillery batteries became the 120th Field Artillery. By 1917, cavalry had become obsolete, while machine guns and artillery had come to dominate the battlefield. Reflecting these changes in warfare, Wisconsin's cavalry units were disbanded and the troops redistributed to artillery and machine-gun units in each regiment, both of which required men knowledgeable in the care and handling of horses and mules for hauling guns and supplies.

Systematic training began at the end of September and lasted until the

32nd Division began its departure for Europe during January 1918. Prevailing military thinking at the time emphasized small, highly maneuverable infantry units relying on initiative and small arms, principally the rifle. This doctrine grew quite naturally out of the experience of fighting relatively simple engagements with Native Americans, Spanish soldiers, and Filipino insurrectionists in the fifty years since the end of the Civil War. Those conflicts were fought in open terrain, at which the skilled rifleman excelled. American doctrine took little account of modern warfare with machine guns, massed heavy artillery, poison gas, and airplanes. Despite the realities of western front trench warfare and the devastating effect of modern weaponry, American doctrine continued to emphasize the superiority of independent infantry units comprised of expert marksmen. At a time when France could deploy 1,700 aircraft, and dogfights, strafing, and bombing runs had become common occurrences on the western front, the United States could only muster fifty-five planes and a comparable number of pilots. American officers would have to experience modern warfare firsthand in 1918 before they began to reconsider their ideas about fighting this war.

At Camp MacArthur and similar military bases across the country, training emphasized long marches for physical conditioning, maneuvers against trenches to prepare for warfare on the western front, and rifle practice to hone marksmanship in keeping with army doctrine. All of these activities improved military discipline, physical conditioning, and marksman accuracy. In addition, officers and sergeants improved their understanding of small unit tactics and how to handle small groups of men in the field.

Brigadier General William Haan took command of the 32nd Division in mid-September. Haan would turn out to be a fortuitous choice. After graduating from West Point in 1889 he spent his career in the artillery and fought in the Spanish-American War and in the Philippines. Later, in France he would quickly adapt to battlefield conditions and understand the importance of using overwhelming firepower in support of the infantry. Haan's first task was to implement the War Department's comprehensive training regimen, including military protocol and discipline, use of machine guns and grenade launchers, trench warfare, and care and use of gas masks. In a December 9, 1917, evaluation of the division, Haan concluded:

"Progress in this Division has been better than I had expected it would be, but it is not intended to indicate that it has been entirely satisfactory." Although he was generally pleased with the progress and attitude of the average soldier, he found that National Guard officers, as well as a significant number of regular army officers, failed to adapt when new work was undertaken: "The officers did not properly connect the disciplinary training which had been given during the fundamental period with the training in the specialties. . . . The men were ready to take any kind of training; to obey any kind of instructions given by the officers . . . so that in my view the relative progress of the enlisted men of this Division has been much greater than that of the officers." Haan concluded, "I have hopes that with a great deal of additional training this Division may be brought finally to such a state of training that it will stand the test of severe battle."

Training for the 32nd Division was hampered by lack of ammunition and equipment. Classroom instruction was on schedule during the fall, but the all-important practice needed by troops to reach proficiency with their weapons and equipment lagged far behind schedule. As Haan reported in mid-December, he had rigorously followed the program prescribed by the War Department "with the exception of Practical Instruction with Automatic Rifles, Machine Guns and live grenades, on account of the lack of this equipment. The actual number of hours prescribed for rifle practice have not been put in, on account of the lack of ammunition." Because the National Guard units brought their own ammunition, they were able to conduct rifle practice until December 8, when the supply ran out. Typical of the logistical problems plaguing commanders, a supply of ammunition had been shipped in late November but had not arrived by mid-December. Machine-gun units had not practiced either, and artillery practice was delayed until the second week of December, when shells finally arrived.[33]

The trench warfare training did not and probably could not train troops for the realities of the western front. "Training has been maintained at a high pitch," Major Garlock wrote to his old friend Eda Landorf in Milwaukee. "Especially have we been busy shooting on the range, marching, living in trenches, and digging trenches." In keeping with army doctrine, those who scored well on the rifle range were sent to "sniper's school" for further training with a variety of rifles at distances of one hundred to one thousand yards. For the longer distances they trained with telescopic sights. Although the members of the 32nd Division learned to build and live in trenches, their training exercises against an enemy trench system seemed focused on infiltration and reconnaissance. Instead of an attack en masse, troops moved out stealthily at night with the goal of getting as close as possible to the defenders before being detected. These skills were useful for night patrols, but there was no way to duplicate the "over-the-top" attack. Troops left Waco physically fit and skilled in the use of the rifle, but unprepared for the realities of modern trench warfare.[34]

As fall turned into winter, freezing weather and a strong north wind made life uncomfortable in Waco. It became difficult to stay warm. Garlock recorded in his diary, "Our men need more woolen clothing. Most of them now have 3 blankets and woolen underwear but still need overcoats and woolen uniforms."[35]

Rumors of departure for Europe abounded in December. On December 11, 1917, Garlock wrote: "Pretty certain Division will begin to move out of this camp on Dec. 23. Our regt. Dec. 26. Sent Anna a long letter on business affairs. Have advised her not to come here. Plans are moving fast to get away. It's said that 57 trains are needed to move the outfit. Still cold." The rumor held a kernel of truth: The division would soon move to Camp Merritt, New Jersey, and then on to their transport ships, but not for another month.

The 32nd Division was a small city. It took sixty-one trains to move the 23,685 men and their baggage, equipment, weapons, livestock, wagons, and trucks. On January 13 and 14, 1918, the headquarters and engineer units boarded trains in Waco and left for New Jersey, where they would ship out to Liverpool. The 127th Infantry left for New Jersey on January 21; finally, on February 3, the 128th Infantry boarded trains and followed.

The first members of the 32nd to cross the Atlantic—engineers, supply troops, and military police—boarded the *Tuscania* on January 24 in Hoboken, New Jersey. On February 7, the 128th's headquarters was forty miles west of Buffalo when news arrived that the *Tuscania* had sunk, hit by a torpedo from a German submarine within sight of Liverpool. The fourteen-thousand-ton passenger liner had been converted to troop transport ship and was carrying more than two thousand passengers. It took four hours for the ship to sink, which allowed most of the passengers and crew to be picked up by the escort destroyers. Later, members of the division would learn that thirteen soldiers from the 32nd were among the dead, but for now they knew only that the division had suffered its first casualties.[36]

Transporting troops to Europe was a monumental task. Shortages of transports slowed the shipment of men during 1917, but the pace picked up rapidly in 1918 as the British devoted greater shipping capacity to transporting American troops and the United States put confiscated German passenger liners into service. The transatlantic crossing also became safer as the United States and Great Britain implemented a convoy system. Typically, a cruiser escorted a convoy across the Atlantic. Approximately forty-eight hours from the destination, a small fleet of destroyers met the convoy, the cruiser headed for home, and the destroyers guided the convoy through the treacherous waters around the British Isles and into port. Between April 1 and October 31, 1918, the convoy system neutralized the German submarine fleet and delivered more than 1.6 million American soldiers to Europe.[37]

The Atlantic crossing could be an uncomfortable trip. In the best of times, soldiers were crammed below deck in poorly ventilated compartments with sweaty, seasick comrades. Company K of the 128th Infantry traveled to France on the *America* (formerly the *Amerika*), a German passenger liner seized when war was declared. The ship had been converted to carry troops. Compartments contained closely placed bunks stacked three high. The fresh air of the deck would have been a welcome change from the warm, close air of the lower decks scented by unwashed soldiers. When Sergeant Walter Zukowski of Greenfield, Wisconsin, embarked "on an old English merchant ship named 'ORDUNA'" with the rest of the 107th Ammunition Train (the unit responsible for supplying ammunition to the rest of the 32nd Division) for transport to Europe on February 1, 1918, he wondered what they were getting into. Neither ship nor crew engendered confidence. Zukowski was assigned a hammock and felt like a sardine in the close quarters. The trip was punctuated by several days of high seas and seasickness, but otherwise proved uneventful.[38]

For Sergeant Gaylord Bradley, from Mauston, the trip was worse. Bradley played trombone in the Wisconsin Third Infantry regimental band. On January 1, 1918, he began keeping a diary. Bradley and the other band members were regular soldiers, but with the added special duties of playing reveille in the morning and retreat in the evening; they entertained fellow troops and performed concerts for visitors and dignitaries. When the division went into battle, band members shed their instruments and became stretcher bearers for the living and the dead.

While at Camp Merritt in New Jersey, Bradley came down with something he called "Grippe"—presumably the conventional flu. On February 17, he was feeling better but was still weak and dizzy when he packed his gear and "staggered" onto the *Covington*, where he fell into his bunk and slept in what he called the "Black Hole of Calcutta." Bradley's accommodations were below the waterline on the fourth deck. Seasickness and the lingering effects of the flu kept his stomach in turmoil. "I stay pretty close to my bed," he wrote. One week into the voyage he wrote: "Our corner of the hold is quarantined for mumps—I only hope I don't get them—I don't know whether I've had them or not. Also someone on our deck has Scarlet Fever. Nice place." Meningitis was also rumored to be on board.

Bradley's convoy consisted of nine ships, six carrying soldiers and one each for nurses and horses. A cruiser provided escort protection. "Some ships are beautifully camouflaged but our ship is painted plain gray." By February 28, they were in the "submarine zone," "which makes it a little more exciting." Daily "abandon ship" drills relieved some of the boredom while keeping nerves on edge. To the troops' concern, the destroyer escort failed to arrive on March 1. Instead, a German submarine surfaced in the middle of the convoy, resulting in a flurry of gunfire from the cruiser and the transport ships. The *Tuscania* was on everyone's mind. But, after fifteen rounds, a shot from the *Covington* sank the submarine. To the relief of everyone in the US convoy, an escort of fifteen destroyers arrived on March 2 to escort them safely into the harbor at Brest. At about eleven o'clock in the morning of March 4, 1918, the convoy docked. Everyone could breathe more easily; they had made it to France. To one soldier, "Land sure looks just as good to us as it did to Columbus."[39]

On a different ship, a converted German liner, Major Garlock had better accommodations, reflecting his rank. He shared Stateroom 72 with Major Ulysses G. Carl, an officer in the 128th Infantry in the 32nd Division. They had their own bathroom, with a tub and shower, although the water for bathing was cold seawater. The ship's officers and the regimental officers of the rank of captain or above ate meals in the aft dining room.[40]

The UB-77 sank the *Tuscania*. It was similar in size to the captured German submarine pictured here. Because of their role in American entry into the war, submarines became a hallmark of World War I. The danger posed by the German submarine fleet prompted the use of convoys to help protect troop transports. WHI IMAGE ID 55665

Moving the 32nd Division to Europe took more than two months, beginning with the departure of the *Tuscania* on January 24 and completed in late March as the final troops trickled into France. The month of March was a period of waiting and boredom while all the elements of the 32nd Division arrived in France and reassembled. The guardsmen were dispersed to some thirty small towns and villages, where they were billeted in private homes, barns, sheds, and any other structure that could be adapted as housing. Bradley waxed poetic about the French villages he saw and complained of boredom, poor food, and erratic pay. He and other members of the band were occasionally asked to play concerts or sweep the village streets. They often passed the time at small cafés; during one evening of drinking, two band members got into a heated debate over the origins of the French language. Only in a Wisconsin unit would a soldier suggest, "Why you know I'm Norwegian, and the French language is derived from the Norwegian and the English."[41]

According to Bradley's diary entries throughout the month of March, it seems the logistics of feeding the army were overlooked in the 32nd Division's planning. On March 9 elements of the 128th boarded a train for a three-day trip to an unrecorded destination. Bradley's compartment of eight soldiers was issued rations consisting of twelve cans of corned beef hash, one can of beans, three cans of tomatoes, and forty-eight boxes of hard tack. By March 12 they had taken up residence in the loft of a barn in a small village. With time on their hands, they "walked all over the village and wished we had some money as things looked good to eat and we were hungry." Bradley became increasingly preoccupied with food. It was several weeks before these logistical problems would be solved.[42]

Sergeant Zukowski and the rest of the 107th Ammunition Train, part of the 57th Field Artillery Brigade, landed at Liverpool on February 16, 1918, and made their way to Camp de Coëtquidan near Rennes in Brittany in northwest France by way of Le Havre harbor. On General Haan's orders, they began a rigorous course of combat training designed to toughen them up. Under the watchful eye of two French officers, they went on long endurance hikes with full packs and practiced hand-to-hand combat with bayonets and the use of grenades. They dug trenches and practiced all aspects of trench warfare, from defense to attack. The process of converting them from raw American National Guardsmen into hardened soldiers had begun.[43]

Shortly after arriving in France, Zukowski sent a reassuring letter to his brother:

> First of all I want to let you know that things in general here are fine and most satisfactory. I'm healthy and feeling good as well as the rest of the boys. Conditions here are fine off [sic] course and most naturally most of our time is taken up here with a lot of training and a whole lot other work [sic]. But we don't mind that we know it's all in the game. . . . We had quite a lot of rain of late but that didn't stop us from our daily routine.

The letter goes on at some length to describe a forty-eight-hour leave during which Zukowski and several other soldiers visited a Polish army unit composed largely of volunteers from other European nations, Canada, and the United States. Sergeant Zukowski concluded his letter with two requests: "Now brother write me a little about friends and Folks. If the folks are worrying much try to quite [sic] them as much as you can." He omitted one major event from the furlough. After a few drinks with his new friends in the Polish army, they decided to visit the "ladies" of a local bordello. In a memoir written in 1978, Zukowski compared the decor of the bordello to that of the Schlitz Palm Garden back home, with a fountain, palm trees, and ferns. The sergeant maintained his virtue, but without judgment he recounted that "some of the fellows decided to go up-stairs." Obviously there were aspects of army life one did not write home about.[44]

As they arrived in France, the 125th, 126th, and 127th Infantry Regiments were reassigned to unload supply ships and build warehouses for the newly formed Services of Supply of the American Expeditionary Force, known as the SOS. Early in March 1918, the remaining members of the 32nd Division learned the dispiriting news that they were going to be broken up and used as replacements for those killed and wounded in other divisions. The 128th Infantry bore the brunt of replacement transfers, as its members were sent to the First Infantry Division to compensate for soldiers killed during fighting in the spring of 1918. In a letter that somewhat surprisingly was not censored, Garlock explained to his wife, "It is a little uncertain just at present as to what will be done with us. Several hundred of our men have been drawn off for service elsewhere also ten of our best captains leaving the regiment in a more or less state of disorganization." Ultimately, seven thousand men, including all of the captains and privates from the 128th, received transfer orders.

General Haan mounted a successful campaign with Pershing's headquarters to reverse the use of his division for replacements. Haan argued that reassignment duty was a waste of a division that was well trained in marksmanship and the tactics of open warfare. In short, Haan argued, the 32nd Division was ready to fight Pershing's kind of war. Haan's arguments seemed persuasive. The beginning of the spring German offensive may also have played a role. The Germans threw all of their resources into the offensive. Pershing may have concluded that he could ill afford to use a division in good order for replacements. Haan then negotiated the release of his men who had been reassigned to work with the SOS.

On March 31, 1918, Haan received orders to reassemble his division. The 32nd Division had arrived in France two thousand men short of full strength. With the losses from transfers, Haan was now short nine thousand men. He reconstituted the 128th by bringing in men from his other regiments. By reducing the size of companies from 200 to 150 men, he preserved the overall structure of the division. He also received an infusion of men hurriedly shipped to France from the United States. When Samuel

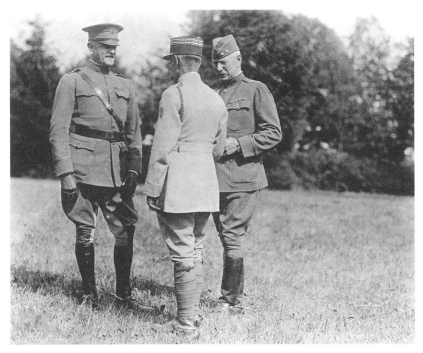

Major General William Haan, commander of the 32nd Division, on the right, conversing with a French officer, middle, and General "Black Jack" Pershing, commander of the American Expeditionary Force, on the left, after inspection of the 32nd while in the quiet zone in Alsace. Initially responsible for the division's artillery, Haan took command of the 32nd in September 1917 and served through the end of the war. He is rightly credited with the leadership necessary to turn the division into a creditable fighting force. WHI IMAGE ID 131017

Kent of Baltimore, Maryland, joined Company K of the 128th Infantry as one of those replacements, he recorded his first impression of the 32nd Division: "These men are from the states of Wisconsin and Michigan—all national guardsmen, and I think I am going to like them very much." [45]

Throughout April, officers and enlisted men received further training in tactics, weapons, and marksmanship. By mid-May, the 32nd Division was on its way to Alsace—a quiet zone on the western front—for further seasoning. This interlude, common for green troops, provided the opportunity to develop an understanding of the rhythms and nuances of trench warfare while learning from the experiences of French instructors. Despite being in a quiet sector, the Germans and Americans routinely engaged in artillery duels, occasionally gas barrages, and raids and counterraids to lethal effect. During the sixty-five days they spent in Alsace between

May 18 and July 21, the division suffered 430 casualties. Approximately 220 would likely return to active duty after recuperation, but the remaining 210 were lost to death or incapacitation.[46]

AT THE FRONT

Germany's last great offensive on the western front ended unsuccessfully in mid-July, and the Allies began a series of offensives that would finally push the German army out of France, breach the backbone of the German defense known as the Hindenburg Line, and eventually end the war. The 32nd Division finished its tour in Alsace and immediately joined the Allied reserves supporting the Aisne-Marne offensive. On July 30 they rotated into the front line and for the next seven days slugged it out with the Fourth Prussian Guards and the German 200th and 216th Divisions, culminating with the capture of Fismes, a small village on the Vesle River in northeast France.

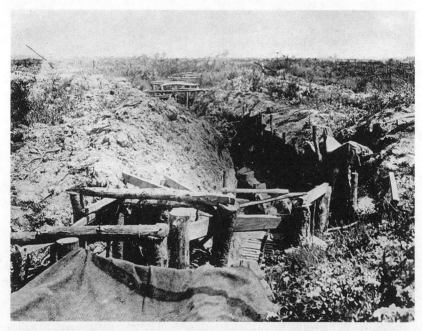

Part of the trench system in Alsace, where the 32nd Division received training in the static form of warfare that had stalemated both sides for almost three years. WHI IMAGE ID 101011

No one could endure the stresses of life at the front and in the trenches for long duration. From the end of July through late October, the 32nd Division, like other units, rotated between being on the front lines and in reserve. In August they spent a week in the trenches, followed by three weeks in reserve; they returned to the front for six days at the end of August and the beginning of September; and finally, they were in the front line trenches for twenty days in October.

Although German infantrymen could attack at any time, the real nemesis of frontline duty was the ever-present threat of an artillery barrage, which could deliver gas or explosive annihilation. Observers could watch for enemy infiltration and signs of poison gas, but there was no antidote for the terror delivered by artillery. A barrage started at the whim of the enemy. If possible, the soldier headed for a bunker designed to protect defenders, but if on duty in the trench or caught in the open, all the soldier could do was hunker down and pray for deliverance. Along with the uncertainty of life or death came the cacophony of sound, shock waves, dirt, and debris all around, followed by the screams of the wounded. The dead lay silent. In a series of bloody engagements between July 30 and August 6, 1918, the 32nd Division crashed through the German defenses, advanced nineteen kilometers (11.8 miles), and took control of the territory between the villages of Cierges and Fismes along a three-kilometer (1.8-mile) front. During seven days of brutal fighting, the 32nd Division took a beating, but prevailed by dint of tenacity. On July 29, the German army controlled the territory between Fismes on the Vesle River and the Ourcq River. During the night of July 29 and morning of July 30, the 32nd Division moved into position to relieve the Third Division along the Ourcq River, some ten miles south of Fismes.

The 127th led the advance on July 30. By evening, they occupied a strategic point overlooking Cierges and held their position, despite a German counterattack that became hand-to-hand combat with bayonets. The counterattack failed, but German artillery subjected the 127th to a prolonged bombardment.

The 128th took the lead on the right side of the line on August 2, 3, and 4 while the 127th rotated to a supporting role. The Michigan 125th led on the left side of the front with the 126th in support as the 32nd Division pushed forward thirteen kilometers (eight miles) in two days. This was a

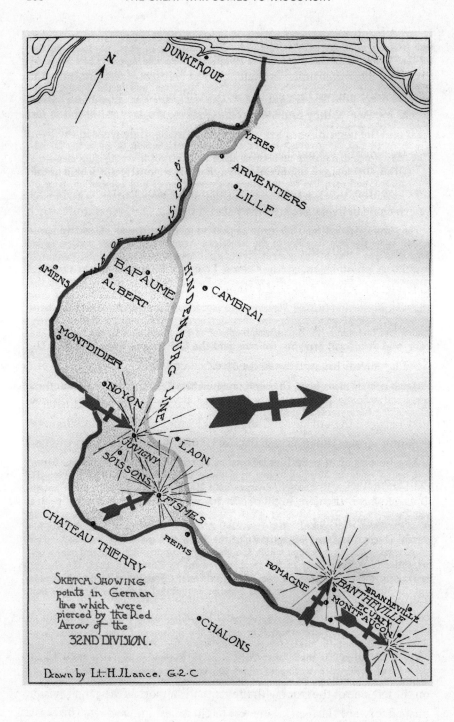

N

DUNKERQUE

YPRES

ARMENTIERS
LILLE

THE LINE OF JULY 15 1918

BAPAUME

AMIENS

ALBERT

CAMBRAI

HINDENBURG LINE

MONTDIDIER

NOYON

JUVIGNY

LAON

SOISSONS

FISMES

CHATEAU THIERRY

REIMS

ROMAGNE

BRANDEVILLE
BANTHEVILLE
ECURY
MONTFAUCON

CHALONS

Sketch Showing
points in German
line which were
pierced by the Red
Arrow of the
32ND DIVISION.

Drawn by Lt. H. J. Lance. G-2-C

remarkable achievement during which the lead units suffered through sniper attacks, machine-gun ambushes, artillery barrages, and gas attacks as they took one objective after another. On August 3, Kent of Company K recorded in his diary:

> [We advanced] thru a terrible barrage, the wounded and dead lying all around us. It was pitiful to hear the wounded crying out in agony and writheing [*sic*] in pain, but ours was the duty of "carrying on" and we had to leave them until the stretcher-bearers came along and carried them back to the dressing station. The air was almost stifeling [*sic*] with the odor of gas and powder, and the ground is literally covered with "mustard-gas." It settles upon the ground, where it is damp and low and in the dark, it shines like Sulphur. In the sunshine it vaporizes and floats in the air, again doing it's work of destruction to those who breathe it. Again, I must agree with Sherman, when he said, "War is Hell."[47]

One Ho-Chunk family paid a high price for the victory that earned the division its sobriquet of *"Les Terribles."* Although beyond normal enlistment age, Foster Decorah and three of his sons expressed their patriotism by joining the 32nd Division. They all served in Company D of the 128th Infantry. Corporal Foster Decorah and Private Robert Decorah both died on August 2, 1918, as Foster led his unit against machine-gun emplacements that were covering the German retreat. " 'Killed in action' was the brief message sent by the war department to members of his family in

FACING: The German Army created a dangerous bulge, called a salient, in the Allied lines during its massive spring offensive in 1918. The 32nd Division played a key role in pushing the Germans back across the Hindenburg Line and closing the salient. Haan chose the insignia of an arrow piercing a bar "signifying that the Division shot through every line the enemy put before it." In fact, the division achieved its goals by brute force and hard fighting. Every foot they captured, every machine-gun nest they overran, was bought dearly with men's lives. During six months of almost continuous fighting, the 32nd Division advanced thirty-eight kilometers (23.6 miles) at a cost of fourteen thousand casualties; 41 percent were killed in action, died of their wounds, were missing in action, or were severely wounded. *THE 32ND DIVISION IN THE WORLD WAR: 1917-1918* ISSUED BY THE JOINT WAR HISTORY COMMISSIONS OF MICHIGAN AND WISCONSIN, 1920

the Winnebago settlement north of Mauston." Mauston held a memorial service on August 27, 1918, for three fallen Ho-Chunk heroes from Company D, Foster and Robert Decorah and Mike Standingwater. At home in Wisconsin, families grieved.[48]

On the afternoon of August 4, the 127th returned to the lead. In brutal fighting that day, the division took Fismes, a key victory in creating a bridgehead across the Vesle River. The final assault cost the 127th Infantry Regiment dearly. The official history, *The 32nd Division in the World War*, tells the story: "In its attack on Fismes, the 127th Infantry was badly cut up, and late in the day Colonel Langdon organized a provisional battalion out of what was left of his regiment and sent this force forward to storm the town. His shattered companies made a desperate assault and finally succeeded, about nightfall, in passing through the town and establishing a position on the south bank of the river."[49]

The next day, August 5, the Third Battalion of the 128th Infantry arrived to reinforce the battered 127th. Despite getting several patrols across the river, the 128th could not hold the bridgehead. Fresh troops were needed for the renewed assault. On the night of August 6, Pennsylvania's 28th Infantry arrived to provide relief for the beleaguered Wisconsin troops. The Pennsylvanians would eventually cross the Verle and hold a bridgehead, but German snipers made the village dangerous and German and American patrols occasionally clashed in Fismes. The village remained disputed territory for several weeks.

In seven days of hard fighting, "which means shooting, marching, rushing, digging, sweating, bleeding, enduring hunger, thirst, exhaustion, cooties and all manner of the manifold hardships of war," as the official history describes it, the soldiers of the 32nd Division "had gained 19 kilometers; captured eighteen villages or fortified farms," and relieved the German army of "trainloads" of ordnance. They had done well in their first major engagement, but the cost was horrific: 777 killed in action or died of wounds, another 1,153 severely wounded or gassed, and 12 missing. An additional 2,009 men suffered slight wounds or gas.[50]

During this fight, the 32nd Division was under the authority of General L. de Mondesir, commander of the 38th French Corps. The general observed the division's inaugural experience at the front. When he learned the American division had captured every German strong point north of

By the time the Americans captured Fismes, it was a shattered imitation of a picturesque French village. WHI IMAGE ID 131013

the Ourcq River, de Mondesir reputedly exclaimed, "*Oui, Oui, Les soldats terrible, tres bien, tres bien!*" General Charles Mangin heard the story. When he asked the 32nd to join his 10th French army in late August, he referred to the division as "*Les Terribles.*" The nickname took on an aura of official sobriquet when Mangin referred to "*Les Terribles*" in a formal commendation for the division's attack on Juvigny at the end of August.[51]

After being relieved in Fismes, the division went into reserve and began a program of rest and training. Less than two weeks later they received orders to join General Mangin's 10th French army near Soissons, where they enjoyed a few days of rest before relieving the 127th French Infantry Regiment at the front during the night of August 27–28. Ahead of them lay five days of hard and continuous fighting. "It was a fight all of the time—every minute. There was no respite."[52]

The division's 63rd Brigade, comprising primarily Michigan National Guardsmen, came close to Juvigny on August 29, only to be forced into a short retreat by German machine-gun fire and artillery barrage. The brigade suffered heavy casualties. During the night they were relieved by

Two companies of tanks were assigned to the 32nd Division to assist in their advance on Juvigny. WHI IMAGE ID 131015

the Wisconsin 64th Brigade, which led a coordinated American and French attack the next day and nearly encircled Juvigny, resulting in the capture of the entire German garrison.

William Haan's creativity and adaptation made him an excellent division commander. His troops had suffered egregiously in the capture of Juvigny. In an attempt to avoid a repeat experience as the division advanced on Terny-Sorny during the first days of September, he ignored army dogma emphasizing the independent infantryman and planned an attack in coordination with artillery. Haan was an old artilleryman, and he had an unusually large number of guns at his disposal. In addition to the 57th Field Artillery, he commanded the artillery of the First Moroccan Division. In conjunction with the commander of the 57th, Haan planned to use the abundance of artillery to conduct a triple barrage. German machine gunners had become accustomed to the double barrage and stayed in their bunkers until it was over. Haan hoped the third barrage would catch the gun crews back in their nests. The strategy eliminated many of the machine-gun positions, softening the German lines for the Allied advance. By nightfall the 32nd Division was poised to take Terny-Sorny the next day, but was relieved by the First Moroccan Division, which took the village. The capture of Fismes and Juvigny cost the division dearly. On July 29, at the beginning of these operations, the division's rifle companies, which comprised the core of its strength, averaged approximately 200 men each. By the beginning of September, the rifle companies each numbered fewer than 100 men.[53]

On September 5, the 32nd received orders transferring it to the newly formed First American Army. They had the luxury of a month of rest and retraining, during which they absorbed five thousand semi-trained replacements. Soon they were on the move to the Verdun area. Even with the infusion of new troops, the division's forty-eight infantry rifle companies were still short fifty men per company, 20 percent of their strength. The division needed another 2,400 infantrymen to have a full complement of soldiers.

Despite the shortage of manpower and the raw recruits, the 32nd went back into action on September 30, slugging it out with German units for the next twenty days. Their goal was to breach the strongly fortified *Kriemhilde Stellung* line—a dense, four-kilometer-deep, layered network of defensive barbed wire, trenches, and pillboxes with overlapping firing positions. Artillery formed the final element of this defensive maze, positioned to rain destruction on attackers. The *Kriemhilde Stellung* formed the eastern end of Germany's Hindenburg Line.

To reach the *Kriemhilde Stellung*, the 32nd Division had to liberate the villages of Cierges and Gesnes. Their first day of action resulted in the quick capture of Cierges near the Meuse River, not to be confused with the village of the same name liberated in the battle for Fismes. They spent several days consolidating positions and shifting units around. On October 4, they were ready to attack German positions in the village of Gesnes, only to find the enemy had spent the lull strengthening their defenses. Dislodging the Germans required a heavy artillery barrage. Pummeled by the American guns, the German defenders retreated from Gesnes and, in turn, directed their own artillery barrage on the village and the Americans. As the American soldiers advanced on the *Kriemhilde Stellung*, the Germans gave ground only grudgingly, requiring the 32nd to eliminate several strong defensive positions. During the hard fighting that followed, the 32nd found that rifle power alone often was not enough to dislodge the enemy, so they called in artillery, poison gas, flame throwers, and tanks. Four days of intense fighting brought them to the doorstep of the *Kriemhilde Stellung* on October 9.

The battles sufficiently depleted the strength of the 32nd that they needed four days to reposition their units before resuming the offensive. A massive five-minute barrage on the German trench system preceded the attack. At 5:30 on the morning of October 14, the Americans rushed the German defenses, hoping to overwhelm the defenders before they could regain their full orientation after the shelling. One function of artillery barrages was to break up defensive barbed wire and allow attacking troops to pass through. The 126th and 128th Infantry Regiments made rapid progress, while the 127th Infantry found itself attacking uphill through intact barbed wire and against withering machine-gun fire. Finally, elements of the 126th and 127th encircled the hill known as Cote Dame Marie and forced the surrender of its defenders. The 32nd Division had breached the seemingly impregnable *Kriemhilde Stellung*.

The 32nd continued its advance for another five days. Finally, during the night of October 19, the exhausted division moved out of its frontline position and went into reserve status until November 10.

Reports of the 32nd published during the war and its immediate aftermath often used the same slogan, "the Division shot through every line the enemy put before it," inspiring the division's insignia of a red arrow shooting through a line. But the Red Arrow Division, as it came to be known, did not breeze through or effortlessly roll over the German lines. To accurately reflect the sacrifices required to "shoot through every line," the slogan should have read, "*With great dedication to duty, perseverance, and courage* the Division hammered through every line the enemy put before it."

ARMISTICE

The German will to fight was undermined by defeat on the battlefield, bread riots at home, faltering supply systems at the front, and, perhaps, the aura of the newly arrived Americans. The battles fought by the 32nd Division formed one piece of major offensives happening all along the front. Their victories and those of other American units in France signified a shift in power that enlivened the Allies and disheartened the German defenders.

As the number of American forces in France grew ever larger and the German army found it ever harder to stay in the field, families and friends of the American servicemen read news from the trenches in their local newspapers. During the summer and fall of 1918, casualty lists reminded everyone of the cost of hard-fought victories. Newspaper coverage of the war reflected some of the hardships faced by the troops and the seemingly relentless Allied offensives.

On September 8, 1918, for example, the *Wisconsin State Journal* carried two articles about the war on the front page. The headline of one told the story: "ALLIES NEARING ST. QUENTIN; FRENCH TAKE ST. SIMON; YANKS GAIN; AMERICAN GAINS PROD THE FOE TO HASTEN HIS RETIREMENT; BRITISH REACH ROISEL AND BEAUVOIS." For the reader back home, the message was clear: the Allies were advancing on all fronts. The second headline read: "RATS! MADISON YANK CATCHES NINE IN FRONT LINE 'ROOM.'" The article quoted a letter from H. D. "Hub" Stevens. "I wish you could see my cozy little 'room,'" he had written to his mother. "I have a nice cot and a table and a big box to keep my stuff in and nails on which to hang my clothes and a curtain for a door. The only trouble is that the rats have been as thick as hair on a dog's back. However I went to town and bought a rat trap and caught nine rats and they kind of leave me alone lately." He then wrote about the airplanes flying over the trenches every day and with almost poetic imagery described the planes' machine guns: "It looks as if they put a hole right through the sky every shot." Finally, he told his mother that when the American artillery targeted a battery of German heavy guns, it was like "the Fourth of July." The sanitized message to the Wisconsin reader: The war is being won and my biggest problem is catching rats.[54]

On the evening of November 10, the 32nd Division prepared to renew their assault on the German lines at 6:30 the following morning. The 127th and 128th Infantry Regiments drew frontline duty that morning and stood ready to go "over the top"—out of the trenches and on the attack. As the sun rose on November 11, artillery on both sides began exchanging their lethal greeting. As 6:30 arrived, so did runners carrying the news that an armistice would begin at 11 a.m. Unfortunately, some units had already begun the attack. It took hours to round everyone up, but the troops were all back behind American lines by 10:45. The war was almost over.

The killing continued until the armistice went into effect at the eleventh hour of the eleventh day of the eleventh month of 1918. The 32nd Division lost nineteen men on armistice day. Ironically, the last soldier from the "*Les Terribles*" to die in action was First Lieutenant William F. Davitt, a noncombatant, a Catholic priest and regimental chaplain for the 125th Infantry—killed by a piece of shrapnel from a German shell targeted at the headquarters of the 125th Infantry Regiment.[55]

These nineteen deaths offer oblique testimony to the terrible cost of victory. The 32nd Division arrived in France with approximately twenty-seven thousand men from Michigan and Wisconsin. Of the nineteen men from the 32nd Division who died on the last day of the war, William Davitt came from Michigan and three others hailed from Wisconsin. The remainder came from Connecticut, Kentucky, Louisiana, Ohio, Missouri, Illinois, Indiana, Arkansas, Minnesota, and North Dakota. In the official history of the 32nd Division, the Joint War History Commissions of Michigan and Wisconsin published an Honor Roll listing the men who gave their lives in combat or died of disease. Page after page lists the names of men from Wisconsin and Michigan, but also from virtually every state from Maine to California. Some of these men joined the 128th to fill the gap created when most of the unit was sent to the First Division in the spring of 1918, but many others were replacement troops assigned to the 32nd Division to fill the gaps left by casualties during the hard months of fighting since the spring.

THE COSTS OF WAR

For Germany, France, and Great Britain, four years of bloodletting cost an entire generation of young men. By contrast, the American Expeditionary Force (AEF) engaged in combat for only seven months and reached a peak strength of roughly 2,084,000, of which 1,390,000 (two-thirds of the force) saw combat. The combat forces suffered approximately 75,900 deaths from combat and disease, a 6 percent death rate. Most of these casualties occurred during the last four months of the war. Although the American force fired its first shot at the enemy in October 1917, it did not join major combat operations in large numbers until July 1918. The AEF suffered an average of roughly 15,000 to 18,000 deaths a month during this period of active combat.

Wisconsin contributed 118,000 troops and suffered 8,000 casualties, including 1,800 who were killed in action or died of wounds. Every community in Wisconsin felt these losses. If the Wisconsin numbers follow a pattern similar to the national scene, approximately 60,000 men saw combat. The experience of the 32nd Division brings the cost into focus. By war's end, the 32nd Division was a heralded unit, but it had paid a heavy price for its string of victories. The 32nd Division suffered the third-highest casualties for an American unit, perhaps as high as 15 to 18 percent. The dead and severely wounded were replaced by men from almost every state in the country. By the end of the war the 32nd was no longer a Wisconsin and Michigan unit; it had become an American division.[56]

Letters from soldiers and war coverage in newspapers created a shared understanding between American soldiers and Americans back home. But that understanding was based on an imperfect reflection of life at the front. Letters home were often written in ways to reassure loved ones. Major Glenn Garlock, whose letters were forthright, articulate, and even poetic, was an unusual correspondent. Garlock set out to create "pen pictures" for his wife, Anna. He did not hesitate to describe close calls, the horrors of war, and even the possibility of his own death. In a letter near the end of the war, Garlock expressed a self-conscious realization of the impact his forthrightness might have on Anna:

> Do my letters terrify you? I hope not. I try to give you pen pictures of the life. It is not all easy, it is not all safe and not entirely healthy and yet neither is the reverse true. The stars shine as brilliantly tonight as ever, the woods are green and alluring, to tired bodies sleep is so welcome and refreshing that even air attacks often fail to break it.[57]

A few days later, Garlock wrote to Anna:

> I have been writing to you with much regularity and hope you have received my many lengthy epistles. There have been times when I have feared that any day might be my last. For this reason I have tried

to keep a steady stream of letters going back so that you would know week by week that I was still alive and kicking. I suppose your feelings have been harrowed by reading long lists of casualties some of which you must have known were ours. If I understand the system aright casualty lists are not issued until 24 hours after the nearest relative has been notified so you need not fear to look over the news in that line if you have not had a telegram from the War Dept.[58]

What the soldiers' family and friends understood about the war experience was shaped by what soldiers chose to communicate in letters home, what censors allowed them to communicate, and the inconsistent and sometimes biased nature of newspaper coverage. Opinions and understandings were also shaped by what relatives, friends, and neighbors shared with each other. The shared understanding often was more about men doing their duty than about the carnage of war. When the war ended and soldiers returned, they brought many secrets with them, but they also returned to communities that had shared some small part of their experiences.

With the end of the war, more than two million American "doughboys" began crossing the Atlantic for home. This time they crossed without fear of submarine attack or need for naval escort. The 32nd Division had become one of the most respected units of the AEF. Instead of orders to return home, the men of the 32nd, along with those of the First and Second Divisions of the regular army, and the 42nd Division from the National Guard, all storied units, received orders to march on to Germany as the army of occupation. The first units of the 32nd finally set sail for home on April 20, 1919. By May 22, the final contingents arrived in New York. As veterans arrived home they were honored for their service and sacrifice.

They returned to a country at once familiar and different. Comrades lay buried in France. Loved ones had sacrificed at home to win the war, and some bore bitter memories of repression because of their political beliefs or ethnic heritage. Soon the nation would enter a period of peace and prosperity, but also disillusionment over the costs of the war. Wilson's great legacy, the League of Nations, would never reach its full potential as American participation collapsed amidst political rankling between the president and the Senate.

Soldiers tried to return to civilian life as best they could. Of the soldiers whose letters, diaries, and memoirs are included here, William Bruce, Glenn Garlock, Samuel Kent, and Walter Zukowski returned home to their families and to long and productive lives. Bruce sailed home on the Italian steamer *America*. Upon arrival home he reveled in his own bed, civilian clothes, and his mother's cooking. He went on to a career as a chemistry teacher and school superintendent in Park Falls and Sparta. Garlock sailed on the *Washington* along with General Haan and the 127th Infantry. He returned to West Salem and edited *The West Salem Nonpareil Journal* for twenty years. He became best known as the historian of the 32nd Division. Kent also sailed on the *Washington*. On May 19, he arrived unannounced at his parent's home in Baltimore to the surprise and great joy of his family. Kent became a mail carrier for the US Postal Service, where he worked for thirty-four years. Zukowski, or "Zucki" as he was known, arrived home to Milwaukee in 1919, worked in retail, and rose to become a divisional merchandise manager and telephone service supervisor for Sears Roebuck Co.

Gaylord Bradley, the young musician, did not come home. He "died of his wounds" on October 6, 1918. We do not know more than this. Was he wounded by machine-gun fire while collecting the dead or injured in no-man's-land? Was he killed in an artillery barrage behind the lines? Was he one of the many for whom a gas attack resulted in a lingering death? We will never know.

CHAPTER 4

LIFE ON THE HOME FRONT

Sunday April 8/17

My Dearest Anna

*. . . Well if you got the papers of Thursday you will see that I with
49 others voted against war. I listened to 17 hours of the 18 hours of
debate & weighed every argument & circumstance & concluded we
should not declare war. I expect to be criticized & branded as a coward
etc. but the future will judge & judge rightly. When the boys are being
conscripted & sent to the trenches in Europe to fight the battles of other
nations our people will begin to question the wisdom of the course
taken. But now that we are at war it is the duty of every loyal citizen
to stand by his government & its flag without faltering or delay.*

*Your Loving
John [Esch]*[1]

Once Congress declared war, the semblance of normal life continued:
individuals went to school and to work, families raised their children,
neighbors shared gossip over the fence, and on Sundays many people went
to church. This normalcy obscured the tensions of home-front life created
by equal parts worry, sacrifice, and patriotism, amidst constant reminders
that the nation was in jeopardy of being overwhelmed by the autocratic,
militaristic Hun.

The war touched every heart in America.

The war reached into every kitchen in America.

The war tapped every pocketbook in America.

The war dominated life in America.

Shaping Public Opinion During the War

Although the declaration of war brought a surge of patriotic fervor, American officials remained concerned about the lack of national consensus. Northeastern states seemed in full support of the war, but the vote in the House of Representatives suggested a lack of unity in the Midwest. Fifty representatives voted against the declaration of war. More than half of the "no" votes came from just six Midwest states: Wisconsin, Illinois, Minnesota, Missouri, Nebraska, and Iowa. Only two votes against the declaration of war came from the Northeast, one each from New York and Massachusetts. The United States entered the war without national unity or, in some regions, any great enthusiasm.

In September 1914 the British Foreign Office created the War Propaganda Bureau, a secret office assigned the task of creating and distributing pro-British propaganda. The bureau's most important subunit was the American Ministry of Information (AMI), which flooded the United States with information favorable to the Allied cause. To target its propaganda effectively, the AMI studied and reported on US public opinion. In an era before public opinion polls, the American Ministry of Information used US newspaper reports, augmented by information from contacts in the United States, as the basis for *American Press Resumes*, weekly reports about public opinion in the United States kept secret from all but the highest echelons of the British government. Washington was not privy to this information at the time, but it is available to researchers today and corroborates the US government's concern about public support for the war. The *American Press Resumes* reported that even after the declaration of war the American people in general were slow in reacting and perhaps even apathetic. Reports from May and June 1917 indicated that US citizens considered the war "with a feeling of its inevitability rather than with any enthusiasm." The report of June 27 reads, "In spite of the President's assurances, doubts still appear in some quarters as to why the United States is in the war, and what she is fighting for."[2]

Without a national consensus about the war and its goals, the government initiated a variety of measures designed to promote loyalty, patriotism, and sacrifice through a mixture of voluntary action and coercion. Much as Wilson had feared, but nonetheless at his own behest, his government became increasingly hostile to ideas and actions that might jeopardize the fragile unity of wartime society. Freedom of speech became something to be controlled and dissent to be crushed. The federal government set out to mold wartime life to the needs of the war effort by controlling the economy, managing the administration's message, and curtailing free speech.

The Council of National Defense, the Food Administration, the Fuel Administration, and the War Industries Board managed and coordinated different segments of the economy and life on the home front. The Council of National Defense had relatively little direct authority over state activities, but in many states such as Wisconsin the council's recommendations were interpreted as orders. As the war progressed, the council wielded

The patriotic surge that came with the declaration of war immediately placed Woodrow Wilson in a hallowed pantheon of war presidents including Washington, Lincoln, and McKinley. *GREEN BAY PRESS GAZETTE*, APRIL 6, 1917

considerable indirect power through the state councils. The Food and Fuel Administrations and the War Industries Board exercised considerable control over the home front as they promoted the conservation of food and fuel and coordinated manufacturing and agriculture. Through these bureaucracies, wartime controls touched everyone.

Under the leadership of journalist George Creel, the Committee on Public Information (CPI) shaped public perceptions of US involvement in the war for both domestic and foreign audiences. Creel used every available mechanism of public distribution: newspapers, film, graphic art, public speakers. He recruited respected writers such as novelist Edna Ferber and journalist William Allen White to write about American life for publication in the foreign press.

Under Creel's direction, during the war the CPI made inspirational documentary films using footage shot by the Signal Corps, and it worked with commercial producers to make additional films. Ranging in length from one reel to a dozen or more, CPI films were designed to be shown anywhere an audience could gather: churches, schools, libraries, meeting halls, and theaters. Film topics included recruiting, military maneuvers, selling bonds, women in the war, and the participation of Native Americans and African Americans in the war effort.

Pershing's Crusaders, for example, was an eight-reel feature film released in May 1918. It was advertised as "telling authentically the story of all our war activities." After the credits the film's first intertitle card told viewers, "The mailed fist of the 'Rule of Might' lies heavy upon Europe. To it no contract is binding, no obligation is worthy of fulfillment, no word of honor sacred." Later, after watching images of Belgian refugees and destroyed villages, viewers read: "Plots, fires, strikes, agitations, fomented by German agents to strike terror in our hearts have but fixed our determination to conquer at whatever cost." The film showed war production, draft registration, troop training, American Expeditionary Force arrival in France, and, at the end, a great mass of French and American soldiers marching on to the war. In the last scene, the viewer saw a smoldering map of Europe overlaid with an American flag. The movie was patriotic and uplifting. Advertising for the film depicted Pershing riding alongside knights in a medieval crusade. The message was absolutely clear: the American Expeditionary Force was fighting for a righteous cause.

Perhaps most memorable, the CPI developed posters and window cards exhorting citizens to do their patriotic duty, for which Creel recruited noted artists to contribute almost fifteen hundred drawings. Some images, such as the one of Uncle Sam declaring I WANT YOU FOR THE U.S. ARMY, became iconic representations of the time. Particularly memorable were the images of flag-draped young women planting victory gardens or urging the purchase of Liberty Bonds, as well as images of apelike Germans ravaging Europe. The posters were designed to move the spirit, inspire patriotic action, and build a national consensus in support of the war effort. They were ubiquitous. Everywhere Americans looked—in libraries, banks, retail stores, government offices—posters promoted wartime causes.

The CPI also organized the Four Minute Men—an organization of seventy-five thousand speakers who delivered hundreds of thousands of four-minute inspirational speeches across the country during the last year of the war. Generally presented in movie theaters as the projectionist changed film reels, these speeches promoted food conservation, bond campaigns, and other patriotic activities. In Wisconsin the Loyalty Legion distributed millions of CPI leaflets and managed the appointment schedule for the Four Minute Men. By the armistice on November 11, 1918, Wisconsin's Four Minute Men had delivered more than five thousand speeches throughout the state.[3]

Wilson's administration need not have worried about unifying American society. The gradual heightening of tensions between the United States and Germany had prepared Americans for war. By the time Wilson spoke to Congress on April 2, the chorus advocating war was reaching a crescendo. The peace advocates were about to be drowned out by a countervailing force that defined loyalty and patriotism as support for the president and the government. In Wisconsin, at patriotic meetings across the state in the months leading up to the declaration of war, speakers helped audiences make the rhetorical transition from esoteric grievances about submarine warfare and international law to the more familiar if less defined reasons for war: protection of rights, defense of national honor, defeat of despotic autocracy, preservation of democracy, and survival of civilization.

When the United States finally became an active belligerent, outward opposition to the war disappeared virtually overnight. The vast majority of Americans seemed to accept the fact of being a nation at war and

Perhaps the most memorable of the World War I posters produced by the Committee on Public Information. Artist James Montgomery Flagg drew inspiration from a similar British poster of Lord Kitchener urging enlistments. Four million copies of the Uncle Sam poster were distributed across the nation. WHI IMAGE ID 32145

Private organizations as well as the government promoted patriotic behavior through poster art. Often depicting heroic figures such as Miss Liberty, posters called on citizens to plant gardens, conserve food, donate to the YMCA, or volunteer for the Red Cross. Posters were part of the ever-present campaign to encourage active participation in the war effort on the home front. WHI IMAGE ID 3548

supported the president as a matter of patriotic duty. With the exception of the Socialist Party and some of its most prominent leaders, those who opposed the war generally fell silent, lest they face the penalties of opposition: community ostracism, judicial scrutiny, government sanction, or retribution from pro-war vigilantes. Others, like Wisconsin Congressman John Esch, supported the war effort as a matter of patriotic obligation. Very few individuals possessed the political support and personal fortitude necessary to critique wartime policies and propose alternatives.

In a sense, going to war was easier than remaining at peace. Going to war meant taking action to control the future. It provided the satisfaction of righting a wrong, of fighting for an idealized democratic world order. In contrast, staying at peace meant reacting to events controlled by others. Wilson had defined the cause with righteous rhetoric. Although peace advocates would have defined a desirable future in equally righteous terms, they were drowned out by those who defined peace as cowardly capitulation to an evil autocracy. Taking action, terrible as the results would be, was preferable to most Americans than the seeming cowardice of hiding behind the Atlantic shield with the sheathed sword of diplomacy at their side.[4]

Headlines shouted WAR IS DECLARED and U.S. ENTERS WAR, conveying in word and style that it was time for everyone to join the war effort. An individual who read a local newspaper during March and April of 1917 as the nation went to war could come to only one set of conclusions: the United States was in jeopardy from Germany and possibly Mexico; the nation was in a righteous fight to preserve democratic government; the future of humanity lay in the balance; and the nation was marshalling unparalleled strength to enter the fray. There were rumors of Mexican armies at the border and German submarines patrolling the coast. The *La Crosse Tribune and Leader-Press* ran a story titled "HUNT FOR SPIES IS UNDER WAY THROUGHOUT UNITED STATES," and the *Wisconsin State Journal* told readers, "8 SPY SUSPECTS TAKEN IN CHICAGO." The *Green Bay Press-Gazette* informed its readers, "GERMAN SUBMARINES READY TO ATTACK UNITED STATES," accompanied by an Associated Press story out of Birmingham, Alabama, about German agents posing as Bible salesmen and Christian ministers, encouraging African Americans in the deep South to migrate to Mexico. In New York, Secret Service agents took into custody "one of the 'master spies' of Germany's vast system of espionage."

Community and business leaders across the country worried about the security of local infrastructure, including bridges, dams, and factories. Federal marshals immediately advised county sheriffs in Wisconsin to increase their vigilance and report any suspicious or seditious activities. In this small way the far-reaching surveillance system of World War I began its evolution. Eventually it would involve not only local law enforcement and federal marshals but also the Bureau of Investigation (the precursor to the FBI) and its volunteer force of local informers known collectively as the American Protective League.

Explicitly and implicitly, news coverage during the first days of the war also conveyed the optimistic message that the once-neutral giant was now angry, seeking justice, and girding for war. With a little hyperbole, headlines on the front page of the *Eau Claire Leader* on April 6 made the story clear: "UNITED STATES BRINGS POWER NEVER EQUALED INTO WORLD CONFLICT—OVER 20,000,000 MEN CAPABLE OF MILITARY DUTY—Army Is Now Small, But Efficient; Navy Will Rank Among Foremost Afloat—Industrial Resources Have Been Mobilized; Labor Will Back President." National Guard units prepared for imminent mobilization.[5]

Most expressions of patriotism went unheralded by public notice because they were small personal actions. In contrast, periodic rallies and parades fulfilled the need for a community expression of loyalty and unity and a public affirmation of faith in the nation. Monroe, Wisconsin, provided a dramatic example of the complexity of community attitudes about war. The city achieved notoriety when residents voted ten to one for an antiwar referendum on April 3, 1917. The referendum clearly communicated that voters in Monroe wanted no part of the war in Europe. Two days later, as the House of Representatives debated the declaration of war, five thousand people marched in a patriotic parade around the Monroe town square and filled the armory. Half the audience was proudly of German heritage. They and their neighbors pledged their loyalty to the nation. The local newspaper hailed the rally as "indisputable proof that the people of this community can exercise the inalienable right of Americans to express themselves on any question of national policy and still remain loyal and patriotic citizens."[6]

The *Janesville Daily Gazette* succinctly placed Monroe's war referendum in context and defended the right of local residents to express their views: "The scene was a most dramatic one, and it was a most fitting answer to the charges of some of the local war fanatics, who charged disloyalty because Monroe people at the polls dared to exemplify the inherent right of Americans to express their opinion on the present crisis by a referendum vote, strongly opposing a declaration of war by congress."[7]

During the earliest days of the war, patriotism was often invoked to boost public participation and demonstrate local devotion to the war effort. When the Eau Claire cavalry troop needed new recruits to bolster its ranks, C. W. Johnson, the troop's commander, wrote an open letter to the newspaper and explicitly made community attendance at a recruiting rally a measure of patriotism.

> The people of Eau Claire should show that they are for America, now and always by turning out tonight and give their support to the men who are offering their service to the country.
>
> Be a patriot![8]

The event was well attended and the troop enrolled more than eighty new men, more than enough to bring its roster to full strength.

The emphasis on loyalty, duty, and patriotism permeated wartime life. Flags flew on street corners, in window displays, and on newspaper mastheads. The war was the topic of discussion everywhere.

In the days immediately following the declaration of war, a few letters supporting John Esch's antiwar vote continued to arrive in his congressional office, but they no longer made up the bulk of his correspondence. Most letters that mentioned the war struck a patriotic note, the greatest number of which criticized the congressman's war vote and urged him to support the president. George Andrews of Baraboo told Esch:

> I hesitated to line myself up to the need of urging War before the final break came, but after the declaration, I stand firmly for ample preparation, and doing it quickly as possible and it seems to me that we can only do it in this manner, by coming out now for the draft system.
>
> We must now use our full force, as promptly as possible, to bring this war to a Glorious Victory for Our Nation.

In wartime, Americans look for symbols around which they can unite. The most natural and powerful symbol is the American flag. During World War I most newspapers sported a flag on the front or editorial page. Woe be to the poor soul who disrespected the flag, as such behavior could get the culprit thrown in jail or beaten by a vigilante mob.

GREEN BAY PRESS GAZETTE, MAY 2, 1917; *GREEN BAY PRESS GAZETTE*, JUNE 14, 1917; *RACINE JOURNAL NEWS*, APRIL 6, 1917

The Flag

By Berton Braley

Against the skies Old Glory flies,
 It's never looked so bright,
For now it seems as if it gleams
 With some strange inner light;
As though each thread of white and red,
 Each filament of blue,
Were spun of spiritual fire,
The flame of that fine high desire,
 Which thrills the nation through.
The flag on high it greets the eye
 And grips our hearts somehow,
Though it has passed through struggles vast,
 Its proudest hour is now;
Now 'tis unfurled to show the world
 That willingly we give
Our lives, our all to Liberty,
That after we have ceased to be,
 The flag, the flag may live!

Esch agreed. After explaining to another constituent that he voted against war out of fear that "our troops would be sent to the trenches of Europe," Esch exhorted that it was time for Americans to "stand behind the government" and work for a "speedy victory." Similarly, he told W. H. McFetridge of Reedsburg: "Now that we are at war, it becomes the duty of every citizen to loyally support the government." Esch planned to support the draft as a way to equalize the burdens and sacrifices of war. He concluded his reply to McFetridge with a cautionary note: "While we should feel charitable towards our citizens of Teutonic decent during these days of stress and strain let us not question their loyalty to the stars and stripes. Their watchword as well as ours should be America for all and all for America."[9]

Robert La Follette is often remembered as a disloyal obstructionist during the war because he opposed conscription, supported free speech, and refused to follow the president blindly. La Follette might have disputed the declaration of war, but in the end he chose to support the troops. Like Esch and others in the Wisconsin delegation, La Follette believed the declaration of war imposed obligations not to be shirked or avoided. In an article critical of Socialist opposition to the war, La Follette made this opinion clear:

> Everyone must admit that we are in this war lawfully and in a constitutional manner. The obligations we, as a people, have assumed in this war have been lawfully assumed and we must lawfully accept them. We can no more repudiate our obligations to prosecute this war efficiently until it can be ended honorably than we can repudiate our obligations to pay the debts we have contracted in the prosecution of the war. Over this proposition there can be no reasonable dispute or controversy.[10]

Judge J. M. Becker, a staunch La Follette supporter and organizer of the Monroe war referendum, made a similar public statement on the day his country declared war:

> Congress, vested with the constitutional authority has deemed it necessary to declare that a state of war exists between the United States and Germany. This mandate is now the law of the land.

As author and instigator of the war referendum, I deem it fitting to state that it is now the duty of every American citizen to stand by the Government.[11]

Near the end of April, an estimated ten thousand to fifteen thousand people gathered in La Crosse's Riverside Park to sing patriotic songs, listen to stirring speeches, and pledge allegiance to the United States. The *La Crosse Tribune* described an almost religious fervor at the gathering, as attendees pledged their dedication to the nation and its war effort. The newspaper told its readers: "La Crosse County Consecrated to America." The crowd

> unanimously rededicated itself to the uttermost service of America and American ideals, endorsed America's stand for freedom and humanity, and committed itself to active service and fullest sacrifice by authorizing the organization of the La Crosse County Council of Defense, to cooperate with the National and Wisconsin Councils of Defense in all steps deemed essential to security at home and to the successful prosecution of the war.

This civic enthusiasm may have waned as the novelty wore off and as the war became part of everyday life, but it fairly represented the initial response to the First World War in communities across the state and nation. In similar fashion, a patriotic mass meeting filled the Milwaukee city auditorium with an enthusiastic audience pledged "to protect American lives and American rights."[12]

A national solidarity was coalescing around an enormous charge: build an army of two million to three million men almost from scratch, keep it in the field for an indefinite period of time, and supply food and materiel to the Allies. To do this, the nation's agriculture systems would need to produce the crops essential for domestic, military, and Allied consumption; family consumption of food would need to match national priorities; industry would need to be harnessed to produce the weapons and supplies of war; and labor would need to be found for the army and for increased agricultural and industrial production. These efforts were going to require a massive overhaul of the economy as well as the national coordination of farm and factory, in ways that demanded vast sacrifices from everyday Americans. Participating in a patriotic rally was easy, but living patrioti- cally was much more difficult. The response often was highly individual- istic. Knowledge, skill, occupation, wealth, family duties, organizational affiliations, race, ethnicity, and myriad other factors helped determine the roles that individuals played in wartime society. A common theme emerged: the declaration of war had brought great clarity, and the question "Will we fight?" was replaced by the questions "*How* will we fight?" and "What will I personally do for the war effort?"

Organizing the state's residents in support of the war effort was the her- culean task of the Wisconsin State Council of Defense. University of Wis- consin history professor A. L. P. (Alfred) Dennis is credited with suggesting that Governor Philipp establish a state council modeled after the Council of National Defense. On Philipp's recommendation the legislature acted quickly. One week after the declaration of war, Wisconsin became the first state to form a council of defense, which quickly established chapters in every county. Other states would soon follow suit, and state councils became the active agents through which the Council of National Defense carried out its work across the country.

The demands of war imposed a thread of sacrifice and uncertainty woven into daily life, composed of military duty, casualties, fund drives, shortages, and conservation. In addition to the tension and sacrifices ex- perienced by everyone in wartime society, German Americans and other ethnic groups whose homelands were at war with the Allies endured public distrust based on the assumption that loyalty followed ethnicity. More than anything else, military service imposed hardships on families, as young men and sometimes breadwinners left home for duty with no release date. As the National Guard mobilized, state and local officials recognized the need to provide financial support to the dependents of men in service. The Wisconsin Soldiers Aid Law, providing modest financial assistance to de- pendents of Wisconsin residents called into service, went into effect in July 1917, four months before a comparable federal program began.

Since 1914 Americans had been reading daily accounts of the European meat grinder. Now, with American boys headed to European battlefields, the news from France took on new poignancy, and casualty lists made the terrible costs all too clear. The unsettling question "Who will be next?"

was on everyone's mind. Whatever one's political beliefs or opinion of the war, the desire to end the carnage and bring the boys home was a powerful motivation encouraging people on the home front to sacrifice in the name of the war effort.[13]

THE WAR COMES TO AMERICA'S KITCHENS

The need for food to feed the army and the Allies, combined with several bad grain harvests, created a crisis. Early in the war, transportation difficulties disrupted the flow of grain from Russia to Western Europe. As the belligerent nations mobilized their armies, large numbers of farm laborers went to the battle front, crippling domestic farm production. An increase in American grain shipments to the United Kingdom, France, and Italy made up some of the deficit during 1917, but at the cost of rising prices in the United States. Inflation plagued US consumers even before American entry into the war. Market pressures drove the price of a bushel of wheat in the United States from $1.42 in 1916 to $3.25 in May 1917. Between 1914 and 1917, the cost of flour rose 95 percent, corn meal 100 percent, sugar 125 percent, beans 150 percent, and onions 250 percent. The cost of the humble potato rose an amazing 300 percent. To help control this inflation, the Secretary of Agriculture recommended "the government be given power to buy and sell products and to license and regulate packing and storage concerns."[14]

The food crisis was well known to Wisconsin consumers. Not only were high prices hitting their pocketbooks, but farmers and home gardeners were being told to grow as much as possible. A little more than a week after the declaration of war, University of Wisconsin agricultural extension agents were called to a meeting in Madison "to devise means of increasing production of foodstuffs." Based on a federal report distributed to the agents, the United States led the world in the production of corn, wheat, oats, cotton, tobacco, and hops. The US harvest in 1916 declined in all of these and most other categories compared to the previous year. In many cases, world production also declined. In 1916 the world corn crop was 85 percent of the 1915 crop. The United States wheat harvest fell to 62 percent of the 1915 harvest. Prior to the war the United States was a net importer of agricultural products. Now, with European production crippled by war, the nation's farmers were being asked to overcome the bad harvests, increase production, and become net exporters.[15]

University of Wisconsin agricultural officials quickly recognized that consumer hoarding was distorting the relationship between supply and demand and creating unnecessary problems in the agricultural delivery system. A month after the agricultural extension meeting, Henry Russell, dean of the UW College of Agriculture, told a gathering of newspaper publishers from across the state that they were on the front line in the fight against hoarding. Russell reassured the journalists that food supplies were ample for domestic needs and argued that hoarding only served to raise prices and hamper distribution to meet domestic and foreign needs. In other words, there was no need to hoard supplies out of fear of scarcity or going hungry. Russell, Governor Philipp, and university president Charles Van Hise all urged the newspapermen to popularize the anti-hoarding message: "Buy as you eat." The university also reassigned faculty as county agricultural advisors and produced posters to promote agriculture. Each poster carried the slogan "More Food This Year Is Patriotism." As in other areas of home-front life, growing more food had become a litmus test of an individual's devotion to the war effort.[16]

Recognition of the food crisis and its relationship to homemakers was so clear that women's organizations tended to identify their members as the solution to the problem.[17] When the Wisconsin Federation of Women's Clubs met in West Allis late in May 1917, Margaret P. Radcliffe, chairwoman of the conservation committee, addressed women across the state when she said:

> Never before has America faced the responsibility of supplying food for its own people and fighting men and also for the nations by whose side we are fighting. We must share with our allies to the last crust.
>
> Food conservation is therefore a duty which every citizen owes to the country—a dictate of patriotism which, in the words of the president, "no one can now expect ever to be excused or forgiven for ignoring."

Radcliffe called on Wisconsin women to help increase production, and to "dry, can, and conserve food products. We can largely control household waste. We can set the example of intelligent economy." As managers of home and family, the argument went, women had a patriotic duty to help solve the food crisis.[18]

Action at the state level was one answer to the growing food crisis, but the nation needed a more coordinated program. Poor harvests, rising world demand, inadequate supply, and inflated prices raised serious concerns within the Wilson administration that greater production and haphazard voluntary conservation would be inadequate to feed civilian and military populations in the United States and the Allied nations. One month after the declaration of war, Wilson appointed Herbert Hoover to head the newly created Food Administration. Hoover's assignment: create an effective system for managing the conservation and distribution of food. Hoover had gained international recognition for helping Americans stranded in Europe in 1914 and for providing relief supplies to captive Belgium. His selection to lead the new agency was no accident. During the first five months of 1917, as it looked increasingly likely that the United States would enter the war, Hoover actively courted major administration figures and met with Wilson in the hope of securing the top position in an agency managing the nation's food supply—an agency that, at the time, did not yet exist.

News of Hoover's appointment was greeted with acclaim by newspapers and politicians alike. Hoover accepted Wilson's offer only after receiving assurances that he would have the authority and independence necessary to succeed. Hoover's Food Administration would work closely with the Department of Agriculture, but he would report directly to Wilson.

Hoover returned to the United States from Europe in 1917 with the experiences of a diplomat, a deep understanding of Allied needs, and faith in the resilience of the American consumer. Hoover rejected authoritarian measures, government regulation, and rationing. He believed prices could be controlled through voluntary restraint exercised throughout the commercial chain, from producer to distributer to retailer to consumer. Perhaps a reflection of his Quaker upbringing, Hoover demonstrated great faith in the ability of average citizens to discern the proper course and follow it. Hoover also was a realist prepared to apply pressure or take punitive action against commercial entities unwilling to cooperate voluntarily. With the authority of the president and informed by faith and realism, Hoover set about harnessing food for the war effort.[19]

Herbert Hoover made a fortune as a mining engineer. When the war started in 1914, he was living in London and immediately turned his attention to helping Americans get home. He then organized an effective Belgian relief effort. By the time President Wilson asked Hoover to manage the nation's growing food crisis, he was one of the most highly regarded private citizens in America and Europe. When he arrived in Washington to head the Food Administration, he already possessed great moral authority. Relying primarily on volunteer cooperation, Hoover successfully harnessed the patriotism of his fellow Americans to eat less and waste less in order to feed the United States and the Allies. WHI IMAGE ID 23792

On June 19, 1917, Hoover explained his strategy to the Senate Committee on Agriculture: "It is our desire to decentralize our administration into the hands of State administrations at every point possible. Our theory of administration is that we should centralize ideas and decentralize execution." This approach was well formed even before he left London to return home. In a press release sent to the *New York Times* Hoover outlined the key elements of what would become the Food Administration's program: increase production, eliminate waste, prevent American products from reaching Germany through neutral nations, and stamp out profiteering. Hoover believed "all these are problems which the capacity and high ideals of self-sacrifice of the American people can solve smoothly and efficiently." Most of all, because 85 percent of "American food is consumed in the household," Hoover wrote, "the women of America thus really control America's food consumption."[20]

The United States had enough food to feed its people. The core issue for the new Food Administration was how to create the greatest possible surplus for use feeding the Allies. By the time the Food Administration began tackling the problem during the summer of 1917 the only immediate way to increase the surplus was conservation. Farmers had completed planting for the 1917 harvest. Increased agricultural production could not play a role in the food crisis until the harvest of 1918. Thus, Hoover's first task was to convince homemakers to pledge their willingness to conserve food and avoid waste as official members of the Food Administration. Hoover launched his first pledge drive in mid-July 1917, using local Council of Defense women's committees as foot soldiers canvassing door-to-door. The campaign lasted roughly eight weeks. The women asked each home-maker they contacted to sign a pledge card. The Hoover pledge read:

> I am glad to join in the service of the food conservation for our nation and I hereby accept membership in the United States Food Administration, pledging myself to carry out the directions and advice of the food administration in the conduct of my household, insofar as my circumstances permit.[21]

In return, people who signed the pledge received a window display card and a card with conservation hints to post in the kitchen. The first pledge drive was hastily organized and reached a minority of homes.

Each state was expected to create an infrastructure through which the Food Administration could work. Hoover appointed Magnus Swenson to be federal food administrator for Wisconsin. At the same time Swenson continued serving as the chairman of the State Council of Defense. This simple appointment created a unified leadership for managing the labor supply, monitoring the Liberty Loan drives, conserving fuel, and managing virtually every other aspect of home front life. In his capacity as Food Administrator, Swenson was able to harness the full power of the state council and its county chapters, creating a robust infrastructure for Hoover's conservation program that reached into every community in Wisconsin virtually overnight. In fact, Swenson had recognized the pending food crisis during the previous spring and began an intensive campaign in mid-March 1917 to encourage farm and garden production. By that summer, local vegetables were readily available in many markets and the Council of Defense turned its attention to promoting home canning and drying.[22]

Hoover's second pledge drive utilized the state infrastructure and was better organized. The campaign began in August 1917 and lasted into November. Although the federal government encouraged a focused effort at

Magnus Swenson took the reins of the Wisconsin Council of Defense and the state food administration. Just as Herbert Hoover did for the nation, Swenson's commonsense approach to managing food and fuel supplies encouraged average Wisconsinites to do their part to win the war. WHI IMAGE ID 5109

the end of that period and beginning of November, state and even county organizations had the authority and flexibility to undertake additional efforts using methods of their choosing. The conservation message reached a population ready to listen. The response was overwhelming. By October 1917, nearly five hundred thousand volunteers were canvassing the United States, going door-to-door collecting Hoover pledges. Approximately fourteen million women across the country signed the pledge and joined the Food Administration.

President Wilson gave the campaign a boost by proclaiming the week beginning Monday, October 29, as Hoover Pledge Card Week. The fall pledge drive demonstrated the wisdom of delegating to state and local organizers. With direction from the State Council of Defense, each county planned their pledge drive to match local conditions. In La Crosse, the *Tribune* boldly announced, "A Message from the Government of the United States to Every Citizen of La Crosse County." The article painted a dire picture of starvation in Europe, forcefully urged people to cooperate with Hooverizing, and warned that rationing would result if they failed. More than two hundred Council of Defense volunteers canvassed every house in La Crosse, and major civic leaders held nightly meetings in rural areas of the county to promote the pledge. Four days into the drive, La Crosse officials estimated better than 80 percent compliance with the pledge drive. When the campaign wrapped up in November, La Crosse reported that an astounding 100 percent of county households had pledged to follow the Food Administration's conservation program, tied with Green Lake County.

Members of the Winnebago County women's committee worked with local women's clubs to recruit approximately seventy-five canvassers to visit every home in Oshkosh not already displaying the Hoover pledge window card. They also met with club women in Neenah and Menasha to organize the canvass in those cities. The first pledge drive amassed only twenty-five hundred pledges from city women and overlooked rural areas of the county. The defense council women also worked with approximately one hundred teachers to secure pledges from rural mothers through their school-age children.

Before beginning their pledge drive, Sheboygan County organizers asked teachers to explain the Hoover pledge to their students, and the *Sheboygan Press* carried Magnus Swenson's call to action: "Our meatless and wheatless days are being observed in many homes, but every table in Wisconsin should serve these patriotic meals on these days. I ask every woman to sign the food pledge card and to live up to it until the war is won."

Dane County enrolled an estimated 87 percent of households, placing it third in the state. Achieving these results required social pressure to encourage enrollment. The first Dane County pledge drive had enrolled 5,249 households, only 29 percent of the estimated 18,088 households in the county. The Dane County Council of Defense decided to rectify this poor showing with a ten-day, whirlwind effort in November. On November 18, the final day of the drive, promoters of the pledge went door-to-door in a manner that made it difficult for housewives to turn them down. Phoebe Ayer, organizer of the drive, reported triumphantly that they added 10,448 pledges. They achieved this result through hard work and concerted effort. Ayer told the Wisconsin Council of Defense, "The last day of the drive we arranged an automobile parade that went through every street in Madison, and at every house where the Food Pledge card was not to be seen in the window an automobile stopped, and one of the women from the automobile went to the house and got the housewife to sign. There was scarcely a house in Madison at the end of the campaign that did not display a food pledge card."

After the pledge drive, the defense council set out to more thoroughly organize the towns and villages across Dane County. Only in the towns of Berry, Roxbury, and Springfield did they have difficulty. Ayer attributed the problem to the fact that those towns were "entirely rural" and "entirely German."[23]

The pledge was updated periodically to keep pace with changing conditions. In each case, the new version was more stringent than the last. Those who signed the pledge during the second national campaign agreed to follow eight basic rules: (1) eat one wheatless meal per day and order bread in advance so bakers would not waste wheat by overproducing; (2) eat beef, mutton, and pork only once a day and in smaller portions; (3) save milk for children; (4) conserve butter by using other fats in cooking; (5) conserve sugar; (6) conserve coal and other fuels; (7) use plentiful fruits and vegetables and can or dry the surplus; and (8) patronize local producers in order to save transportation costs and fuel.[24]

Once again, each woman who signed the pledge received a card to post in her kitchen. One side of the card explained the reasons for conservation; the other side provided directions regarding what should be conserved, as well as helpful substitutions for use when cooking.[25]

Although the act of signing was technically voluntary, house-to-house canvassing and the public display of window cards made taking the Hoover pledge almost compulsory. When patriotism failed, public pressure helped achieve widespread compliance.

Wheatless and meatless days soon became synonymous with "Hooverizing" and the system became ever more regimented. Homemakers and restaurants were instructed to observe "wheatless" Mondays and Wednesdays plus one wheatless meal each day, "meatless" Tuesdays, "porkless" Saturdays, as well as breakfast each day without meat. Meat was defined as beef, pork, or mutton. Fish, poultry, eggs, and cheese could be substituted in a "meatless" meal. To the modern mind accustomed to vegetarian diets and to chicken as the dominant meat, the meat restrictions seem to be a minor sacrifice. But for Americans during the second decade of the twentieth century, meat—especially beef or pork—was an important part of every meal, considered by many people to be essential for good health. As wheat restrictions forced consumers to rethink the texture and flavor of bread, the limits on meat consumption represented real sacrifices as families carried out their patriotic duty.[26]

A hotel proprietor or restaurant owner who ignored the Food Administration's conservation measures risked public shaming or prosecution. When Frank Smith, the Brown County food administrator, began receiving reports from federal authorities that some smaller hotels and boarding houses were ignoring meatless and wheatless days, he wasted little time before placing a notice in the newspaper: "We are watching hotels and other eating places which have violated the food administrator's orders, and prosecutions will be made if the proprietors continue to serve meat on Tuesdays or wheat foods on Wednesday."

Hoover relied heavily on the nation's newspapers to carry the conservation message across the nation and into every community. The Food Administrator, state governors, and councils of defense also encouraged ministers to influence the behavior and attitudes of their congregations. The Portage County Council of Defense solicited help from Polish priests in the county to encourage Polish farmers to build silos. Rock County pastors were asked to use their positions to promote food conservation and preservation in their congregations. The La Crosse County Council of Defense declared September 2, 1917, "Hoover Sunday" and urged pastors to preach on the subject of the Hoover pledge.[27]

Hoover's message of patriotic conservation was impossible to miss; it was everywhere. Posters in stores and streetcars, conservation advertising by food companies, and local newspapers all promoted the cause. The La Crosse Tribune played a role typical of what Hoover envisioned for community newspapers. The Tribune regularly carried Hoover's messages and encouraged compliance with each new conservation measure as a patriotic duty.

Although the Allies believed rationing would be necessary, Hoover believed the "spirit of self-sacrifice of the American people could be relied upon for so great a service as to accomplish the necessary results on a voluntary basis." A true rationing system would have required the creation of a large bureaucracy to categorize food, give it numeric values based on such factors as scarcity and resources needed for production, issue ration coupons to every American, police the system, and fight the inevitable black market. Widespread cooperation with food conservation efforts prevented the need for the complexities of formal rationing, but restrictions similar to rationing proved necessary for several important commodities, particularly sugar and wheat. By August 1918 Wisconsin residents were being warned that two-person families who had already received a canning allotment of twenty-five pounds of sugar would receive no more; families of more than two people but fewer than five could receive ten extra pounds of sugar; while larger families were eligible for forty-five pounds of additional sweetener. This was not rationing in the strict sense, but it had similar repercussions. To conserve sugar and stretch available supplies, La Crosse candy factories agreed to "Hooverize" by ending evening overtime work. To meet the demand for orders, each factory had been running a partial evening shift using day shift workers paid double for their overtime. Ending this practice saved coal and sugar by producing less candy and curtailing the number of hours during which lights and machines were in operation. For Christmas 1917 the *Tribune* urged parents to substitute popcorn, nuts, and fruit for their usual bags of Christmas candy. And a local ice-cream social featured sugarless ice cream and wheatless and sugarless cakes sweetened with corn syrup.[28]

By early 1918, the acute need for wheat both overseas and in the domestic economy forced the Food Administration to begin requiring food production companies to increase their use of substitute flours. Swenson implemented new rules at the production, wholesale, retail, and consumer levels emphasizing use of at least 50 percent substitute flours. Makers of products such as pasta, crackers, and breakfast foods were limited to purchasing only 70 percent of the wheat flour they had purchased during the same period in 1917. Wholesalers were required to follow the same rule. For each pound of flour sold to consumers, retailers were expected to sell a pound of substitute flour or meal such as rye, corn, or barley. In an attempt to control prices, those selling flour and flour substitutes were instructed to set prices at a level yielding a profit margin equivalent to that of the prewar period. County food administrators instructed millers to distribute their output geographically in the same proportion as their prewar distribution, to prevent producers from increasing shipments to geographic areas of greater profit. The rules governing prices and distribution created a fabric of interconnected practices designed to conserve wheat for shipment overseas while preventing imbalances in the distribution system or price increases in response to market shortages. Without concerted action by the Food Administration the natural forces of supply and demand would have created a disastrous inflationary cycle. Hoover's system of voluntary compliance and limited controls proved wildly successful at limiting consumption, increasing surpluses, preventing serious inflation, and virtually eliminating profiteering related to the food supply.[29]

The United States successfully fed the nation's civilian population and the American Expeditionary Force and supplied surplus food commodities to meet shortfalls in Allied supplies. Hoover's faith in the American people paid great dividends. Although the Food Administration and the Wisconsin Council of Defense could impose serious sanctions on offenders who refused to comply voluntarily, the conservation program worked because of voluntary compliance by commercial concerns and private citizens alike. The housewife who took the Hoover pledge and the grocer who adjusted his prices to comply with each new regulation were the quiet patriots of the home front. They represented the best of wartime society.

Fighting Famine in the Fields

Conservation could supply only part of the agricultural commodities needed to win the war. Greater agricultural production was the second half of the solution. The message to farmers was clear: produce more! When farmers worried about labor to plant and harvest, students were enlisted to help. When they worried about selling their crop at a good price, they were reassured that the government was prepared to set prices. The Council of Defense would help with marketing, promotional materials, newspaper articles, and advertisements and offer classes on home gardening and how to get the most from the land or a particular crop. Every newspaper, every class, every meeting conveyed a clear message about what was expected as a social norm. The mildest form of this social pressure was conveyed by advice articles and advertisements promoting home gardening. The Sheboygan County Council of Defense went a step further. In a poster encouraging everyone to do their part, the council reinforced its message by defining "slackers": "(1) Those who are physically able to work, but are idle because they have means of support, and (2) those who loaf about town and absolutely refuse to work." The message: support the war effort or be labeled a slacker. For farmers that meant growing more; for everyone else it meant planting a garden.

The Brown County Council of Defense took a more direct and possibly intimidating approach. Beginning on April 18, 1917, the council "called farmers to colors." The language was designed to convey an obligation for farmers similar to the obligation felt by soldiers reporting for duty. Farmers belonged to a land army and needed to fight the war with food. The Brown County Council of Defense sent thirty speakers, each with a volunteer automobile driver, to speak to farmers in thirty different county locations about the need for maximum agricultural production. The meetings were all scheduled for Sunday, April 29, 1917. Each speaker was equipped with a uniform set of talking points designed to reassure farmers that despite the government's request to grow more wheat, potatoes, navy beans, corn, and rutabagas, there was no danger of overproduction or collapse of the market because the government had "practically consented" to establishing minimum prices. The speakers also tried to dispel farmers' concerns about labor shortages. They promised the Council of Defense would enlist high school and college students, rural children, and "others" to help with farmwork; encouraged farmers to plant all available land, including roadsides; and proclaimed "that it is a patriotic duty of every farmer to raise as big crops as possible to cope with war time conditions." The speaking tour inspired hundreds of farmers to sign on to increase production and to grow wheat. Although the tour was conducted with great seriousness and purpose, this outcome was never in doubt. Other less dramatic means could have been used to recruit farmers' support—but as home-front theater, and as a way to unify the community behind the war effort, it was a valuable exercise.[30]

By 1918, Wisconsin farmers had brought approximately ninety-four thousand additional acres under cultivation. Production of corn, potatoes, oats, and barley had increased by 10 to 15 percent over prewar output. Farmers more than doubled wheat and buckwheat production, which had been relatively uncommon crops in Wisconsin before the war.[31] Yet state and national Food Administration officials worried these improvements would not be enough to forestall famine in Europe. Throughout 1917, conservation worked wonders to secure a surplus for Europe, but predictions for 1918 presented a challenge to the United States. Between domestic needs and existing commitments to the Allies, the United States projected virtually no wheat surplus for 1918. At the end of January, Lord Rhondda, British Food Controller, cabled Herbert Hoover with a bleak assessment: "Unless you are able to send the Allies at least 75,000,000 bushels of wheat over and above what you have exported up to January 1st, and in addition to the total exportable surplus from Canada, I cannot take the responsibility of assuring our people that there will be enough food to win the war."[32]

As the Food Administration prepared to tighten consumption controls further, farmers faced a conundrum. On the one hand, they understood the need to produce more than ever before, but they faced a fundamental manpower shortage. The armed forces siphoned approximately 118,000 men out of the Wisconsin labor force, 40,000 of whom came from the agricultural sector. The military demand for men created a labor shortage at the very time farmers needed to increase agricultural production and factories needed an influx of labor to produce war material. Wisconsin farmers faced critical shortages during planting and harvesting. The seasonal nature of this work made it difficult to find workers, and special recruiting was needed to fill the shortage. One option was to solicit industrial firms and schools to temporarily assign employees and students to local farms. In April 1917, in anticipation of spring planting, more than three thousand men in La Crosse promised to participate in the fall harvest. To supply this workforce, companies assigned employees to work several days in the fields: Listman Mill pledged 150 men for three days; Wisconsin Pearl Button Company, 150 men for three to six days; National Gauge and Equipment Company, 150 men for one, two, or three days. In Calumet County women and girls took work in canning companies so men could work in the fields. Oconto County merchants and clerks were encouraged to devote their vacations to farmwork, especially at harvest time.

In almost every county, students, often boys, assisted agricultural concerns. In Jefferson County former governor William Dempster Hoard employed schoolboys on his farm and encouraged others to do likewise. In Milwaukee, 110 schoolboys signed up to harvest cherries in Door County, while others elected to work in canning and sugar beet factories. The La Crosse superintendent of schools organized five hundred students to help with planting and harvesting; the added help allowed farmers to plant every available acre.

In Oneida County the sheriff assigned prison labor wherever needed, and Rock County law enforcement officials and judges were "doing their best to put all idle people at some kind of work in the county."[33]

The Wisconsin Council of Defense and state agricultural officials had encouraged farmers to expand production of potatoes, and local councils of defense promised to help famers by securing the necessary seed potatoes and recruiting volunteers, many of them students, to supply labor for planting and harvesting. Often the recruiting of volunteers became a communitywide affair. Eau Claire delayed the start of school for two weeks in the fall of 1917 and all of the schools in Ashland County closed on October 17 and for the remainder of that week to facilitate the use of students to harvest the potato crop.[34]

Farmers occasionally complained that bringing businessmen, retail clerks, and students to the farm was counterproductive. Many agricultural tasks required existing knowledge or skill, and urban volunteers often required training and supervision not needed by experienced farmworkers. Nonetheless, no serious attempt was made to redirect these volunteers. Short of reversing the draft and bringing farmworkers home, no other labor force existed to meet the seasonal needs dictated by planting and harvesting. Perhaps most important was the fact that this farmwork could be done by an auxiliary workforce and filled an important social need to be involved in the war effort.

The drumbeat for greater production succeeded, but occasionally the system broke down in unpredictable ways. When Wisconsin potato farmers completed their harvest in the fall of 1917, they discovered a shortage of rail cars to transport the potatoes to market. In March 1918 a group of Wisconsin potato growers sent two representatives to Washington to plead for more rail cars. Growers complained that the lack of railroad equipment was threatening the harvest. Results of the visit are not known, but three weeks later, a joint Wisconsin Assembly and Senate committee on marketing had taken note that potatoes had not been shipped from central Wisconsin the previous fall. Concerned that potatoes were being hoarded by farmers or by profiteering middlemen, the committee came north to investigate. At hearings in Barron, Madison, and Waupaca, hundreds of

unhappy potato farmers, dealers, and shippers testified to their dissatis-
faction about the lack of transport equipment and about prices below the
cost of production. The legislators concluded that half of the crop was stuck
on the farms because of the rail car shortage. The farmers had planted
potatoes in patriotic good faith and now could not get them to market.
The *Wisconsin State Journal* turned the issue into a political football. After
reporting the committee's findings, the newspaper twisted the complex
issue of railroad logistics and transformed it into a simplistic, even simple-
minded, example of war profiteering. The paper blamed the lack of rail
cars on the brewing industry's hoarding of refrigerator cars to ship beer.
With a good deal of hyperbole the *State Journal* asserted: "No more scan-
dalous war profiteering has been recorded in this country!"[35]

The scandal was of the newspaper's own making, and the problem of
getting Wisconsin potatoes to market was more complex than even the
growers understood. A small potato harvest nationally in 1916 resulted
in high prices the following spring. By the time the United States went to
war, farmers had already planted the regular potato crop. With encour-
agement from federal and state officials, and with good market prices,
farmers nationally agreed to plant an estimated seven hundred thousand
extra acres of potatoes. They used whatever seed potatoes they could get.
Shippers agreed to sell farmers three hundred carloads of potatoes from
their warehouses for use as seed, but some of the seed potatoes were low
quality and produced small potatoes that were difficult to market. The
record crop in Wisconsin and nationally glutted the market in the fall of
1917, and prices plummeted. In anticipation of strong demand and better prices in the spring, many farmers kept their crop in storage over the
winter. Approximately half the crop was still on Wisconsin farms. Farmer
reluctance to sell their crop at a loss was reflected in low shipping rates.
Normally fifty thousand carloads of potatoes should have been shipped
by February 1, 1918. Only twenty-eight thousand carloads had left the
nation's warehouses. In February, the Food Administration warned of a
serious lack of rail cars to transport agricultural goods. By spring farmers
worried that the previous harvest would rot before they could get it to market. Growers probably did encounter problems getting the necessary rail
cars in February, but by the end of March that problem had been solved,
although farmers were still blaming the railroads. At the same time the

legislature's marketing committee released its findings, Governor Philipp issued a contradictory statement. As a railroad man himself, Philipp had already secured the necessary rolling stock. He noted the real problem lay in the fact that bad roads and spring mud kept the potatoes from getting to market. In addition the glutted market was still not conducive to sales and many of the remaining potatoes in Wisconsin were of lower quality.[36]

The state and county councils of defense, Wisconsin Department of Agriculture, University of Wisconsin, and county agriculture agents all worked to encourage a record harvest of potatoes that wholesalers, retailers, and consumers would want to buy. They encouraged farmers to standardize within a region on one or two of the half dozen best potato varieties so they could develop a common marketing strategy and benefit from a growing reputation for high quality. Similarly, the governor, the councils of defense, and newspapers across the state emphasized the importance of replacing wheat products with potatoes at the family table. In many rural communities, the local agriculture agents formed "potato clubs" in the schools and worked through the children to reach the parents. There would always be ups and downs in the harvest and the market, but farmers who produced desirable potatoes would weather the unpredictable nature of agriculture.[37]

In spite of all the problems associated with growing potatoes in 1917, Wisconsin farmers grew 32,518,000 bushels of potatoes in 1918, a 13 percent increase over the prewar years. By any reasonable measure Wisconsin farmers met their wartime obligations. Although the wheat crop increased 112 percent, it was a minor crop with only 7,931,000 bushels produced. More remarkable was the 15 percent increase in oats to 94,349,000 bushels in 1918, the 18 percent increase in cheese production, the astounding 75 percent increase in sugar beet production to 70,000,000 pounds, and the doubling of milk to 800,000,000 pounds in 1918. If, as the slogan said, "Food Will Win the War," Wisconsin had done its part.[38]

Major commodities like wheat and sugar were being shipped to Europe, and surrogates for wheat such as barley, corn, and oats were products of commercial agriculture. Although war gardens sometimes supplied local markets, they served a broader function as well. War gardens brought squash, carrots, turnips, spinach, and a panoply of other produce to the family table, easing some of the strains on commercial agriculture. From the beginning of the war, families were advised to plant gardens wherever they could: on their own property, in vacant lots, on street medians. Perhaps the most important aspect of war gardens was the sense of participation in the war effort that gardeners felt when they grew their own food. In a society so totally committed to the war effort, gardens gave the young and old a sense of belonging.

Virtually every newspaper ran gardening columns that instructed readers when, what, and how to plant a garden, such as "Poultry and Garden" in the *Janesville Daily Gazette* and "Everyone Have a Garden" in both the *Green Bay Press Gazette* and the *Sheboygan Press*. Articles written by university professors, federal officials, and master gardeners reaffirmed that gardening was patriotic. The *La Crosse Tribune* and the La Crosse Chamber of Commerce sponsored a program that matched people in need of garden space with people who had unused land. Participants clipped forms printed in the newspaper and mailed them to the newspaper's "Garden Department." Civic organizations such as the North Side Progressive Club, the La Crosse Women's Club, the Twentieth Century Club, and the public schools joined forces to turn every foot of vacant space into a producing garden. With the World War I motto of "Every Scout to Feed a Soldier," the area's Boy Scouts also took up gardening. Home gardens were touted not only as a way to augment the food supply but also as a way to fight the rising cost of living.[39]

CHILDREN IN THE WAR EFFORT

Organizing society in support of the war effort required everyone's cooperation. The role children played is easy to underestimate and overlook. Once children reached adolescence they became a ready source of farm labor, but even younger children learned about and participated in patriotic activities. In La Crosse a committee of "school men" signed boys up for summer farmwork. The rural schools of Brown County hosted fairs to exhibit the produce grown by schoolchildren. These fairs not only promoted gardening but also aroused the patriotic spirit of the community. By one account, almost every child in Outagamie County had a war garden by the summer of 1918. Jean Jackson, chairwoman of the war garden committee in Appleton, reported that the city had 910 war gardens. Although her claim of "almost every child" probably was an exaggeration, it suggested that war gardens were readily embraced by many families.

Schools promoted patriotic fervor and sacrifice. Students learned the pledge of allegiance, practiced patriotic songs, and read moralistic lessons in textbooks. In September 1917, the Wisconsin legislature mandated that "Every pupil in the upper grades and high school should know by heart and be able to sing the leading patriotic songs. The singing of such songs should be a frequent school exercise." Teachers encouraged students to "Hooverize" at home and to buy thrift stamps, the children's version of war bonds.

In Green Bay, the Women's Committee of the Council of Defense trained older children to deliver four-minute speeches to students in lower grades and to audiences in theaters and public gatherings. They held patriotic essay contests in the seventh, eighth, and high school grades, and the winning essays included, "What Are You Going to Do for Uncle Sam?," "Keep Old Glory Waving," and "Why It Is Our Duty to Buy Liberty Bonds." In honor of Liberty Day in April 1918, eighth graders in Green Bay's Howe School wrote and presented a play, "The Trials of a Bond Seller," which portrayed the different types of people met by a bond seller.[40]

Some high schools, such as those in Appleton and Onalaska, instituted military training for male students. E. T. Berg, president of the Onalaska Board of Education, was an enthusiastic proponent of the training. In addition to military training for boys, Berg said, everyone, "even the little tots and the girls," was learning

first aid, camp cooking, and to shoot, all alive with patriotic enthusiasm to be ready to do our part to preserve peace, to defend our flag, to make America the standard-bearer for righteousness, to defend the principle of America for Americans, a country of the people, for the people, and by the people. . . . We are sure that this training will increase the efficiency of our students by cultivating more respect for our flag and country—to make them loyal, patriotic, liberty loving Americans, increase their respect for our government and its ideals, to become self-reliant young men and women.[41]

Many apolitical events easily could become overtly political reflections of the contentious nature of wartime society. Henry N. Sherwood, a professor of European history from La Crosse State Normal School, presented a "loyalty proposition" to the Wisconsin county school superintendents' 1918 annual meeting in Wausau. "Be it resolved: That we condemn the disloyal expression of our senior senator, Robert M. La Follette, and recommend that he be dismissed from the United States Senate." After "considerable debate and bickering," the superintendents adopted the resolution 23 to 13.[42]

Families, schools, and houses of worship have traditionally been among the primary sources for inculcating values in children. At no time has this been more true than in times of "total war," when all of society is marshaled to support the war effort.
GREEN BAY PRESS GAZETTE, JUNE 9, 1917

A BOX FROM HOME

Drawn by Gahr Williams, Division of Pictorial Publicity.

Food savings of millions of Americans during our first year of war enabled this government to send enormous food shipments abroad for our fighting forces and the Allied nations. Our savings in cereals—out of a short crop—amounted to 154,900,000 bushels; all of which was shipped to Europe. We increased our meat and fat shipments 844,600,000 pounds. This was America's "box from home" to our army abroad and the civilians and military forces of the Allied nations.

The cartoonist's message was clear: Food saved on the home front nourished the body and soul of Allied troops on the western front, whether they were French, American, British, or Italian. *EAU CLAIRE LEADER*, AUGUST 16, 1918

CRISIS IN COAL AND TRANSPORTATION

Food conservation and home gardens did more than emphasize family sacrifice and self-sufficiency. They had the ancillary value of promoting consumption of local produce. This change in buying patterns conserved coal that would have been needed for processing and transporting produce from remote farms to distant markets. In 1917 and 1918, the importance of conserving fuel and transportation resources became all too clear as coal shortages and transportation problems struck the nation.

The fuel crisis in Wisconsin was less about coal than about shortages of railroad cars to transport the coal to the upper Midwest and the logistics of ensuring even distribution across the nation. Problems in the distribution system became evident at least as early as November 1916, when the staff at St. Francis Hospital in La Crosse blamed a scarcity of coal on the shortage of railroad cars. The following year the *La Crosse Tribune* observed there was an ample coal supply but a shortage of railroad cars. The problem was not unique to La Crosse. During the summer of 1917, Governor Philipp anticipated fuel and transport shortages in the coming winter. He relied on a variety of allies to help him secure critical fuel for Wisconsin's furnaces. In August, he sent William N. Fitzgerald, a Milwaukee businessman, east to arrange for special shipments of coal to Wisconsin. Hoover soon named Fitzgerald as the federal fuel administrator for Wisconsin. The close relationship between Philipp and Fitzgerald served the state well during the bitterly cold winter of 1917–1918. Because of Philipp's foresight, the state began the winter months with a reasonable supply of fuel, although not adequate for the entire season. W. H. Groverman was a second ally. Groverman was the federal fuel administrator in Superior and Duluth and had previously worked as secretary of the Coal Dock Operators Association. As fuel administrator, he focused his attention on the equitable distribution of the coal supply to the upper Midwest from the stockpile on his docks.

By mid-October 1917 it was obvious that coal demand was going to outstrip the supply secured by Fitzgerald during the summer. Supplies in Appleton, Berlin, Neenah, and Oshkosh all were running low, and Chicago had only a three-day supply. Although the impact of the supply/demand imbalance was self-evident in rising prices, "the question of the price of coal is not bothering officials or the people of cities in the Fox River valley," reported the *Green Bay Press Gazette*. "The only thing they are concerned about is how to get a supply of coal at any price."[43] Officials began counseling consumers to conserve fuel and use wood as an alternative. Municipalities took various steps to ensure residents had fuel to heat their homes. Marinette purchased a large quantity of hardwood and sold it to residents at cost. In Grant County, seventy-seven-year-old twins John and Chris Kleibenstein cut sixty cords of wood for use in Platteville, and officials in DePere purchased extra coal for municipal purposes and sold the excess to the poor at cost. Coal dealers limited deliveries to one ton per customer to ensure fair distribution of existing supplies.

Philipp took a personal interest in the fuel crisis and on numerous occasions intervened to secure coal for a Wisconsin city or village facing cold weather with little or no coal on hand. On January 2, 1918, Philipp learned that Hartford was on the verge of running out of coal to heat homes. He immediately contacted Fitzgerald and asked for his help. A few days later an emergency supply of coal was on its way to Hartford "borrowed" from the Milwaukee Western Fuel Company, which had a surplus of coal. A similar sequence of events provided La Farge with emergency coal. With a clear tone of urgency, three prominent citizens of the village wired a plea to Philipp: "The town entire out of coal. Dry wood practically depleted. Twenty-eight below zero. People suffering. Please see what you can do for us at once. Two cars of soft coal would relieve the situation for a few days. Letter to follow. Answer."

Coal fields in Illinois and Kentucky normally supplied Madison via Chicago. On January 15, Chicago officials protected supplies for their city by sequestering more than three thousand coal cars destined for Wisconsin, northwestern Illinois, and southern Minnesota. To avert disaster, Philipp wired Groverman and received a commitment of twenty carloads of coal stockpiled in Duluth/Superior. From the St. Paul, Minneapolis, and Omaha Railroad, Philipp secured a special train to bring the coal to the capital. On January 15, Groverman wired Philipp that he could expect twenty-eight railroad cars of coal in Madison by about 10 p.m. the following day, a scant twenty-four hours after the crisis began. Expedited shipments averted disaster, but they could not solve the fundamental problem that the Midwest, along with the rest of the nation, suffered from fuel shortages and distribution problems.

The logistics of supplying the nation with coal for domestic purposes broke down as coal was diverted to fuel the ships carrying troops and supplies to the Allies, and as railroad cars were at a premium to carry supplies, troops, and coal to eastern ports. In mid-January 1918 one of the worst blizzards in years snarled rail traffic across the Midwest, and a wage dis-

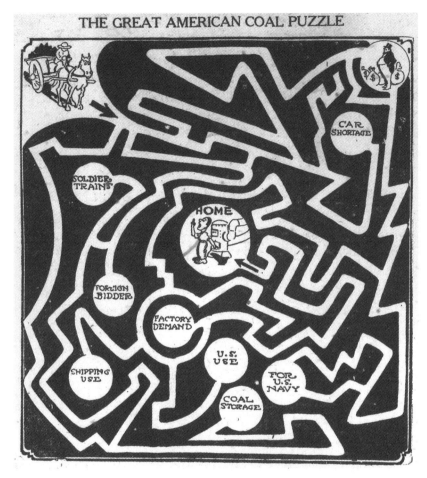

During the winter of 1917–1918, the demands of the war pushed the coal production and distribution systems almost to the breaking point. Emanuel Philipp and and fuel administrators William N. Fitzgerald and W. H. Groverman undertook valiant efforts to secure adequate coal supplies and the rail cars needed to bring the coal to Wisconsin. They succeeded in preventing a catastrophe, but just barely. Some communities almost ran out, and there were times when coal was distributed a ton at a time to individual customers to ensure there was enough to go around. *GREEN BAY PRESS GAZETTE, OCTOBER 22, 1917*

pute between miners and owners in Illinois reduced production just when it was needed most.[44]

In an attempt to stretch existing fuel supplies, Harry Garfield, the nation's fuel administrator, ordered lightless nights on Sundays and Thursdays of each week beginning December 15, 1917. Streetlights could remain lit, but business and theater districts needed to turn off their bright "white way" lighting, and advertising, display windows, and store showrooms had to go dark at night.[45] As the shortage worsened, Garfield imposed new conservation measures. He ordered most factories to suspend their use of fuel, principally coal, for one week beginning January 18, and then every Monday thereafter through most of March, to ensure an adequate coal supply for essential factories. Garfield's order effectively idled 125,000 workers in Milwaukee and thousands of others across the state of Wisconsin: an estimated 7,000 in Madison, 5,000 in La Crosse, and 1,800 in Green Bay. The fuelless days were particularly hard on the working class because a day without work was also a day without pay. Some municipal leaders tried to offer temporary work for those idled by the fuelless days. The mayor of La Crosse provided work and helped alleviate the coal shortage by hiring idled workers to cut cord wood in city parks. Facilities with major war contracts, such as Nordberg and Allis-Chalmers in Milwaukee, remained in operation, as did factories that operated on electricity generated by water power or burning wood, such as those in Marinette and Menominee. In towns across the state and nation, theaters, bowling alleys, and other places of amusement could remain open on Mondays to offer people a diversion, provided they closed on Tuesdays.[46]

The restrictions on fuel were not rationing in a formal sense, nor were they truly voluntary. The penalties for fuel violations were more concrete than the public scorn faced by people who flouted the Hoover pledge to conserve food. Businesses that violated fuelless Mondays risked incurring a ban against receiving any fuel for the duration of the winter. Such a penalty could easily drive a shopkeeper out of business.

Wisconsin's careful planning and management of its resources paid off. On a visit to Madison, Charles McCarthy, Hoover's assistant who previously had led the Wisconsin Legislative Reference Bureau, said, "Wisconsin is the only state I have seen where the people are warm." Draconian as some of these measures seemed, they allowed 480 ships carrying more than 2 million tons of supplies to set sail for Europe January 17–26, 1918. As the severe winter came to an end, officials at all levels of government began planning a new round of conservation measures for the coming winter season and hoped they could avoid a repetition of the congestion and shortages experienced during the season just past.[47]

A semblance of normal life continued during wartime. Not only did people try to maintain a sense of normalcy, but commercial enterprises turned the fuel shortage into an advertising opportunity. Your factory is closed to save fuel, you have nothing to do, why not buy a phonograph or billiard table and take entertainment into the home? *GREEN BAY PRESS GAZETTE, JANUARY 19, 1918*

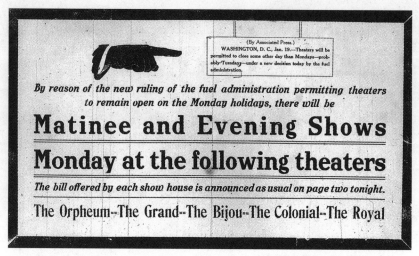

(By Associated Press.)
WASHINGTON, D. C., Jan. 19.—Theaters will be permitted to close some other day than Mondays—probably Tuesdays—under a new decision today by the fuel administration.

By reason of the new ruling of the fuel administration permitting theaters to remain open on the Monday holidays, there will be

Matinee and Evening Shows
Monday at the following theaters

The bill offered by each show house is announced as usual on page two tonight.

The Orpheum--The Grand--The Bijou--The Colonial--The Royal

As cities wrestled with fuel shortages and the government-imposed heatless Mondays, theaters received a waiver. Across Wisconsin, theaters stayed open to provide a comfortable, heated environment for people whose places of employment were without heat and closed for the day. *GREEN BAY PRESS GAZETTE*, JANUARY 19, 1918

In 1918, daylight saving time provided one answer as government and industry sought solutions to the fuel crisis. In the 1890s a New Zealander named George V. Hudson promoted a new idea called daylight saving time to make better use of available light during the summer for work and leisure. Farmers would nominally have an extra hour to work their fields, home gardeners would have more time to cultivate their plots, but most importantly, manufacturers would use one less hour of energy to light their factories. It took a world war and a fuel crisis for the idea to catch on. Germany and Austria-Hungary implemented daylight saving time in 1916, followed shortly thereafter by Great Britain, France, and Russia in 1917, and the United States a year later.

The concept of shifting hours of work to save energy did not spring forth with the catalyst of war. An organization supporting daylight saving time held its fifth annual convention at the Astor Hotel in New York on January 31, 1917. Delegates were heartened by a letter of support from Wilson, and the convention adjourned optimistic that Congress would soon pass the necessary legislation. Supporters had to wait another year before daylight saving time became a national war measure in 1918.

Officials in Green Bay were particularly aggressive at implementing daylight saving time. Only days after Congress adopted the war declaration, the Green Bay Association of Commerce appointed a special committee to promote daylight saving time to the cities of the Fox Valley and Lake Michigan shoreline. Employers who had tried the scheme tended to be enthusiastic supporters. Others were either cautious or supported the plan only if it was implemented universally. Despite pockets of opposition, Green Bay Mayor Elmer S. Hall proclaimed April 29, 1917, as the day to change the city's clocks. National implementation remained haphazard until March 19, 1918, when Congress passed legislation calling for federal implementation at the end of the month.[48]

Focusing the Economy—No Detail Too Small

As it attempted to focus the huge American economy on the war effort and eliminate inefficiencies and waste, the Council of National Defense took an interest in such prosaic issues as the return of unsold loaves of bread to wholesale bakers and the home delivery practices of retail grocers. As a customer service, wholesale bakers generally accepted unsold loaves from retailers and then donated them to charitable institutions. Imprecise retail orders led to this overproduction, which wasted both wheat and labor. The Commercial Economy Board, a subunit of the Council of National Defense, sought to tighten up the system. The board instructed state councils to solicit pledges from wholesale bakers to cease accepting unsold bread from retailers beginning June 25, 1917. The Wisconsin Council of Defense, with help from county councils, readily undertook the task of seeking compliance from the state's bakers.

Henry A. Burd, executive secretary of the Wisconsin council, reported excellent results to federal officials after a flurry of activity during June 1917. Members of the county defense councils interviewed bakers in their counties to secure cooperation. The state council then mailed postcards to every retail and wholesale baker in the state, asking them to sign the pledge on the card and return it to Madison: "I hereby pledge myself for the duration of the war not to accept the return of unsold bread." Burd proudly reported, "To date we have had responses from 90% of the bakers, covering all of the wholesalers and virtually all of the retailers. The few stragglers we are still after and have no doubt that every card will be in by the end of the week."[49]

Achieving the cooperation of wholesale bakers was relatively easy compared with reorienting retail grocery delivery systems to make them more efficient and less labor intensive, freeing the energies of workers who could otherwise help with the war effort. During the early years of the twentieth century, grocers routinely offered credit and delivery services to regular customers. A patron could visit the grocer when convenient, place an order for delivery later, and run a credit tab commonly paid off once a month. Depending on the size of the city or village, grocers often ran regular deliveries to customers on an established schedule and made special deliveries when needed. If both parties happened to have telephones, orders could be placed with a call to the grocer, recorded on the running credit tab, and delivered to the customer's door. In an era when automobile ownership was not yet ubiquitous, home delivery was an important service that could be a deciding factor for consumers in a competitive environment.

The national discussion about a more efficient grocery delivery system revealed a certain social schizophrenia regarding women and their roles at home and in society. Hoover imagined an intelligent, patriotic housewife, manager of the household economy, at the center of his plan for food conservation; without her, his plan would collapse. In contrast, when Anna Howard Shar, chairperson of the Council of National Defense Woman's Committee, described the importance of reforming the old delivery systems, her explanation relied on a clear assumption that credit accounts and home deliveries served housewives who were lazy and frivolous. In a letter to state council of defense chairpeople across the country, Shar acknowledged that reform depended on the commitment of housewives to accept the changes, but she explained the need for change in demeaning terms: "No man ought to be taken from essential war industries to carry parcels which women might carry for themselves, or be required to make repeated and unnecessary trips at the call of improvident house-wives. This is the time when every act of men and women must be made to count definitely in the prosecution of the war and every bit of useless effort must be eliminated."[50]

The Commercial Economy Board, anticipating labor shortages as the draft siphoned men into the military, sought to decrease the number of delivery drivers by promoting once-a-day deliveries and multistore cooperative delivery services. Beginning in July 1917, the Wisconsin Council of Defense began promoting these new delivery models, as well as the concept of "cash and carry" systems, in which patrons purchased products with cash instead of credit and carried them directly home. Grocers who failed to cooperate could anticipate a visit from the state defense council for their evident lack of patriotic spirit.

By fall 1917, the Wisconsin Council of Defense reported promising developments, but implementation of the Commercial Economy Board recommendations proved to be a complex and moving target. In Green Bay, department stores had adopted a reduced delivery plan, but the local grocers and butchers did not trust each other and made little progress on an agreement. Kenosha merchants were reluctant to adopt new delivery patterns because their delivery services helped set them apart from the Atlantic and Pacific Tea Company (A&P), which undercut their prices. Merchants in Madison were working on a cooperative delivery plan, but the geography of the lakes made working out the final details difficult. La Crosse and Oshkosh had fully implemented reduced delivery schedules, and in Sheboygan implementation was slow but steady.[51]

Early approval came from the state grocers association, but achieving full cooperation required vigilance. Outliers created by factors such as unique geography or unusual competitive demands could make cooperative agreements and delivery efficiencies difficult. As of March 1918, six out of seven grocers in Viroqua had agreed to a cooperative delivery program. They streamlined their services, sold most of their horses and mules, and relied on five automobiles for their shared delivery service. Their cooperative service was 50 percent less expensive than when each grocer worked alone. In turn, they reduced the cost of some of their items. Unfortunately, not everyone cooperated. Viroqua grocer C. E. Mullen refused to join the cooperative service, claiming he could deliver more cheaply and effectively than the other grocers in town. Upon investigation, the Vernon County Council of Defense concluded that, although the other grocers were satisfied with their cooperative program, Mullen was taking their customers by offering a more frequent and flexible delivery service. Going alone clearly gave Mullen a competitive edge.

Henry Burd of the Wisconsin Council of Defense gave him a choice:

> Under the conditions, however, it will be necessary to require you either to join the central delivery system or to confine your deliveries to the same number and the same routes as the general delivery system does, that is, if they make two deliveries a day, you must not make more than two. If they make a delivery in one end of the city at one part of the day and at another end of the city at another part of the day, you must make your deliveries in the same section of the city at the same time. This will equalize matters and make it fair allaround.[52]

In some cases, gaining full compliance required interstate negotiation. The merchants of Hurley, Wisconsin, competed for customers with merchants in Ironwood, Michigan. Their Upper Peninsula counterparts worked without delivery restrictions, and the Wisconsin merchants feared they would lose business to their Michigan competitors. Burd explained the problem to the Commercial Economy Board and wrote to the Michigan Council seeking their cooperation. Melvin Copeland, secretary of the Commercial Economy Board, followed his communications with Burd by writing to Major Roy C. Vandercook, secretary of the Michigan War Preparedness Board. Copeland made it abundantly clear that implementing once-a-day deliveries on all routes or a cooperative delivery system between Hurley and Ironwood was a matter of extending "loyal and patriotic support to the Nation's important needs in this emergency."[53] Sacrifice and patriotism created the context of daily life during the war. Even the smallest of issues, such as the delivery of groceries, was a measure of loyalty.

FINANCING THE WAR

Just as the Food Administration reached into virtually every kitchen in the United States, the Liberty Loan drives and the Wisconsin Council of Defense reached into most bank accounts. Liberty Loan campaigns to sell war bonds, and charitable drives to fund the war work of organizations such as the YMCA and Red Cross seemed almost continuous.

Normal revenue from federal taxes fell far short of funding the nation's wartime needs. To fill this gap the government began selling Liberty Bonds directly to the citizenry, turning the American people into creditors for the nation's war debt. Treasury Secretary William McAdoo could have relied on commercial investors to underwrite the war debt, but instead he appealed directly to the patriotism of average Americans. By making bond purchases a patriotic duty, McAdoo believed it would be possible to sell bonds at a lower interest rate than would be possible if he sought commercial credit through the nation's banks. In essence, he used patriotism as an incentive to encourage public purchases of low-interest bonds and thereby decrease the cost of the war. He also hoped that public sales would siphon money out of the economy and lessen demand for scarce peacetime goods: "What is of superlative importance in the readjustment that must take place is that our people shall be impressed with the necessity of economizing in the consumption of articles of clothing, food, and fuel, and of every other thing which constitutes a drain upon the available supplies, materials, and resources of the country."[54]

Beginning in the summer of 1917, the US Treasury Department floated four bond issues sold directly to the public nationwide in Liberty Loan drives. Each drive was an intense affair lasting approximately a month. In the past, government debt was sold to financial institutions as a secure investment. Organizers had never sold bonds directly to the public before and found themselves in uncharted territory. In Wisconsin, the first two drives failed to meet their quota, but with each succeeding drive, organizers refined their solicitation methods.

In one of the most significant political achievements of the early twentieth century, Congress responded to a series of financial panics in the late nineteenth and early twentieth centuries by creating the Federal Reserve in 1913 to provide the nation with a central bank capable of maintaining a more stable national economic system. As the government's fiscal agent, it fell to the twelve Federal Reserve Banks to organize the Liberty Loan campaigns. William L. Ross of Chicago was chairman of the Federal Reserve Bank of Chicago, District Seven. He supervised the bond drives for approximately the southeastern two-thirds of Wisconsin. The northwestern part of the state answered to the Federal Reserve Bank of Minneapolis.

Frank Hixon, a La Crosse businessman, banker, financier, entrepreneur,

The use of bestial imagery not only sold bonds but also used stereotypes to reinforce a sense of the rightness of the Allied cause. This type of imagery helped Americans believe the United States was in mortal danger from an evil force. WHI IMAGE ID 107585

politician, and member of the Federal Reserve Bank of Minneapolis board of directors, supervised the bond drives in Wisconsin's northwestern region. The first drive was disorganized and run by trial and error. Because the government set a low interest rate on the war bonds, they were not particularly good investments. In Wisconsin, the first drive fell $10 million short of the state's $44 million quota. For critics, who were inclined to see pro-German sympathizers at every turn, the state's weak response seemed proof the people of Wisconsin were "slackers," if not outright traitors. In fact, eight counties (Ashland, Douglas, Kenosha, La Crosse, Lincoln, Milwaukee, Oneida, and Racine) surpassed their quotas in this first drive. With the exception of Douglas County, all of the high-performing counties had Germanic populations of 20 to 48 percent. In contrast, of the four poorest-performing counties (Adams, Vilas, Walworth, Waushara), each of which sold less than 10 percent of their bond quotas in the first drive, Waushara County had a Germanic population of 23 percent, and the other three had Germanic populations below 20 percent. The failure of the first campaign was hardly a mark of ethnic sabotage. Rather, it signaled the need for education and a different approach to sales.

Across the country, the first and second Liberty Loan campaigns suffered from a fundamental flaw: organizers centered the sales operation on banks. But bankers lacked a clear understanding of the role expected of them and, because it was a poor investment, they were generally apathetic about the product they were expected to sell. In many cases they failed to push the bonds as vigorously as Hixon would have liked. The first campaign also suffered from the public's lack of understanding of the need for the bonds and the system for purchasing them. At first, Hixon even had trouble securing enough county organizers to make the system work, and he received numerous reports that banks were trying to reduce their quotas. In response Hixon wrote to William B. Banks, his primary lieutenant in northern Wisconsin: "The big problem in my mind is to overcome indifference and bring in slackers." After the first drive was completed, Hixon told a bank colleague that he was "bitterly disappointed over the results shown in some sections."[55]

The Wisconsin Council of Defense took a direct interest in the management of the bond drives. Working closely with the Federal Reserve banks in Minneapolis and Chicago, the council used its authority to enforce bank participation in the first and second campaigns. Council officials investigated numerous reports of uncooperative banks submitted by patriotic citizens. They attempted to maintain an objective position when communicating with allegedly wayward banks, but letters from the council carried an intimidating tone and demanded an immediate reply. In the vast majority of cases, banks promptly denied the charges, and very few cases seem to have been forwarded to federal authorities for legal action. The fact that investigators found relatively few cases of wrongdoing or unpatriotic behavior demonstrated the hazards of any system of security based on public informants.

During the second Liberty Loan drive, in the fall of 1917, Mr. P. E. Ibach, president of the German American Bank in Alma, received an inquiry typical of the Council of Defense:

> It is reported to this office on good authority that you refuse to have little or nothing to do with the sale of Liberty Bonds; that your attitude is unpatriotic, and that you are not co-operating in any way with the men who are working so hard to subscribe for the Buffalo County quota. We wish to know if these facts are correct.
>
> An immediate reply is expected.[56]

The council sent similar letters to other Buffalo County banks that had been slow to sell bonds during the first and second Liberty Loan drives. The phrase "you refuse to have little or nothing to do with the sale of Liberty Bonds" is a double negative that means the opposite of what the council intended. Despite the lack of clarity, recipients of these letters clearly understood the council's meaning: get in line, and sell more bonds.

Mr. Ibach consulted with his lawyer, who advised him to sell bonds. In short order, he sold one thousand dollars' worth of bonds to bank customers and promised his bank would subscribe to another thousand dollars.

Bank customers seemed to have had a mixed view of the government loan program. The vast majority of Wisconsin's urban residents accepted the duty of buying Liberty Loan bonds and thereby lent their money to the government to fight the war. But farmers were more apathetic toward the cause, and rural areas were harder to organize than cities. Andrew Melville, executive secretary of the Council of Defense, attributed the failure to meet quota in the first two bond drives to the issues of rural resistance.

In some areas the problem was not just apathy but hostility and suspicion about the government's ability to live up to its war-related obligations. Some people worried the government would confiscate their money if they refused to buy Liberty Bonds. Others withdrew their money from local banks to avoid the pressure to participate in the drive.

The Council of Defense heard rumors of this happening in Sauk City, Waunakee, DeForest, Marshal, and Alma, and the council unsuccessfully attempted to pressure banks into disclosing the names of customers withdrawing funds.

Concerns about pro-German sentiment also ran rampant in rural areas. John Chase of Oconto wrote to the state defense council:

> There has come to me as Chairman of the County Council of Defense considerable information with reference to certain people in this county who are showing very marked pro-German activities. It has been particularly noticeable during the drive we are making in this county for the second Liberty Loan Bonds, and I wish you would kindly let me know just whom I shall write to in order to get the services of a secret service man in this community for a short time.

T. S. Saby of First National Bank of Alma told Magnus Swenson, "Six of our nine banks failed to raise a finger toward selling bonds during the sale of the last issue. They feared antagonism of their Pro-German clients."

After a poor showing in the first drive, Frank Hixon complained to a colleague that German Wisconsinites were "not going to furnish money to be sent to England." Hixon blamed the German newspapers *Nord Stern* and *Abend Stern*, published by Adolph Candrian in La Crosse, for inspiring sedition. Hixon tried to bring Candrian's perceived "unpatriotic" behavior to the attention of the federal district attorney to no avail.

As the second drive began, Hixon complained to Governor Philipp that some banks had not sold a single first-issue bond, while others made sales only when customers demanded it. As a reprisal Hixon urged the state to withdraw deposits and refuse to cooperate on loans with any recalcitrant bank. Philipp responded by assuring his friend that all in his power would be done to rectify the problem.[57]

Hixon recognized early on that the bank system was ill-suited as the vehicle for selling bonds. In May 1917 he recommended that larger cities use more direct door-to-door solicitation, which became the predominant sales strategy in future campaigns, and he decided to publish the names of bond purchasers. Hixon hoped "that in places where there is a large German population, the subscribers of German birth might be glad to have their subscriptions advertised as a sort of demonstration of their loyalty."[58] These published subscription lists became a measure of loyalty, not just for German Americans, but for the general public as well.

Each succeeding bond campaign made improvements in methods and results. By the third drive, in the spring of 1918, fund-raisers used Hixon's door-to-door approach. Instead of having the buyer come to the seller, Hixon sent the solicitor to the people. Success resulted less from a spontaneous upsurge of patriotic spirit than from a well-organized machine and intimidating tactics.

Well before the start of the third campaign, newspapers began carrying extensive coverage about the importance of buying bonds, the goals of the campaign, and patriotic duty. Communities presented patriotic speakers, held rallies and parades, and hosted the "battle trophy train," which exhibited an American antiaircraft gun, a French 75 mm gun, a ten-inch artillery shell, grenades, torpedoes, and other Allied equipment. The train exhibit also presented a number of German battlefield artifacts, including barbed wire and military helmets.[59] Campaign advertising was everywhere: in the newspaper, on posters in store windows, in Sunday sermons, at the doorstep. The pressure was incessant, the advertising ubiquitous. Behind much of this propaganda were George Creel and the Committee on Public Information, using poster art to advertise the Liberty Loan drives as well as war gardens and food conservation.[60]

The most innovative Liberty Loan advertising came in the form of four-minute speeches delivered in public places, most often movie theaters, by the Four Minute Men, the group organized nationwide by Creel and the CPI to support the bond drives and other wartime efforts.

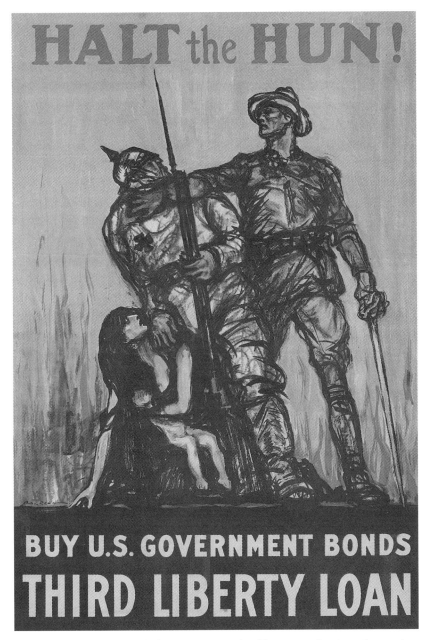

To sell bonds during the third Liberty Loan campaign, illustrators often brought together the rape of the innocent, the bestial Hun, and the heroic Doughboy to remind the home front of the stakes for which they were fighting. WHI IMAGE ID 107568

The methods used to encourage bond purchases became more sophisticated with each new campaign and included community events such as parades, displays in retail windows, and door-to-door canvassing. WHI IMAGE ID 61766

Although they most often spoke in movie theaters, these four-minute patriots could show up in any public space. Occasionally their Liberty Loan messages would be diverted for a week to promote food conservation or to encourage people to file their income taxes on time.[61]

By the third Liberty Loan campaign, Hixon had built an organization of dedicated volunteers, including Boy Scouts, to go door-to-door selling bonds. This canvassing effort touched virtually everyone with its patriotic, if sometimes coercive, hand. In its mildest form, La Crosse Boy Scouts conducted a wrap-up canvass in April 1918. If a household's occupants had already subscribed, they informed the Scout and he would depart. On the other hand, "if there are any members of the family who have not subscribed and who desire to aid Uncle Sam in financing the war, they will be asked merely to fill out one of the subscription cards for the amount of bonds desired."[62]

The person who failed to buy bonds quickly became known as a "slacker." The success or failure of a bank or community to meet its quota on a bond drive became a measure of its loyalty and patriotism. In Brown County, organizers made the link explicit and personal. They adopted the slogan, "A Liberty Bond in every home" and told local residents, "Let every citizen of Brown County do his duty. Enlist your dollars, and express your unmitigated patriotism. The enemy is watching. Any slack in the subscription for the Liberty loan gives aid and comfort to the enemy. Buy a Liberty bond now and show your patriotism."[63]

An army of volunteers canvassed the state, armed with information about each person or family they solicited to buy bonds. Data collected from questionnaires sent to every adult in Wisconsin became part of an alphabetical card file documenting the financial status of each person or family in the state. In many cases, the door-to-door canvassers had the benefit of knowing the client's contributions to other wartime fund-raising campaigns, their ability to pay, any property valuation, and the amount assessed by the Liberty Loan Allotment Committee. Based on this information, volunteers had a stated figure the subscriber was expected to purchase. If the subscriber refused to buy the proper amount, the canvasser would present the card with its stark facts. If this failed to loosen the pocketbook of the recalcitrant, the volunteer would try intimidation and "tell him the card will have to be referred back to the Executive Committee with report of the facts."[64]

These threats were not taken lightly. Tales of being whisked off to Madison in the middle of the night, of "disloyal" citizens losing their jobs, and of terror tactics such as forced flag-kissing rituals and house paintings were all too prevalent. A citizen faced with public ostracism as a "slacker" could ill afford to treat the bond solicitor flippantly.

Even when vigilantes were not involved, official sanction could be just as intimidating. Hixon's strategy of publishing the names of everyone who bought bonds was turned on its head after a number of communities decided to publish the names of the "slackers." Appleton decided not only to publish the names but also to make this knowledge permanent in the Outagamie County war history. At the end of the final wartime bond drive, the Milwaukee County Liberty Loan Committee and a fleet of twenty-five cars visited six farmers who had refused to participate in the bond drive. Three farmers were home that day, and one can imagine the intimidation of watching some of Milwaukee County's most prominent citizens disembark from a caravan of cars. The committee gave each farmer two choices: buy their "fair share" of bonds or be publicly shamed by posting the following yellow placard on their property:

Public Notice
The occupant of these premises has refused to buy his fair share
of fourth Liberty loan bonds. Do not remove this sign.

All three farmers immediately subscribed to their "fair share" of bonds.[65]

Although the bond drives were the most significant wartime fund-raising campaign, additional appeals for money saturated the home front. The cliché "give until it hurts" could never have seemed a more accurate description of realities. The good people of Wisconsin were asked to contribute to separate drives for the Red Cross, the YMCA, and the Knights of Columbus, as well as umbrella canvasses such as the United War Work Campaign in 1918. One particularly busy period in 1917 included a YMCA drive in mid-November, a YWCA campaign in late November, a Knights of Columbus drive in early December, and a Red Cross fund-raising project in mid-December.[66]

The Red Cross was an easy organization to support. In communities across Wisconsin, Red Cross volunteers, mostly women, knitted large numbers of socks, mufflers, and sweaters; made hospital garments and surgical supplies; and assembled comfort kits for the troops in France. The Red Cross assisted military and civilian officials with the work of providing support for soldiers in the field and war relief to the families of military personnel at home. As with many other aspects of life on the home front, meeting the monthly quota for medical supplies, comfort kits, or knitted goods became a matter of personal, organizational, and community pride. It also became another barometer for a community's patriotism.

Sometimes the work of the Red Cross took on a particularly personal tone. During October 1917 volunteers in Brown County worked diligently to make eight hundred sets of knitted goods for the troops in France. As soon as they completed that task, they made knitted sets for the members of artillery batteries B and E, whose members came largely from the

By World War I the YWCA had a long tradition of helping young women with housing, classes, and counseling services. Approximately a million women took up war work in the United States during the war. When the war work took women away from home, the YWCA was there to provide help. Like the YMCA and the Red Cross, YWCA fund-raising became an integral part of the war work campaign. WHI IMAGE ID 36644

Brown County area. The Red Cross was proud that "Brown County boys are to be furnished with sets made from wool from Brown County sheep, sewed in Brown County and made by Brown County women." Sophomore girls at West High School in Green Bay made hospital bed shirts, comfort kits, and sweaters and scarves for the troops in France.[67]

The Red Cross enjoyed almost universal support and even possessed some of the protections afforded the government in defense of the war effort. Refusal to help the Red Cross led to the arrest of at least one young man, a Pentecostal minister named Karl Jacobson, on charges of violating the state's "disloyalty" act.[68]

The Red Cross in Brown County began its second big fund-raising campaign only days after the third Liberty Loan drive ended. Red Cross organizers adopted the bond campaign's local slogan, "Your share is fair," and expected residents to make donations based on the Liberty Loan allotment plan. The campaign easily met its goals, in part because zealous guardians of patriotism chose to enforce their sense of what constituted an appropriate donation. In the small town of Sharon, a group of about forty people visited three farms. John Westphal, an "enemy alien,"[69] had already purchased $1,800 in war bonds and pleaded with Red Cross volunteers that he had no money for another donation. In response, they decorated his home with yellow crosses. The home of a Civil War veteran was decorated in similar fashion when he refused to make a donation, and George Dullam's farmhouse was spared when he made a midnight donation of $15. A person identified as a "slacker" in a Red Cross campaign easily could be targeted by vigilantes in the same manner as someone who failed to buy war bonds. In Stevens Point, for example, a wealthy retired farmer who donated twenty-five cents to a Red Cross fundraising drive found the exterior of the house painted yellow along with the inscription "$.25."[70]

The bond and fund-raising drives of World War I involved all people in the war effort. They could be confident they were aiding the boys "over there." Whether collecting money or scrap paper, these campaigns directly involved individuals in the war effort and helped regular people answer the question, "What can I do to win the war?" The war drives emphasized the nature of a "total war" that demanded sacrifices of everyone.

American Industry Realigns for War

Sacrifice was certainly necessary in order to redirect American industry away from civilian production to support the military production essential to win the war. As the army and National Guard mobilized, General Pershing told the War Department that he planned to enlist one million men in the American Expeditionary Force by May 1918 and recommended a longer-term goal of raising and equipping an army of three million men. When Wilson signed the declaration of war, the United States lacked the supplies necessary to equip and arm a force this size. Civilian production would need to be redirected on a massive scale to meet military needs.[71]

That redirection got off to a slow, uncoordinated start. Shortly after the United States joined the Allies, Secretary of War Newton D. Baker described the monumental task facing the nation as "stupendous." His critics had "no real comprehension of how hard it is to expand industrially an unmilitary country into any sort of adequate response to such an emergency as we are now facing."[72]

In April 1917 a general staff of fewer than twenty officers was responsible for the planning necessary to expand, train, equip and arm a modern force capable of fighting in Europe. Although this general staff would eventually grow to almost eight hundred officers, the structure of the prewar army hindered the army's growth. While the military draft effectively drew the desired numbers of men to the army, American industry proved much more difficult to harness in order to house soldiers in training and supply them with uniforms, equipment, and weapons. During the summer of 1917, the army set out to build housing for 1.2 million men in thirty-two camps, small cities of forty thousand inhabitants each distributed across the nation. This massive new army was going to need unheard-of quantities of uniforms, boots, gas masks, rifles, machine guns, and artillery. The Mexican incursion of 1916 had depleted supplies, requiring the Quartermaster Corps to rush orders into production. Officers estimated they could uniform a million men by the end of 1917. Remington and Winchester factories currently producing Enfield rifles for Great Britain would need to expand to produce millions of rifles for the United States. As war began, the army had not yet identified a suitable standard-issue machine gun and

chose the experimental Model 1916 three-inch gun as its standard light artillery piece. The nation's capacity to produce aircraft and tanks was almost
nonexistent. Going to war was going to require a massive reorientation of
American industry.[73]

Wisconsin military production during the war reflected the diversity
and geographic distribution of the state's manufacturing concerns. Across
the state, companies rapidly retooled to make woolen cloth, boots, rub-
berized rain gear, TNT, artillery, trucks, and ships. Milwaukee, a manufacturing hub with a skilled labor force, had war contracts to manufacture
steel, iron, heavy machinery, motor vehicles, packed meat, and tanned
leather. In 1917, war contracts boosted the value of Milwaukee's finished
products over the half-billion-dollar mark for the first time.[74]

Many companies adapted existing skills and equipment to make new
products. Before the war, Milwaukee's A. O. Smith revolutionized bicycle
manufacturing by developing a method for converting sheet metal into
tubing. The company also invented methods for mass-producing lightweight pressed-steel automobile frames. It was a short leap to make bomb
casings. A. O. Smith became the largest of ten bomb-making companies in
the United States and employed twenty-four hundred men at this task.[75]

Other companies simply expanded existing operations to meet new military demands. In Clintonville, Kissel began turning out camouflage trucks
by the hundreds, and the La Crosse Rubber Company made boots for the
army. In Manitowoc and Superior, existing shipyards built approximately
thirty cargo ships. In an age of steel ships, the Hartman-Greiling Company
of Green Bay and the Burger Boat Building Company of Manitowoc built
wooden patrol boats, fast, agile 110-foot boats designed as submarine chas-
ers. Equipped with listening devices and loaded with depth charges, they
could be just as lethal to a German submarine as a much larger destroyer.[76]

Pershing's incursion into Mexico served as a testing ground for Harley-
Davidson, when motorcycles with machine guns mounted to sidecars were
used in the expedition across the border. During the war approximately
one-third of the company's production, or twenty thousand vehicles, went
to the army. Early in the war the army used civilian models, but the company soon developed models specifically for use by the army in rugged
conditions.[77]

The manufacture of motor trucks was still in its youth in 1918, and dozens of companies produced vehicles for the government and commercial markets. In September 1917 the Oneida Motor Truck Company announced it had secured a contract with the New York firm Hamilton and Hensell worth between $8 million and $10 million for the delivery of forty-three hundred trucks between 1919 and 1923. One month later the company received another large order, this time for one thousand trailer chassis per month for use by the army to haul field kitchens. In 1914, the war had begun as a horse-and-wagon war. By 1918, as orders for motor trucks mounted, it was becoming clear that modern warfare depended more on horsepower than on horses.[78]

Just south of Washburn, in Bayfield County, the DuPont dynamite plant opened in 1905 and produced just under three million pounds of dynamite that first year. They began making the highly explosive trinitrotoluene— TNT—experimentally in 1912. Between 1913 and 1918, DuPont turned out 130 million pounds of TNT and 90 million pounds of commercial explosives. When the United States entered the war, the Washburn plant expanded what it had been doing for the Allies since 1915. The plant eventually employed about two thousand men, and, in classic boomtown fashion, Washburn's population ballooned from three thousand to nine thousand.[79]

Any assessment of the United States' wartime manufacturing must be a mixed review. Although delivery to troops in Europe was delayed and haphazard at first as the army worked out the complex logistics of placing orders, delivery to dock, transport to France, and eventual delivery to soldiers in the field, American manufacturers successfully produced food, uniforms, and small arms and ammunition for the American Expeditionary Force. These were relatively simple items to produce. American industry also produced more complex items, such as artillery, airplanes, and machine guns, although very few of these items reached the front, thanks to the technical difficulty of producing precision equipment, the relatively short duration of US involvement in the war, and army orders requiring additional work before mass production could begin.

Alfred Lawson's attempt to build safer military training planes illustrated the difficulties faced by many new and existing businesses as they retooled for new production with unprecedented speed. Lawson, a former professional baseball player from Detroit, came to Green Bay in March 1917 to find investors for his plan to build planes for the army. Two days before the United States entered the war, Lawson had amassed the backing he needed and filed the paperwork to incorporate the Lawson Aircraft company with initial capital of ten thousand dollars.

By May, Lawson's mechanics were preparing a factory on Green Bay's South Pearl Street for airplane production, with plans to have a plane ready to fly in 90 to 120 days. Four months later, Lawson climbed into the cockpit of the company's first military trainer prototype and took the plane on a fifteen-minute test flight. Lawson flew at five hundred to six hundred feet and pushed the plane to seventy miles an hour. He was impressed that "this machine handled with the greatest ease and controllability. In other words she flew faultlessly." After further testing that fall and winter, the company planned to turn the prototype over to the War Department for evaluation.

Once the company had a working prototype, Lawson rented a hundred-acre field for use as an airfield. By mid-October, workmen were busy leveling the field and constructing a variety of hangars and other buildings to create an "aviation field."

Lawson carefully controlled the company's publicity to convey the image of an active company of the most modern sort. He boasted that the company employed the best men, in the best facilities, to produce the best military plane in the world. On December 15, 1917, the company took possession of a new facility on the corner of Pearl and Howard in Green Bay. Lawson published a full-page ad in the newspaper, describing the building whose "extraordinary number of windows . . . permits an abundance of daylight" to flood into the "spacious halls" that could house up to five hundred workers. Night work would be illuminated "by innumerable electric lights of all sizes and descriptions." "Bubbling fountains" throughout the facility would allow workmen to get refreshment without interrupting work. A central "auditorium" was "commodious" enough to house construction of up to a dozen "whole airplanes" at the same time. Balconies overlooking the auditorium provided ample space for offices and drafting rooms. Through "a most intricate system of handling material" the company would track "every ounce of raw material from the time it is received" through the east door until it left as a finished airplane out the north door. The company had already designed and built a second training aircraft and would soon build a "pursuit" plane capable of flying at the "astounding speed" of 175 miles an hour. Lawson anticipated the War

IT'S A

LAWSON

The M. T. One — Primary Training Type

BUILT BY THE

LAWSON AIRCRAFT CORPORATION
GREEN BAY, WISCONSIN

The Lawson Aircraft Corporation illustrates the plight faced by American corporations and the government as they tried to bring the might of the nation to the battlefield. A company already producing rifles for the British could add production capacity relatively easily; an automobile company could convert to military truck production with some difficulty; for a new company, such as Lawson Aircraft, it was almost impossible to get product to the battlefield before the end of the war. Had the war stretched into 1919, the German army would have been crushed under the great weight of American manpower and war production. America's war lasted only eighteen months and ended before Lawson could produce any aircraft for the military. WHI IMAGE ID 125349

Department would need at least a "couple of hundred thousand airplanes" and envisioned a lucrative future for his company.

Lawson met with military officials during the winter of 1917–1918, but he failed to sell them the results of the first prototype, known as the MT 1. The army wanted an aircraft with a higher performance capacity, so Lawson's engineers went to work perfecting the next iteration, known as the MT 2. Their new aircraft was twelve miles an hour faster than the MT 1 and could reach a speed of ninety miles per hour. The army placed an order for one hundred planes, but canceled it shortly thereafter when the war abruptly ended. Green Bay never produced the fleet of aircraft Lawson had envisioned. After the war Lawson became an innovator in aviation when he designed a passenger airliner in Milwaukee, but his hopes for commercial success collapsed with the crash of one of his airliners on its maiden flight in 1921.[80]

SOLVING THE LABOR SHORTAGE

New companies like Lawson Aircraft and established firms like Allis-Chalmers shared a fundamental problem: not enough workers. The gap left by men drafted into the army could be filled from two sources: men who were not otherwise gainfully employed, such as jail inmates, and women. Wisconsin's Huber Law, passed in 1917, authorized sheriffs to furnish laborers to employers. The mantra became "work or fight." By late spring 1918, the need for factory and farm labor had become so great that the governor told sheriffs to aggressively arrest men known at the time as "vagrants, tramps and loafers" and put them to work. At the same time, Congress adopted a draconian change to the Selective Service law to channel the "unproductive" into the farm and factory labor pool. Effective July 1, 1918, every male of draft age employed in a "non-useful" occupation was to be brought before the draft board and given the choice of a new job or the army. Non-useful occupations included not only professional gamblers, race track and bucket shop (illegal brokerage firm) attendants, and fortune-tellers, but also waiters, bartenders, theater ushers and attendants, passenger elevator operators, other attendants, domestic employees, and retail store clerks. Under the new rule, deferments on account of dependents were disregarded. To solve the industrial labor crisis, the nation had gone dangerously down an autocratic path.[81]

The most practical solution to the labor crisis was to bring more women into war industries. Manufacturers of aircraft, automobiles, and weaponry hired women in record numbers. Wherever one cared to look, women were doing industrial work uncommon in the prewar period. As production in machine shops expanded to meet war needs, and as men left for the army, women moved away from their traditional roles in the textile, clothing, and candy industries and flooded into new areas of heavy manufacturing and machine shops to make war supplies. In 1914 women comprised 3 percent of the workforce in the iron and steel industries. Women comprised 6 percent following the first military draft call and 9 percent after the second draft. By the end of the war, women made up a full 20 percent of the industrial workforce.[82]

The performance of female employees during the war upended the stereotypes of those who doubted women had the mental and physical capacity to work in almost any industrial environment as male workers. Nonetheless, a variety of persistent misconceptions interfered with a clear understanding of the potential of women workers. Employers and many social reformers continued to believe that male workers should be given preference over women, who could be supported by a spouse or other family member. Men were breadwinners, they argued, while women were working for "pin money." This assumption ignored the obvious fact that many female workers were supporting themselves and/or their families. Many progressive reformers and employers also assumed women needed protections or modifications to safely do the work. All too often, assumptions about female knowledge, ability, and fragility became the justification for paying women less than their male counterparts.

For most of the war, farmers dealt with the agricultural labor shortage by cobbling together a solution composed of hired farm hands when available, family members, and untrained work crews of businessmen and high school students. As 1917 came to a close, leaders of major women's organizations thought they had a better solution. A few days before Christmas, leaders of the National League for Women's Service and the Women's National Farm and Garden Association met with representatives from the General Federation of Women's Clubs, the YWCA, the Association of Collegiate Alumnae, the National American Woman Suffrage Association, and a wide array of other professional and educational organizations at New York's Hotel Astor to discuss solutions to the growing farm labor shortage. The meeting attendees adjourned after committing themselves to founding the Woman's Land Army. The Woman's Land Army offered a solution to the agricultural labor shortage, the problem training farm-workers, and the seasonal nature of the work.

The Land Army grew out of prewar experiments in the northeast, principally New York, to create units or work gangs of trained women who could take up significant farm chores without placing a financial burden on farmers or requiring extensive training by the farmer. Volunteers in the Land Army would undergo several weeks of training, would live communally in camps, and would work on nearby farms as needed by local farmers. Farmers would pay the women for their work but not be responsible for their upkeep.

January 1918 brought a flurry of activity as the new organization rushed to build a national base. From offices in New York, the Land Army sent its first communication to Wisconsin and other states on February 9, 1918, on hastily typed letterhead. The Land Army's first publicity heralded the organization's patriotic mission. By April 8, eighteen states had joined and ten states, including Wisconsin, were in the process of establishing Land Army programs.

As with so many other areas of Wisconsin wartime life, organization of the Land Army began with the Wisconsin Council of Defense. On April 16, 1918, Mary P. Morgan, chair of the Woman's Committee of the state Council of Defense, informed Louise Peters, executive secretary of the Woman's Land Army, that renowned home economist Nellie Kedzie Jones had agreed to lead the Wisconsin Land Army. Morgan also informed the national headquarters that Wisconsin was not planning any agricultural camps until an indefinite time in the future because "more men have been secured to work the farms in Wisconsin than there are need of, so that this year women will not be needed." The exception to this generalization seemed to be cherries in Door County and berries in northern Wisconsin. These crops always required a large seasonal workforce, often from the state's Native American communities, to bring in the harvest. Growers worried they might not have the necessary workers to harvest the 1918 crop and asked for help from the Land Army.[83]

By August 1918, the state Council of Defense was no longer so sanguine about the agricultural workforce, and Kedzie Jones began developing a one-week training program to be taught at the Wisconsin State Fair in early September. As she wrote to Morgan,

> The telegram from Mr. [Christian] Norgord [director of the State Department of Agriculture] followed by his letter made me think we can have something which we may call a "Land Army Preparatory School" perhaps! Mr. Norgord thinks it well to combine the Land Army ideas with those of a "State Fair School of Opportunities" for Rural Teachers.

As Kedzie Jones warmed to her topic, the pace of the letter quickened and a rush of ideas flowed forth. "We must see to it that we get our young women to come," she told Morgan.

> My idea is this, to have those young women get a vision of what a "Land Army" might mean if called for in this state.
>
> I want to have them live in tents—do their own cooking (in divisions of course) then have about four lectures a day for five days, one hour each will give twenty lectures—on many farm problems. I want to secure a lecture, or two, on the usual care of horses—then let them see how the fine horses at the Fair are cared for—one or two on feeding calves—their usual rate of growth—and what good care will do for them—lectures on raising pigs for market—on care of brood sows and little pigs—some on raising chickens for market—and for eggs—some on rotation of crops and farm management. Some on cows for milk—and steers for beef—then in all those cases there are the examples to be shown. Probably the lecturer will take the pupils to the hog house and explain many things!
>
> These Land Army women will go home after seeing, not only the best our state can show—but the best in many lines from several other states, with visions of what may be done on the individual farms.

If Wisconsin needs to mobilize her Land Army next year—we shall have these women for captains.[84]

Eighty-one women attended the first Land Army training course at the State Fair. The course was not perfect, but organizers considered it a great success. In keeping with Kedzie Jones's vision and the Land Army concept of "units" rather than individuals, the women stayed on the fairgrounds in a large, 120-foot-long tent outfitted as a classroom on one half and sleeping quarters on the other. A second tent was outfitted for cooking and dining. The women lived, cooked, ate, and learned together and created a bond essential to the future success of the Land Army. At mealtimes, in particular, the women "grouped themselves about the tables or benches and visited while they ate. Not only was this free and easy fellowship fine, but it was a powerful factor in forming an esprit de corps that will be valuable later." As the war ended, Kedzie Jones was planning a two-week course for the next State Fair, and was preparing to mobilize the Wisconsin Woman's Land Army for service in 1919.[85]

Although the Land Army played a minor role during the war itself, its very existence marked a distinct departure from the past and reflected an important way in which the war influenced American society. Young women had almost always worked for pay in the past to support themselves or their families, at least until marriage. Cultural norms placed an emphasis on women managing their household once they married. Managing a family was much more than the stereotypical scrubbing, cleaning, and cooking. The domestic boundaries were defined by the ethic of creating and maintaining a nurturing family environment that would result in children thriving physically and intellectually, playing meaningful roles as adults in the future. The demand for labor in factories and farms forced a rethinking, a least temporarily, of cultural norms. Perhaps women did not need protection from heavy labor or long hours; perhaps they could do complex mechanical tasks; perhaps they could play roles other than those of homemaker and caregiver; perhaps all workers deserved protection from dangerous conditions. The very concept of the Land Army expressed a different way of thinking about the roles of women. The Land Army was led by women and trained by women. It was based on the concept of women living together in camps or units and employed on farms in teams.

The war presented a fundamental challenge to the concept of domestic subservience. The roles women played during this time were part of the general and unsettling effects exerted on society as a result of the war. As brothers and fathers left for the army, women's new activities meant radical, if temporary, changes to family relationships and interactions. For example, women engaged as Red Cross volunteers or war plant workers often found themselves doing double duty as war workers and managers of the home. No matter how many hours they worked or volunteered, their other job as homemaker was always waiting. As would happen again during World War II, many women who entered the paid workforce, whether for economic or patriotic reasons, went to work each day in factory, store, or farm and came home to complete the day as manager of home and family. With less time for themselves and their families, the countervailing demands placed on women, demands that could not be reconciled fully, contributed to the tensions of wartime life.

THE SPANISH FLU

As Americans entered combat in large numbers, news reports told of victories purchased at great human cost by the Allied armies. The news optimistically implied the war was being won, as communities mourned the deaths of their young men. Other sobering news came from Europe as well. Soldiers were dying in large numbers not from battlefield wounds, but from illness. In addition to common ailments such as infection, dysentery, and pneumonia, newspapers began to carry stories of a lethal ailment sweeping through the armies of Europe in the summer of 1918. It was called the Spanish flu. It attacked young, otherwise healthy adults, killed quickly and often, and leapt from Europe to Wisconsin with unimaginable speed. Its cause was unknown; its mode of transmission was unknown; how to stop it was unknown.

The epidemic probably arrived in North America on a troop ship returning home. On September 14, 1918, doctors in Boston diagnosed the first case in the United States. Less than two weeks later the Spanish flu pandemic was wreaking havoc in Wisconsin. During the last five days of September, the number of new cases reported by health officials rose from 6 to 97. One week later, officials reported 256 new cases. Although no one knew it at the time, the epidemic crested on October 22 with a report of 588 new cases.

Midwestern states generally suffered fewer casualties from the Spanish flu than the more densely populated eastern states. Wisconsin was the only state in the nation to take aggressive and uniform action to limit spread of the epidemic. During a forty-year period the Wisconsin legislature had built the infrastructure for a modern public health system. In 1876 it created the State Board of Health with the power to issue statewide quarantine orders. In 1883 the legislature required every municipal unit to appoint local health boards and health officers. When the flu epidemic hit Wisconsin, the state had an existing public health framework within which to order and implement protective measures on a statewide basis.

Without knowing how to stop the epidemic, Wisconsin took one of the few effective steps to curb transmission: it limited the places people congregated. On October 10, 1918, Cornelius Harper, the state health officer, consulted with Governor Philipp and then issued an order instructing all local boards of health "to immediately close all schools, theaters, moving picture houses, other places of amusement and public gatherings for an indefinite period of time." The order effectively closed every public establishment and gathering place, including churches, except for places of regular employment. In many communities, schools and theaters closed for four weeks and churches locked their doors for three weeks.[86]

Nearly comprehensive statewide implementation took less than twenty-four hours. Failure to comply brought a swift response from Harper. For example, when Father J. M. Naughtin refused to close St. Rose Church in Racine, Harper called Archbishop Sebastian Messmer of Milwaukee, and the church quickly closed its doors.

Confusion over the nature of the order brought a tragic delay in Wausau. Although Harper intended his order to be mandatory, he also wished to give local officials latitude regarding how they implemented his instructions. He created confusion when he telegraphed the state's school boards: "Order issued as an advisory order. Local boards of health to use own judgment in closings." Shortly thereafter, Harper received a call from Walter Heineman, one of Wausau's most prominent citizens, complaining that the local health board planned to keep the schools open another week. Through Heineman as an intermediary, Harper clearly instructed the board to close the schools immediately. Heineman relayed these instructions to the mayor of Wausau by telephone, followed by a letter to the mayor in which he claimed Wausau was the only city out of compliance with the closure order, that the board risked an order quarantining the entire city, and that failure to comply "would lay any community open to criticism as being pro-German." For good measure, he also sent the letter to the *Wausau Daily Herald* for publication. Heineman's slight to their patriotism angered members of the local board of health. Harper was working to clear things up when the epidemic hit Wausau and made the board's course clear. Unfortunately, the misunderstanding gave students and teachers an extra week to spread the contagion, and Wausau officials found themselves fighting one of the worst outbreaks in the state. Nonetheless, effective cooperation between the Board of Health, the county Council of Defense, state officials, and a small army of volunteers limited the death toll and placed Marathon County in the lowest death rate category with only 0 to 20 deaths per 10,000 people.

For reasons still unclear, Ashland, Iron, and Kenosha Counties suffered the most severe epidemics and experienced death rates of 50 to 60 deaths per 10,000 people. In contrast—probably a result of advanced public health practices at the time—Milwaukee's tightly packed population experienced only 20 to 30 deaths per 10,000 people. The state's prompt response to the epidemic and the willingness of residents to abide stringent restrictions limited the spread of the disease. This cooperative spirit mirrored the ways in which they were conserving food, buying bonds, and volunteering for war work.[87]

Though new cases would continue to resurface and confound health officials, the epidemic was in decline by the end of December. In total the Spanish flu afflicted an estimated 103,000 Wisconsinites and killed 8,459, either from the flu itself or from related pneumonia. In the end, the Spanish flu epidemic killed more than four times the number of Wisconsin residents than did the fighting on the western front.

The War's Bigger Picture

Wisconsin's experience during the Great War is best visualized as a web of tangled, intersecting strands. This narrative attempts to separate some of these strands into discrete topics for clarity and discussion. To truly understand the war years, one must step back and see them as a whole.

At the end of July 1918, the 32nd Division entered its first major battle, and men died. These were not the first deaths of troops from Wisconsin or from the 32nd Division, but this battle marked a turning point in the war, after which the fighting would be relentless and the casualty lists would grow ever longer. Why did Americans who had steadfastly opposed involvement in the war so wholeheartedly devote their time, energy, and money to winning the war? Why did housewives and businessmen alike voluntarily conserve food and buy bonds? What fueled the typical patriotic response to the war and the super patriots' impulse to require everyone else to respond to the war in the same way they did? The answer to all of these questions lay in the deadly fact that friends, family, and neighbors were dying in Europe.

Daily life during the war retained a familiar but slightly off-kilter rhythm. People went to work, school, and church; they bought their groceries from familiar people; they went to the movies, bought new Easter clothes, visited with their neighbors. But at the theater, a local businessman who belonged to the Four Minute Men might deliver a quick exhortation to buy war bonds. At the grocer's, their regular purchase of four pounds of wheat flour was no longer possible thanks to Food Administration rules, so they bought oat flour instead. Instead of driving to the next county to visit with family, a college student might stay home to save fuel, to help with the harvest, or to visit with a friend home on furlough.

War insinuated uncertainty and worry into day-to-day life: Worry about loved ones fighting overseas. Worry about the massive changes to the economy and to social mores. Worry about the nation's future. Worry about being labeled a traitor.

The war ended on the eleventh hour of the eleventh day of the eleventh month of 1918. For the United States the war had been short, the path to victory had been swift, but the price had been high. Home-front sacrifices made in the name of patriotism were important contributions to the war effort. Although coercion influenced the behavior of some individuals and demonstrated how thin the veneer of civil order could be, the remarkable fact of the home front was that most people willingly and wholeheartedly gave of themselves and their wealth to help win the war and bring their friends and family home as soon as possible.

Charitable war work, food and fuel conservation, bond and fund-raising drives, and farm and factory production all succeeded because average people voluntarily did what they were asked to do. The true mark of patriotism on the home front was not the great heroic act; it was the small sacrifices made every day to win the war.

CHAPTER 5

POLITICS ON THE HOME FRONT

President Wilson had desperately hoped to avoid war, but the German resumption of unrestricted submarine warfare on February 1, 1917, had made that increasingly difficult. Wilson possessed a clear understanding that entry into the war would exact profound human, social, and political costs from the country. After a Cabinet meeting on February 2, Wilson expressed his reservations to Navy Secretary Josephus Daniels. The president did not want to send a generation of young men to the trenches of Europe, and he feared resurgent business interests would roll back his progressive reforms. "More than that," he told Daniels, "Free Speech and the other rights will be endangered. War is autocratic."[1] Wilson feared the war would jeopardize American liberty. Recognizing that danger, he nonetheless curtailed civil liberties and did little to prevent abuses of power by his own government, by local officials, or by self-appointed guardians of loyalty. The war demonstrated the fragility of civil liberties in the face of patriotic fervor and intolerance. Finding the balance between productive disagreement and obstructionism became difficult as super patriots cloaked the war in the American flag, and any negative remark became a disloyal act warranting investigation and sanction.

The declaration of war created a patriotic benchmark against which personal and political behavior was measured. What had once constituted vigorous debate was now considered traitorous speech. This change became a defining element of life on the home front, especially in Wisconsin. Opposition to the war by most of Wisconsin's congressional delegation was a legitimate part of the political discussion as late as April 5, 1917. After war was declared one day later, anyone who questioned the war declaration, presidential decisions, war aims, the draft, or war finance risked censure or legal action for their "traitorous" behavior, in Wisconsin and elsewhere. Daily behavior often was judged by a patriotic litmus test, but what constituted patriotic behavior was defined anew in each situation, and by each person involved in that event. A misplaced word, miserly donation to the Red Cross, or political disagreement could result in a visit with the police or intimidation by vigilantes. Most "unpatriotic" behavior was nothing more than a failure to meet social norms or conduct oneself within boundaries set by wartime society. All too often, the exercise of free speech became "unpatriotic" behavior; criticizing government policy in any way during a war easily took on the aura of yelling "fire" in a crowded theater.

Distinguishing between real threats to national security and imaginary ones was complicated by the fact that there were real spies and saboteurs. The nation's newspapers regularly carried stories of spies and saboteurs arrested by state and federal authorities. Two days after the war declaration, the *Sunday State Journal* reported on a series of federal raids that had happened the day before in New York, Pittsburgh, Cleveland, Chicago, and San Francisco in an attempt to crush or cripple the nation's German spy network. Hundreds of people were being arrested in the roundups.[2]

In wartime, when the threat of domestic sabotage and subversion is real, it often can be difficult to maintain the boundary between what is free speech and what is criminal subversion. The Bureau of Investigation, the Secret Service, and the US Marshals Service all had agents in Wisconsin looking for spies and saboteurs, investigating sedition and espionage, and arresting draft evaders. The Bureau of Investigation maintained a civilian volunteer force whose members spied and informed on their neighbors. Finally, some local citizens became vigilantes to enforce their own perception of justice. The only things holding the nation's security apparatus within lawful bounds were agents with common sense and thoughtful political leaders devoted to maintaining the fragile balance between constitutional rights and national security.

Social Issues in a Wartime Society

In the debate over major social issues such as woman's suffrage and Prohibition, patriotism and patriotic behavior quickly became a test of the

The spy-hunting rat terrier conveyed a variety of meanings to the *Wisconsin State Journal*'s readers: The Secret Service was on the job catching spies, and there were lots of spies to catch. Herein lay a conundrum. How does one protect the security of the nation in a free society at war? The threat was real, but never as serious as super patriots thought. There was no clear or easy answer to the question, What is the right balance between surveillance, repression, and free speech when fighting a total war?
SUNDAY STATE JOURNAL, APRIL 8, 1917

worthiness of the cause. Supporters of a suffrage amendment pointed out repeatedly that women were participating in all aspects of the war effort as nurses, factory workers, volunteers, and, most of all, as managers of the home and as foot soldiers in Hoover's Food Administration. If women could be trusted with all of these critical patriotic jobs, why could they not be trusted with the vote? The roles women played in the war effort made it increasingly difficult to ignore or resist their claim to suffrage.

The war also provided the impetus for passage of one of the most ill-conceived measures in American history: Prohibition. The World War I food crisis turned a marginal issue into a patriotic cause, and demonstrated how cavalierly the advocates on both sides of the debate were willing to bludgeon their opponents with the patriotic club. In Wisconsin, on one side of the argument stood the anti-saloon league and many Protestant churches. On the other side stood the Wisconsin Brewers Association and much of the German community, represented by the German American Alliance. Initially, Congress took a number of steps to limit the availability of liquor. It created "dry zones" around military facilities and prohibited the sale of liquor to military personnel. The Lever Act banned production of distilled spirits made from commodities that could be used as food. Wilson issued a proclamation limiting the alcoholic content of beer. As the war progressed, pressure mounted for a Prohibition amendment to the Constitution. In December 1917, Congress sent the Eighteenth Amendment to the states for ratification. It prohibited the manufacture and sale of alcoholic beverages. By the end of the war, numerous cities and villages had exercised local prerogatives and banned the sale of liquor.

Emblematic of wartime political debate, the "wet" and "dry" forces each relied on patriotism as the underpinning for their solicitation of support. Each side conveniently charged opponents with disloyalty or unpatriotic behavior. Wisconsin's spring election in 1918 not only focused on electing a new US senator, but in many communities included a referendum on whether to license saloons. Prohibition advocates argued that curtailing access to alcohol would protect servicemen from the lethal effects of liquor. The Anti-Saloon League equated a vote against saloons with being a "real American." The Federated Trades Council of Green Bay attacked the proposal to close saloons as "undemocratic and unnecessary." Later in the summer as the campaign for a constitutional amendment gained steam, the Wisconsin Brewers' Association attacked temperance advocates for creating a diversion from the real issue of winning the war. In an advertisement titled "Patriotism" the association criticized the Anti-Saloon League for disrupting national unity by forcing Prohibition, a measure unnecessary to win the war, on a reluctant nation. In a clear attempt to delay action until after the war, presumably in the hope that support for Prohibition would wither outside the hothouse of wartime society, the Brewers' Association declared: "Let national prohibition wait until the country is normal again. Let us fight a united fight against a united enemy."

In contrast to this rather staid critique, the advocates of Prohibition mounted a righteous onslaught. On one occasion the Brown County Dry League declared every aspect of the production and distribution of beer a treasonous waste of resources. Every acre of grain, every ounce of sugar, every pound of coal, every hour of labor, every rail car used by the "un-American beer brewing industry" was a treasonous use of resources better spent supporting the war effort. The ad concluded, "The liquor traffic is the hope of the Hun, the enemy of our flag, the source of selfishness, the corrupter of politics and the debaucher of Democracy. It is the **Arch Traitor**." One Prohibitionist named the enemy explicitly: the nation was fighting German enemies abroad and at home, "And the worst of all our German enemies, the most treacherous, the most menacing are Pabst, Schlitz, Blatz, and Miller."[3]

THE PRICE OF "DISLOYALTY"

In the rhetorical war on the home front, brewers were not alone in being targeted as disloyal and unpatriotic. The legal system could exact harsh retribution from individuals too indiscreet, stubborn, foolish, angry, stupid, or inebriated to avoid slurs or actions insulting to the president, the flag, General Pershing, or any number of other targets associated with patriotism and the American role in the war. Law enforcement was particularly suspicious of "enemy aliens"—German residents of the United who had not become citizens. The day war was declared, a blunt headline in the *Monroe Evening Times* left no doubt about the precarious position "enemy aliens" faced: "ALIEN RESIDENTS ARE WARNED AGAINST ALL ACTS OF VIOLENCE; DRASTIC PUNISHMENT ORDERED FOR ALL VIOLATIONS

DETECTED." This warning explicitly applied to Germans who had not become citizens, but by implication would have been threatening to all 630,000 members of the German American community, 27 percent of Wisconsin's population, including legal citizens, who had either been born in Germany or had German parents.[4]

The wartime rules restricting noncitizen Germans produced some unusual results. The federal government required them to carry identification cards, obey a 9 p.m. curfew, and remain at all times within one mile of their homes. People who had lived in Wisconsin for most of their lives suddenly found themselves labeled "enemy aliens," including a Union army veteran and at least one Republican town leader. Many had come to Wisconsin as young children, with parents who had never sought citizenship. As a consequence, once the war began, they were restricted as if enemies in a foreign land.[5]

People looked for signs of disloyalty everywhere. Postal inspector William Esch wrote to his brother in Congress: "Throughout my territory the Germans have been conducting themselves very orderly. I have had some matters to investigate but found there was no cause for action." A short time later, he wrote his brother again: "A few of the radicals have been quietly warned and the result is a very peaceable sentiment when we might look for the opposite. The worst feature is scandal mongering . . . but I think even this has about run its course."[6]

The effect of all this attention was to cause dissent to go underground. As Frank Blodgett of Janesville told Congressman Henry Cooper, "The citizen who has wanted War; who wants to send a big army to Europe; who wants to destroy the German Government has no hesitation in expressing his views publicly and is acclaimed as a patriot. Those who do not agree with him hesitate to express their opinions, not being desirous of being branded as traitors or unpatriotic."[7]

Whether from an "enemy alien" or a citizen, a careless or injudicious word could result in dismissal from employment or entanglement in the machinery of justice: a professor fired for a critical comment in the presence of the wrong person; a student expelled from the university for a draft violation; a teacher fired for a lunchroom jest about ammunition plants; and a janitor fired because he was a socialist.[8]

Carefully considered words do not always come naturally to politicians.

On April 24, 1917, with the declaration of war still fresh in memory, Frank Raguse, a state senator from the Eighth District in Milwaukee and a socialist, told his colleagues, "Patriotism can be created only in two ways: First, you must either destroy people, or, second, you must destroy property." This inarticulate and incomprehensible statement implied that patriotism could be created only through destruction. When several senators took umbrage at his remarks, Raguse protested that he had expressed himself poorly and his meaning was being misinterpreted. He meant to contrast true patriotism with a false patriotism created by individuals who would benefit from war and stir up the public with false patriotism. His explanation was aimed at war profiteers. It did not mollify his opponents, however. With their hackles raised and perhaps relishing the opportunity to oust a socialist from their midst, his fellow senators would only accept a retraction. Unwilling to disavow what he considered a valid point, Raguse found himself expelled from the state Senate by a vote of 30 to 3. Raguse and the other two socialists in the Senate were the only votes against his expulsion. He promised to be back after the next election. A special election was held to fill his seat in January 1918, but the Socialist Party slot on the ballot was taken by Edward Melms, who lost in a close vote to Republican businessman Louis Fons.[9]

Although a politician and state senator, Raguse shared with everyone else the jeopardy of living in a wartime society. With a misspoken word, a flippant comment, or the perception that an individual was not sufficiently supporting the war effort, a person's comfortable life could disintegrate overnight. A farmer from the town of Eaton in Brown County stopped in a local saloon for some refreshment. According to the bartender, the farmer stood at the bar "decrying the strength of the American navy and army, and sneering at the fighting ability of the soldiers." In June 1917 the American navy was quite strong, but the farmer's comments about the army were completely accurate. Nonetheless, the barkeep found the remarks intolerable, in part perhaps because the farmer was an "alien." As he told municipal court officials the next day, "I reached over and hit him. Then I hit him again and threw him outside. I told him nobody could say that in my place and get away with it." The story came to light because the saloon keeper had gone to the municipal court to find out if a warrant had been sworn for his arrest. Having admitted to assaulting the farmer, the barman walked away from the courthouse a free man. The farmer was unlikely to be so lucky. Municipal court officials were going to report the matter to "the Federal authorities."

Officials sometimes found it difficult to differentiate between a minor indiscretion and a serious threat to the war effort. In La Crosse, Private Jack McPeak of Sparta's Company I, Third Wisconsin Infantry, got drunk and made "deprecating" remarks about the flag. He spent ninety days in the county jail. An army court-martial treated a drunken prank even more harshly. Corporal R. Miller, Private R. G. Brown, and Private Russell Mock, members of the Engineering Corps of the Ohio National Guard, went on leave in Kenosha and got drunk. In their revelry, they tore down several flags and insulted the flag and the government. Miller received a sentence of four months in the Fort Sheridan guard house and forfeiture of two-thirds of his pay for that period. Brown and Mock were sentenced to six months' hard labor at Fort Leavenworth, forfeiture of pay, and dishonorable discharge.

On the morning of May 10, 1918, residents of the town of Amberg, near Marinette, woke to find their rural school festooned with pro-German placards. Three signs were posted on the schoolhouse and one on the flagpole. The signs read: "Hoch Der Kaiser," "We Love the Kaiser," "Germany forever," and "Wanted[:] a German flag for this pole." It was believed that the signs were posted "as sort of revenge" for schoolteacher Alice Sweeney's active war work. One hundred years later, this feels more like a school prank perpetrated for amusement than a malicious act. Be that as it may, the district attorney investigated in the hope of finding the "traitors" who posted the signs.[10]

Widespread suspicions of disloyalty eventually had an impact on children. Across Wisconsin the study of anything German was under critique beginning in April 1917. Particularly, the use of the German language was criticized as an agent of what was known as "German Kulture." Wisconsinites were encouraged by super patriots and pundits to avoid using or teaching German. German-language education plummeted after the declaration of war, not just in Milwaukee where the number of German teachers dropped from two hundred to just one, but all over the state. Into this hostile environment came young Bobby Bizzell of Kaukauna. One day he was playing with friends when two workmen walked by, speaking to each other in German. Bobby picked up a large club and struck one of the men with a hard blow. When taken into the house for punishment, his little sister chided him, "Bobby, you shouldn't have hit that man; how do you know but he was Jesus in working clothes?" To which Bobby replied, "Jesus; do you think He'd be talking German?"[11]

Newspapers routinely carried articles about people who ran afoul of authorities because of a misspoken word or behavior interpreted by others as disloyal. The authority of government agencies to investigate suspicious behavior, augmented by the Espionage Act of 1917 and the Sedition Act of May 1918, had the effect of silencing critics of the government or the war. The Espionage Act made it illegal by word or deed to interfere with recruitment or military operations or give support to the enemy. Congress amended the Espionage Act to prohibit any expression critical or abusive of the government, the war effort, or the American flag. In a measure designed to hamstring dissemination of "seditious" ideas, the Postmaster General was given authority to refuse to deliver seditious materials. These amendments are commonly called the Sedition Act of 1918.

A person could easily be indicted for criticizing the United States or praising Germany. Decrying the conflict as a "rich man's war" could be equally hazardous. In normal times, expressing a simple opinion critical of the president, the YMCA, the draft, or the Liberty Loan drives might spark a debate. During the war a verbal misstep or failure to behave patriotically could result in jail time, a barn painted yellow, or more severely, a coat of tar and feathers.

During the war, ninety people in Wisconsin were indicted for a total of 183 violations of the Espionage Act. The most common infractions (103 violations) were for praising Germany, criticizing the United States, or calling the conflict a "rich man's war." The remaining eighty indictments were handed down for criticizing Liberty Bonds, the Allies, charities, or food laws; obstructing military recruiting; insulting the flag or uniform; or praising a ship's sinking.[12]

The Justice Department's Bureau of Investigation pursued a wide array of cases that more often than not involved speech rather than action. It received tips and assistance from many different sources. Scott Goodnight, a dean at the University of Wisconsin, helped to investigate fellow faculty and students, as well as the Wisconsin Forum, a student organization dedicated to intellectual discourse that had invited socialist and liberal speakers. Milton Potter, Milwaukee superintendent of schools, volunteered to help investigate a teacher at the Center Street School. Across the state, local Council of Defense officials, sheriffs, and prosecutors worked with investigators to uncover disloyalty. When a complaint sent to the State Council of Defense required investigation or legal action, council officials readily forwarded the case to the bureau for investigation.

To supply local information and investigation assistance, the Justice Department created the American Protective League, or APL, a volunteer civilian organization comprised of individuals willing to provide information about suspicious activities. The league amounted to a surveillance system composed of neighbors watching neighbors. APL members supplied information on suspicious behavior, provided the Bureau of Investigation with local assistance, and sometimes conducted investigations on their own. Although the membership lists that have survived almost certainly are incomplete (they list members primarily from the eastern half of the state and do not include Superior, Eau Claire, Stevens Point, La Crosse, Platteville, or Prairie du Chien), the APL had at least 170 "operatives" living in cities large and small across the eastern half of Wisconsin. Just under half of the operatives lived in Milwaukee. The Bureau of Investigation had a limited number of agents in Wisconsin, but the APL gave them "eyes and ears" in every county and in many small towns and cities.

The APL was a key component of a surveillance system that may have been more intrusive to the average American than at any other time in American history, more so than during the "Red Scare" of the 1920s, World War II, or the McCarthy era. One can certainly find examples of groups subjected to extreme surveillance measures during each of these later eras—organized labor in the 1920s; Japanese Americans in the 1940s; Hollywood actors, directors, and writers in the 1950s; civil rights and anti-war activists in the 1950s, 1960s, and 1970s—but none of these examples targeted average Americans the way the APL did in the brief period of World War I. Fennimore had six operatives watching their neighbors, Baraboo had four, Sheboygan had three, Siren had one, and Milwaukee had eighty-one operatives. By the end of the war, members of the Loyalty Legion, a successor to Wheeler Bloodgood's Wisconsin Defense League, were supplying information to the bureau as well.[13]

One of the higher-profile investigations focused on Bishop Joseph M. Koudelka of the Superior Archdiocese. Three priests had reported Koudelka for unpatriotic comments or actions. They alleged Koudelka had expressed concern that Germany's defeat might bring the demise of the Catholic Church in the United States. They claimed he lacked patriotic fervor and limited their patriotic activities. After a thorough investigation, Willard Parker, a bureau investigator based in Madison, concluded the charges stemmed from long-standing tensions between Irish and German priests in the diocese. Koudelka was Czech, and his detractors were Irish. The tensions probably predated the war, but because Koudelka hailed from the Austro-Hungarian Empire, his detractors found it convenient to report him for disloyalty. In a report that reflected the circumspection with which agents carried out investigations, Parker concluded the Justice Department "should not in any way whatsoever mix in the fight involved between the nationalities of the Priests of the Diocese of Superior."[14]

DANGEROUS CONFRONTATIONS

People suspected of disloyalty faced retribution not only from law enforcement, but from local vigilantes as well. Vigilante justice is, by its nature, unjust. In the state's most notorious case, the four Krueger brothers of Clark County paid a dear price for running afoul of the Selective Service Act. In 1884 Louis (originally Ludwig) Krueger, his wife, Caroline, and their young son, Frank, settled on eighty acres of uncleared land a mile and a half south of Withee in Clark County. Louis worked hard, bought an additional 160 acres, and prospered. In due course he and Caroline had four more sons, Robert, Louie, Leslie, and Ennis. Louis cleared the land, built a large home, and bought a portable sawmill to rent out when neighbors were clearing land. Tragedy struck the family in 1910 and 1911 when first Louis and then his son Robert died of pneumonia. The oldest brother, Frank, a strapping young man of thirty, took responsibility for the family, which continued to prosper.

Caroline Krueger was an outspoken woman of strong religious beliefs. After Louis's death, she alienated members of the Congregational churches in both Withee and the nearby community of Owen. The family drifted into community isolation and home Bible study. Their isolation grew deeper as Caroline came under the influence of religious leader Charles T. Russell, alienating friends and neighbors. The Russellites (today known as Jehovah's Witnesses) rejected military service and believed the Great War was the biblical Armageddon.

In a relatively brief period, the Krueger family had gone from being a leading family in Clark County to a status similar to that of outcasts. Caroline made no secret of her antiwar beliefs. Once the nation went to war, her beliefs were no longer just unpopular; when acted on by her sons, they quickly ran afoul of the law.

The draft required men between the ages of twenty-one and thirty to register on June 5, 1917. Ennis and Frank were exempt; Ennis was too young and Frank too old. On June 5, Louie arrived at the Longwood town hall to register and filled out the required form. The last question asked if there was any reason the registrant should be exempt from the draft. Louie gave no indication of the desire for a religious or any other exemption. He simply wrote: "none." Explaining that Leslie was ill, he filled out a form for his brother. To the exemption question he answered, "lame knee."

Nine months later, Louie received orders to report to Neillsville on March 1, 1918, for a physical. Instead of reporting, he headed west to the farm fields of the Dakotas and Montana. Leslie received orders to report for a physical on June 5. He did so, but he took the unusual step of bringing along his mother, who proceeded to berate the draft board and medical examiner. She made it clear that her son would not fight. The doctor found Leslie fit and ordered him to report for induction on June 24. Leslie did not show up for induction and became the second Krueger wanted by the law. Authorities were unable to find either brother. On August 31 Congress expanded the age range of men eligible for the draft. Men who were as young as eighteen and as old as forty-five were ordered to register on September 12. Neither Ennis nor Frank registered. Now all four brothers were wanted men.

When the station master at Withee intercepted a crate of ammunition addressed to Ennis, law enforcement officials became concerned the brothers were planning for a fight. On the afternoon of September 14, a group of men arrived at the Krueger farm with the intent of arresting the Krueger brothers. The group included Joe Gantz, of the US Marshals Service, a Bureau of Investigation agent, the Owen village marshal, and a local businessman acting as driver. Gantz, who had no field experience, was nominally in control.

The encounter went bad almost immediately, when Ennis fired on the lawmen. Gantz sent for help, and soon a posse of 150 armed men arrived from Withee and Owen. At this point Gantz lost whatever control he may have possessed. The posse was more mob than an organized agent of the law. The battle of the Krueger farm lasted into the evening hours. When it was over, hundreds of shots had been fired at the house and barn; the north wall of the house alone had 140 bullet holes. Harry Jensen, Withee station master, lay dying in the dust; Frank Krueger was wounded and in custody; three posse members were wounded; and Ennis and Leslie had escaped. Louie played no role in the shootout; he was still in the West. Home guards from Neillsville and Colby arrived to patrol the farm.

Gantz eventually found Ennis in a Minnesota barn and allegedly shot him when Ennis reached for a pistol and tried to evade arrest. That was the official story, but evidence suggests Ennis was unarmed and asleep when he was killed. Leslie was arrested in Minnesota for carrying a concealed weapon. Under questioning, he admitted to being Leslie Krueger. He and Frank received life sentences for murder. They were pardoned in 1934. The fourth brother, Louie, was recognized and arrested in Chippewa Falls in 1920 but was never tried for a crime. He had not participated in the shootout and was only guilty of failing to show up for his physical. The three brothers lived out their shattered lives in the isolation of the old family farm.[15]

GOVERNING IN WARTIME

The study of six high-profile Wisconsinites can give modern readers a deeper understanding of the full range of political responses to the war, the sacrifices people made to preserve American liberty, and the fragile nature of basic rights in wartime. Governor Emanuel Philipp successfully carried out his duties as a war governor while protecting civil liberties. Daniel Hoan, Milwaukee's socialist mayor, navigated the fine line between faithfully administering Wisconsin's largest city and the Socialist Party's opposition to the war. Victor Berger, founding member of the Socialist Party of America and a leader of its antiwar faction, paid a high price for his defense of free speech in wartime only to be vindicated in the years immediately following the war. The stubborn, bullheaded, indomitable Robert M. La Follette weathered intense criticism in Wisconsin and nationally while giving voice to his conviction that the government had chosen the wrong methods of raising and financing the army. Wheeler Bloodgood of Milwaukee was a businessman and founder of the Wisconsin Defense League; Roy Wilcox of Eau Claire was a prominent state senator. Bloodgood and Wilcox were pro-war super patriots who believed that Hoan, La Follette, and Berger were traitors and that Philipp was soft on loyalty and too considerate of his German constituents.

As elected officials responsible for governing effectively, Philipp and Hoan faced the immediate task of reuniting a divided city and state behind the war effort. They reflected the patriotism of the practical politician; they shared a commitment to govern effectively and to represent all of their constituents, regardless of their views on the war. The price of their patriotic moderation was the undying hostility of the super patriots.

Berger and La Follette represented what one might call the loyal opposition. Their patriotism was manifest in their willingness to advocate unpopular policies in the face of immense pressure to capitulate and support the war on the government's terms.

There was no shortage of patriotic behavior in Wisconsin, but for super patriots like Bloodgood and Wilcox, Wisconsin was a hotbed of pro-German sentiment and La Follette was a traitor. Super patriots did not sit comfortably at the table with democracy, the free flow of ideas, or debate about goals or methods. Their patriotic fervor led to a simplistic view in which the war was a struggle between good and evil, right and wrong, democracy and autocracy. Wilson had predicted just this type of behavior, for war itself does not sit well with democracy.

Governing in Wartime: Philipp and Bloodgood

Governor Philipp exemplified a tolerant interpretation of loyalty and patriotism, rooted in his understanding of the state's German and Scandinavian populations, as well as the many constituents who identified as progressives. In general, they had opposed entry into the war, as had Philipp, who understood that many residents could be ambivalent about the war and completely loyal to the United States at the same time.

Philipp was a stalwart Republican. He had little in common with the

A railroad executive and Wisconsin's wartime governor, Emanuel Philipp was more interested in governing effectively than in hyperbolic charges aimed at political opponents. He played a large role in creating smoothly running government systems to manage the state's war effort. A devoted advocate of the rule of law, he had no patience for inflammatory patriotic rhetoric or vigilante justice.
WHI IMAGE ID 62414

socialists or the progressive Republicans, except for a belief in fair, honest government and the rule of law. In most Wisconsin elections between the Civil War and 1930, the Republican Party was so dominant that the important election was not the general election but the primary. By the beginning of the twentieth century, the Republican Party had split into two factions: the progressive or liberal wing dominated by Bob La Follette, and the stalwart or conservative wing. Progressives occupied the governor's chair between 1901 and 1914 when Philipp regained control for the stalwarts.

Philipp maintained control of the governor's office throughout the war. He had little patience with the socialists or pacifist organizations, but he also could not abide the self-righteous super patriots—those self-appointed patriotic watchdogs who saw traitors or slackers in anyone who disagreed with war policy, criticized the flag, spoke fondly of anything German, or, frankly, disagreed with them on any issue. Philipp recognized these attitudes required only a slight twist to be converted into vigilante justice. By its very nature a society at war drifts toward authoritarian control, and Philipp knew super patriots exacerbated this trend. He believed deeply in the concept of being governor for all the people of Wisconsin and not just for chosen groups. Charges that cast aspersions on German Americans or any other group violated the comprehensive nature of governing. Besides, he knew the people of Wisconsin and knew any generalization about disloyalty was going to be false. As he was fond of telling audiences, "There is nothing wrong with Wisconsin." Philipp was a practical politician. He was not an ideologue.

A week after the declaration of war, the Wisconsin Legislature created the nation's first State Council of Defense and gave it immense authority to coordinate and control home-front life. Philipp's first major wartime action was to appoint the council's eleven members. In this effort he came into direct conflict with Wheeler Bloodgood and the Wisconsin Defense League.[16]

Bloodgood led a group of prominent Milwaukee men to form the Defense League shortly before American entry into the war. The league's goal was clear: promote their narrow concept of patriotism, and counteract pro-German and antiwar sentiment in Wisconsin. A patriotic rally of seven thousand people in the Milwaukee city auditorium on Saturday, March 17, 1917, became the catalyst for the league's creation. The *Milwaukee Journal* story about the rally reported triumphantly: "Milwaukee is loyal." The crowd was in no mood for "unpatriotic" behavior and cheered every statement of support for Wilson's foreign policy.

Wheeler Bloodgood was a supporter of Theodore Roosevelt and a founder of the Wisconsin Defense League. Bloodgood became a staunch advocate for intolerant "patriotism" and the curtailment of free speech and civil liberties in the name of the war effort. He worried Wisconsin was in jeopardy of betraying the nation and feared that pro-German immigrants, socialists, and progressives would undermine the state's war effort. He was convinced that Daniel Hoan, Victor Berger, and Bob La Follette were traitors and that Governor Philipp lacked the backbone to effectively deal with disloyal elements. WHI IMAGE ID 60818

The first speaker was A. M. Vogel, chairman of the Wisconsin branch of the National Security League. When a man in the audience interrupted Vogel and said, "Mr. Vogel, as a true American, I ask you, are you going to enlist?" the man was quickly removed by Secret Service agents while the crowd "hooted and hissed." Why there were government agents in the audience remains something of a mystery. Vogel told the audience he was too old to enlist but expected his sons to do so if the current crisis resulted in war. The crowd responded with raucous applause. Vogel called on everyone to "avoid all manner of speech and action which places in doubt our loyalty." In essence, he was asking the audience to practice personal preemptive censorship. Senator Paul Husting, a Democrat, followed Vogel on the stage. He told the audience it was time to unite behind the president. "This is no time, then, for differences of opinion, for dissention, for opposition, for obstruction. This is the time for unity in all things—in thought, word and deed. We are all Americans." Congressman Irvine Lenroot, a progressive Republican from Superior, followed a similar theme: "Wherever the interests of America are concerned, we must be one people, in thought and action. We must stand ready to support America against the world." Each speaker was calling for conformity, for an end to debate and discussion, for joining together in support of the president. This was a call for unity based on unwavering loyalty defined as adherence to a particular point of view. Individuals who questioned the loyalty of their neighbors, community, or state often did so based on whether the person under scrutiny adhered to the observer's definition of acceptable thought or action. This super patriotism could easily become the catalyst for witch hunts and superficial security. Seldom, if ever, did it identify a true traitor to the United States.

The loyalty rally's organizers met a week later to form a permanent organization, the Wisconsin Defense League. Bloodgood, a wealthy Milwaukee industrialist and adherent of Teddy Roosevelt's bellicose views on the war and patriotism, served as secretary to the organizing committee and then chairman of the league. They launched the organization with substantial financial resources and an aggressive program. A little more than a month after the declaration of war, the league had raised fifty thousand dollars; had organized chapters in sixty of the seventy-one counties, half of which had members working at the precinct level; and had supplied speakers and literature to encourage enlistment and farm production. It was an impressive start.

When, under Philipp's direction, the Wisconsin Legislature created the State Council of Defense, Bloodgood wanted to protect and strengthen the league's authority by linking the league's voluntary activities with the council's state-sanctioned authority and power. Here, Philipp drew a line. Philipp was highly suspicious of individuals and organizations that seemed focused on finding traitors in Wisconsin. He also had no intention of sharing the authority of the council or the power of the governor's office with anyone, let alone self-appointed super patriots from one corner of the state. In making the eleven appointments to the council, Philipp chose prominent figures from the university and business communities, as well as a socialist. None of his appointees were connected to the Wisconsin Defense League nor had "patriotic" credentials.[17]

The Defense League sought to find traitors in Wisconsin and encouraged the citizenry and "apathetic" local and state officials to do the same. League members saw signs of disloyalty everywhere: among socialists, anyone expressing pro-German sentiment, and followers of La Follette and Berger. Bloodgood complained about slow military recruiting and implied it was caused by the state's ambivalence toward the war effort. When journalist Ray Stannard Baker visited Wisconsin in June 1917, he found the state "really the most backward state I've struck in its sentiment toward the war."[18]

These concerns were oddly out of sync with reality. Steady recruitment quickly brought National Guard units up to war strength. As Congress declared war, the call went out for ten thousand recruits for the National Guard and seven thousand for the regular army and navy. By the middle of May, seventy-five recruiting stations had opened across the state. The recruiting effort went better than anyone expected. The First, Second, and Third Regiments reached war strength quickly, and the state organized three new regiments. On August 1, Adjutant General Orlando Holway announced that the Wisconsin National Guard had reached war strength with 15,266 men on the roster. The mobilization of troops across the country stretched federal logistics to their limit, and Philipp allocated $780,000 to equip the National Guard.

When the United States declared war, volunteers made up the ranks of the regular army and National Guard. As the president contemplated how best to grow the armed forces from roughly two hundred thousand men to over 4 million, he rejected a volunteer system in favor of a system based on the draft. Major political figures voiced their opposition to conscription or their support for a volunteer system. Teddy Roosevelt wanted to form and lead his own volunteer division and head straight to the front, something Wilson's military advisors adamantly rejected for fear it would pull good men from units where they were needed and for fear the aggressive, compulsive Roosevelt would be difficult to control. La Follette railed at conscription as unconstitutional, autocratic, and destructive of democracy. More judiciously, Philipp advised Wilson: "The volunteer system will leave a good feeling at home, while conscription at this time would, in my judgment, have a tendency to make the war unpopular." Ultimately Wilson accepted conscription as the best way to raise the large number of troops needed and prevent throwing the economy into disarray as men left the civilian workforce.[19]

Madison draftees at the Northwestern Depot preparing to leave for training in 1918. Some ninety thousand young men from Wisconsin entered military service as draftees during World War I. WHI IMAGE ID 11039

Unlike the Civil War, during which the Union army administered the draft, local civilian draft boards now had the responsibility for screening young men selected by the lottery and determining their best role in the war effort—whether to keep him home in a critical occupation or send him to the military. Before the draft could occur, every eligible male needed to register with the Selective Service. June 5, 1917, was designated registration day.

Wisconsin's large German population, its influential Socialist Party, and the opposition to conscription by Philipp and La Follette gave federal officials cause for concern that registration day in Wisconsin would fail because of unrest. In addition, Democratic Senator Paul Husting suggested Philipp was pro-German and would be ineffective in dealing with protests. To help, General Enoch Crowder, provost marshal of the army and administrator of the Selective Service, offered Philipp the use of federal troops to maintain order on June 5. Philipp replied with a polite "no, thank you"; he had full faith in the people of Wisconsin. Without fuss or fanfare, 218,700 men registered for the draft—106 percent of the number estimated as eligible.[20]

Governing in Wartime: Philipp Defends Wisconsin's Loyalty

At times it seemed like open season on Wisconsin. Despite a sterling home-front record during the war, outsiders and visiting pundits repeatedly called Wisconsin's patriotism into question. All too often, instead of critiquing reality, critics saw what they wanted to see. Wisconsin, the "traitor state," was a mirage of their own making.

On March 21, 1918, for example, the *New York Sun* published the Wisconsin "Sedition Map" prepared by the Loyalty Legion. The legion focused on finding disloyal individuals in Wisconsin. Their primary tools were the loyalty petition to Congress and loyalty pledges. In both cases, individuals were asked to pledge their loyalty to the government and support of the war effort. Those who refused to sign or pledge were, by implication, suspect. By the end of the war, the legion was sharing its information with the Justice Department's Bureau of Investigation. Based on voting patterns from the US Senate primary election on March 19, 1918, the legion identified areas in which James Thompson, the "La Follette" candidate, and

Victor Berger, the Socialist candidate, had polled well. By implication, the legion identified those areas as pro-German and seditious.[21]

Philipp, Hoan, Berger, and La Follette all felt the blows of unreasoned super patriotism. Even the University of Wisconsin—which had fired "unpatriotic" faculty, censured La Follette, sent approximately two hundred faculty and 2,150 students to war, and created an officer training

The Wisconsin Loyalty League's "Sedition Map" purported to show disloyal regions of the state based on "pro-German" voting patterns during the 1918 spring primary election for US senator. As far as the League was concerned, a vote for Berger (the Socialist candidate) or Thompson (the La Follette progressive candidate) was a vote for Germany. WHI IMAGE ID 40882

program—became the target of critics whose sense of reason had been replaced by preconceived expectations.

Carl Schurz Vrooman, assistant secretary of agriculture, came to Madison in November 1917 as the keynote speaker for the Wisconsin Potato Growers' Association's annual convention. The university was planning a loyalty rally for the afternoon and invited Vrooman to address

University of Wisconsin students created this massive service flag to honor their classmates who had gone to war. The flag included 1,750 blue stenciled stars, each embroidered with the name of a student. The flag first went on display in Bascom Hall on Decoration Day, May 27, 1918, but was soon moved to the grander and more public space of the University Reading Room in the recently completed Wisconsin Historical Society building on the eastern edge of campus. The flag served as a visible reminder of the university's support for the war effort and a rebuke to those who criticized the university's commitment to the American cause. WHI IMAGE ID 72204

the assembled students. After reviewing the officer cadets on the parade ground in front of the Wisconsin Historical Society, Vrooman walked across the street to the red brick armory with its two imposing turrets meant to remind the viewer of a fortified facility. He found his student audience unresponsive and was surprised that campus administrators had waited until late November to hold a rally. That evening his talk to the Potato Growers' Association made headlines not because of some great agricultural wisdom, but because he questioned the patriotic fervor of campus leaders. As he told the potato farmers, "A patriotism that is not militant is contemptible." Richard Lloyd Jones, editor of the *Wisconsin State Journal*, wrote to Vrooman with undisguised glee: "You stirred up the lions here and you did a good piece of work. The University is now busy defending itself."

Students and administrators were not so pleased. The student newspaper, *The Daily Cardinal*, delivered a rebuke to Vrooman. They chided him for judging them in fifteen minutes and for not staying for the whole rally. They compared the "studious, constructive, positive, determined view of patriotism which the students take" to his preference for a patriotism displayed in raucous fashion. Instead of "brass bands and bonfires," the students chided the secretary, "we oversubscribe the war fund, we subscribe $119,000 to the liberty loan, we send hundreds of men to the service, we do all in our power to aid these men. This may not be patriotism according to Mr. Vrooman's definition. It is the kind which we prefer. It is the kind which produces results!"[22]

One of the most publicized attacks on Wisconsin loyalty occurred during a massive rally in Madison on April 6, 1918, to commemorate the first anniversary of the declaration of war. It was an overcast and dreary day. At two o'clock in the afternoon, church bells heralded the start of the parade. The beginning of a long, cold rain failed to dampen spirits. Cheering spectators lined the route as marchers wound their way almost two miles from the Capitol Square to the Stock Pavilion on the western edge of the University of Wisconsin campus. Everyone was in a festive mood. The *Wisconsin State Journal* reported:

It was an inspiring sight. Ten thousand men, women, and children following the colors. It was a sight that translated for the boys in the trenches "over there" gave this message:

WE ARE WITH YOU! . . .
Everywhere along the line of march old glory flapped in pride—
from the tops of lofty flag-poles, from windows—everywhere—the
stars and stripes—the emblem of freedom—played approvingly in
the wind.

Once marchers arrived at the Stock Pavilion, a variety of public officials
and dignitaries spoke to the crowd about patriotism and support for the
troops in France. The rally lasted three hours. The audience welcomed
Senator-elect Irvine Lenroot with an enthusiastic standing ovation. Lenroot had just won his Senate seat as the loyalty candidate. He told the crowd
that nothing short of civilization was at stake in this war.

When Robert McNutt McElroy, Princeton professor of history and
economics and education director for the National Security League, came
to the podium, he complimented Wisconsin for electing Lenroot to the US
Senate and then delivered a lengthy speech declaring, "We are fighting
today for the same principles our fathers fought for, translated into higher
terms. The doctrine of the rights of man can become the rights of nations."

McElroy's opening remarks were cordial, but he droned on for another hour and a half, in a voice so low it was largely unheard by the audience in an era before loud speakers. Seated prominently at the front of the
Stock Pavilion was a group of military cadets from the university who had
marched in the rain without coats. Still wet, they had dutifully taken their
seats in the drafty, cold building. As McElroy's speech showed no sign of
ending, many in the audience began to leave and the cadets grew restless.
Finally, according to his own account, which appeared on April 17 in the
New York Tribune, McElroy lost his temper.

To the consternation of many back in Wisconsin, the rally McElroy
described bore little resemblance to the event Madisonians remembered.
According to McElroy:

For the most part, once they [student cadets] had learned that American patriotism was my theme, they sat with folded arms, staring
wearily at the ceiling. From time to time they'd turn and look at each
other and smile superciliously, sort of pityingly. There was a good
deal of fidgeting and shuffling of feet. Several times, generally at the

most strongly patriotic portions of my talk, sounds which bore every sign of being subdued hisses could be heard. Later it was offered to me in explanation there were warnings to the noisy ones to be quiet; but they didn't sound that way to me.

When I began to quote from some of President Wilson's messages . . . the rattle of snapping rifle triggers throughout the audience—the men, being under compulsory military training, have guns—sounded very much like an attempt to break up the speech.

Finally, I couldn't stand it any longer. I determined to find out whether it was my fault or whether it was the American point of view that these young men objected to. So I leaned forward and I deliberately insulted them.

"Do you know what I think of you for your conduct tonight . . . I think you're a bunch of damned traitors!"

To McElroy's surprise, the students did not react. He was "thunderstruck." He called them a "Prussian audience" and got no response. He concluded with a tirade:

I hesitate . . . to accuse an entire University of disloyalty and many people have since tried to reassure me as to Wisconsin. They insist that it's absolutely all right, and I certainly hope that it is. But to my mind that episode stands out as one of the most disgraceful things I have encountered, especially coming from a state in which 100,000 disloyal votes were recently registered. I say that a thing like that should be investigated.

Here was super patriotism in destructive form. McElroy felt perfectly comfortable branding the entire audience as disloyal based on his perceptions of their failure to receive his remarks with proper attention and decorum. In fact what he remembered as a ringing insult directed at the cadets was delivered almost under his breath. Faculty near the podium reported that his declaration of traitors in the audience was barely audible beyond a few feet. McElroy's willingness to impugn the loyalty of the entire university illustrated a trait endemic to the world war home front: a willingness to interpret normal behavior by friends and neighbors—a joke, a comment critical of the war effort, the failure to buy "enough" Liberty Bonds—as a sign of disloyalty. Ultimately, the misplaced patriotism of McElroy and many others diverted attention away from productive support of the war and dissipated home-front energy against the ramparts of imaginary enemies.

McElroy's criticism sparked a heated exchange with university officials that left little resolved. The charge of traitorous behavior remained in the public media even as the university mounted a campaign to defend its reputation.[23]

Likewise, Philipp routinely found it necessary to defend the people of his state. Many of his domestic speeches included a lengthy recitation of Wisconsin's war record. In a speech delivered late in the fall of 1917, Philipp made clear the obligation of every citizen and his faith in the people of Wisconsin. First, he addressed a rhetorical question raised by super patriots and newspaper editors: What is wrong with Wisconsin?

"Of course there is nothing wrong with either the people or the state government. I charge that all the criticism that has been made of Wisconsin and its people, its state government affecting the loyalty and good citizenship of the people of the state has been inspired by politicians for selfish political purposes." Later, he appealed "to you citizens to give the state and the government your fullest cooperation. Whatever your thought may have been before war was declared by this country you have only one duty now and that is to your own country."[24]

In a May 12, 1918, article for the *Chicago Herald and Examiner*, Philipp denounced the havoc caused by rumors of sedition and disloyalty. He recounted having to calm three normally rational residents of Milwaukee who came to his office with a series of alarming rumors. First, they "insisted I send a military force to the City of Milwaukee immediately to watch the Germans." They explained "that there were 10,000 German reservists in the City of Milwaukee, armed and ready to destroy the city in the interest of Germany." They could offer no proof or information on how to find these German reservists. As Philipp reasoned his way through the first problem, his informants expressed concern that enemy soldiers were being trained in a tannery at night. This rumor developed because a light was on at night in a Milwaukee tannery, and cars were seen coming and going. In yet another rumor, a Milwaukee gun dealer had allegedly sold ten thousand rifles to an organization for use against the United States. The gun shop in question had sold fewer than one hundred guns of all types during the previous year. Finally, again without proof, they expressed concern that 250 Milwaukeeans were pledged to reap a harvest of death and destruction until they themselves were killed.

These and many other stories of disloyalty came to Philipp from around the state, all false and unsubstantiated. The governor expressed confidence that the state's war record ultimately would put to rest stories of disloyalty; he closed his article philosophically: "To undertake to fight all the falsehoods that have been circulated concerning the state is not unlike fighting the wind."[25]

Governing in Wartime: Philipp and Wilcox

Because of Philipp's rational approach to rumors and his insistence on maintaining the rule of law, the governor was unable to avoid criticism that he coddled pro-Germans. Samuel Hopkins Adams, a journalist working with the Committee on Public Information, accused Philipp of being a pacifist with an unusual "tenderness" toward the feelings of German constituents, who had supported the war only under duress. Even Philipp's friend John M. Whitehead criticized the governor as a "weak sister" in the loyalty work. This colloquial insult provided an easy way of saying, without specifics, that Philipp was soft on Germans, not vigorously hunting traitors, and unconcerned for the security of the nation. All such charges were absurd, but when repeated often enough and loudly enough, they acquired the aura of reality.[26]

Philipp found attacks from Roy Wilcox of Eau Claire particularly galling. Wilcox was a rapidly rising state senator with ambitions to be governor. An attorney, Wilcox was well regarded in Wisconsin legal circles. In his first bid for elected office, he ran for the state Senate as a Republican in 1916 and won by a landslide with more than twice the votes of his opponent. As a state senator, he was something of a political hybrid, neither stalwart nor progressive, but with tendencies toward both. Almost immediately Wilcox became a leading voice in the legislature as a critic of La Follette; an advocate of patriotism, loyalty, and vigorous prosecution of the war; and an opponent of the governor's legislative agenda.

When an Assembly resolution expressing the state's loyalty and commitment to the war effort came before the Senate, Wilcox offered an amendment that converted the resolution into a direct attack on La Follette for opposing entry into the war, advocating a volunteer army and financing the war through taxes on the war merchants. In a fifteen-page speech, Wilcox defended the righteousness of the cause and chastised La Follette for sowing the seeds of sedition. His simplistic recitation of La Follette's views and actions was designed to convince his colleagues of La Follette's wayward course without representing any of the nuances of the senator's views. Wilcox concluded that La Follette

> has been at the forefront all over this land as the one man who was obstructing the nation. . . . Our president is saying today, "he that is not with me is against me;" . . . . He has referred to our senator as the leader of a little group of willful men, obstructing our government. We must choose, senators, "Are you for La Follette, or are you for our commander-in-chief, Woodrow Wilson, the president of the United States?"[27]

On the evening of February 25, 1918, the Wisconsin State Senate voted 22 to 7 to censure La Follette. Through a series of parliamentary maneuvers, progressives in the state Assembly delayed a vote on the resolution until March 6, when it finally passed on a vote of 53 to 32.[28]

Wilcox had been developing the themes evident in his Senate speech since the beginning of the war. On July 4, 1917, he told an audience at Half Moon Lake Island, a city park in Eau Claire, that the United States has, "since her inception, been foremost in every battle for liberty and every real struggle for the preservation of individual rights as against autocracy and the exaltation of the few." He portrayed the United States' past wars as a series of conflicts in a process of ever-expanding freedom. "Today, my friends, in this great world crisis, when a carefully and scientifically organized war machine has been let loose upon the free peoples of the world, the United States of America is once more called upon to preserve democracy; to see to it that liberty's torch be not extinguished and submerged in the roaring flood of militarism which threatens to engulf the world."

Wilcox was careful in most speeches to emphasize that the nation was not at war with the "imaginative, kindly, sympathetic people" of Germany. Rather, the United States was at war with the Prussianism, and freeing the German people from their Prussian masters was "one of the great purposes of this war."

While portraying Wisconsin's German community as completely loyal, he took to task politicians who hid behind the wishes of their constituency as an excuse for not supporting the war. This jab was almost certainly directed at La Follette and probably Philipp as well. It was time to stop criticizing the president and his policies and go forth united.[29]

From the very beginning Philipp and Wilcox seemed to have a visceral dislike for each other, which did not improve as Wilcox became a major critic of the state administration. In 1918 these two politicians clashed explosively over Philipp's plan to cover the debt incurred when he spent roughly $780,000 in 1917 to properly outfit the Wisconsin National Guard as it mustered into federal service. Philipp had asked the legislature for a bill authorizing a $1 million bond issue with a fourteen-year maturity to cover the expense and to fill a deficit in the state budget if necessary. Although he had asked for the bonding authority, Philipp was confident the federal government would reimburse the state before he would need to resort to the bonds. The governor's bill was unpopular in the legislature, and Wilcox offered an alternate bill authorizing bonds that would mature in one year, pay 5 percent interest, and be paid off with a surtax on incomes over fifteen thousand dollars. Wilcox dubbed his bill as an "excess profits tax" even though it made no attempt to apply it to excess profits. The measure passed readily and Philipp vetoed it as unconstitutional. Because he could find no relationship between high incomes and war profiteering, Philipp viewed the "excess profits tax" as a soak-the-rich scheme dressed up to look like a war measure. Wilcox could not overcome the veto and the legislature passed Philipp's original bill. During this struggle the senator began referring to his nemesis almost derisively as "the war governor."[30]

Wilcox planned to run for governor in 1918. Although Philipp would have preferred to retire from politics, he could not countenance a Wilcox victory and threw his hat in the ring for a third term. On June 27, Philipp delivered a well-crafted campaign speech defending his record. He distinguished himself from Wilcox by emphasizing his experience, his defense of judicial process, and his opposition to those who would judge the patriotism of others. He then threw down a challenge to the Eau Claire senator: "If my opponent, Mr. Wilcox, wishes to stand before the people as the Tar and Feather Candidate, he may do so. I shall stand for law and order."[31]

Not surprisingly, Wilcox opened his bid for governor with a full-throated attack on Philipp's record and fitness to be "war governor." On July 12, 1918, in Menomonie, Wisconsin, just up the road from his home town of Eau Claire, Wilcox quickly went on the offensive. To win "the greatest war the world has ever known," he told the audience, "we must prepare ourselves here at home to stand loyally by the administration of the United States of America. . . . What can we do to help win the war? Loyalty is the paramount issue." He called for party unity and an end to factionalism, and ridiculed the claim that Philipp "has been such a great war governor." With complete disregard for the context of 1915, Wilcox attacked the governor's prewar neutrality, and his support for an embargo of goods going to the belligerents. An effective embargo, Wilcox told his attentive crowd, would have starved the Allies of food and ammunition; it would have produced a rapid "victory for Prussian arms." He continued: "It would have meant that the flaming torch of liberty would have been forever extinguished in the world and that the United States of America would have come next. . . . That is what an embargo meant; that is precisely why it was advocated by all of the Germanistic agencies and influences within this country and abroad. They were for an embargo."

Lest anyone in the audience miss his meaning, Wilcox made clear "that this man who now claims to be a war governor tried to make an embargo on bread, ammunition and guns for the Allies." In short, the governor was either a dupe or an agent of the enemy. Wilcox went on to ridicule Philipp's support for a volunteer army as well as his request that the Wisconsin National Guard be allowed to conduct their initial training in the north instead of being sent south in the heat of summer. He vigorously rejected the moniker of "tar and feather" candidate, but never disavowed vigilante justice.[32]

Wilcox's speech in Menomonie set the tone for the primary campaign. As summer passed into fall, it became obvious Wilcox was attracting support not only from super patriots but from a significant number of progressives as well. Leaders of the "La Follette progressives" began to worry that Wilcox might have generated enough support to win the Republican primary and threw their support to James N. Tittemore, president of the American Society of Equity, in the hope that if he lost, he would at least draw enough progressives away from Wilcox to secure the election for Philipp. The gambit worked. Philipp defeated Wilcox in the Republican primary by 440 votes.[33]

Philipp had little tolerance for Wilcox's form of patriotism especially when it led to vigilante justice. More than anything else, he believed it was his duty to govern responsibly. Time after time he demonstrated his willingness to chastise super patriots for behavior that derailed rather than facilitated governing the state in wartime. He believed in the loyalty and patriotism of the entire state regardless of ethnicity and believed, as governor, he should represent all the people.

In his most strident denunciation of super patriots, Governor Philipp told an audience that the willingness to charge others with disloyalty "is a type of impudence that is indulged in by a class of self-asserted patriots who are the greatest menace to the country today, because they discourage what the country needs above all things during a crisis, and that is the hearty cooperation of all the people in support of the war."[34]

During his 1918 campaign for reelection, he explained his inclusive interpretation of the governor's responsibilities:

> I feel that I am bound by my oath of office to protect the people of this state in the exercise of their constitutional rights of freedom of speech, and I propose to protect that right as long as their speech has the right American ring.
>
> I am equally bound by my oath of office to protect the people of this state in the exercise of their constitutional right of freedom of religion, and I shall not interfere with their worship unless their church is used as a propaganda [sic] for our enemy.
>
> I have proceeded upon the theory that patriotism is an individual responsibility, and I have declined to condemn people on racial lines. I maintain that one patriot is as good as another, I care not where he comes from. He who promotes the spirit of cooperation to the end that every citizen do his part to aid the government in the prosecution of the war is rendering a real service to his country at this time.

> Our government is a government of parties, and I maintain that
> the minority party of this country is rendering a service to the people
> by holding the majority to strict account for its actions. [35]

Philipp's belief in civil order and the rule of law gave him a foundation on which to base governing the state in wartime with justice and humanity. A case of vigilante justice in Ashland tested his patience.

The Loyal Knights of Liberty in Ashland became the most notorious vigilante group in the state. They struck at least four times to chasten those they deemed disloyal. Late at night on Sunday, March 31, 1918, nearly a dozen masked men barged into E. A. Schimler's boarding room and swiftly abducted the Northland College professor of modern languages. They drove into the countryside about a half mile outside of Ashland. After stripping Schimler of his clothing, the Knights applied "a substantial coat of tar and feathers," their weapon of choice. Schimler was left to recover his undergarments and walk back to his boarding house. He resigned his position at the college, prompting the rumor that he had been fired for disloyalty. In a statement to the press, Schimler protested that he had, in fact, resigned and that Northland College accepted his resignation only upon his insistence. Not surprisingly, Schimler then left town. An investigation uncovered no evidence of disloyalty, and concluded "that Professor Schimler had not made seditious remarks or taught disloyalty either in the class room or on the college premises."

Using the *Ashland Daily Press* as its mouthpiece, the Knights of Liberty published a lengthy explanation of the indiscretions that led to Schimler's abduction and punishment. According to John J. Haupert of Ashland, Schimler had defended Germany's use of submarine warfare on the grounds that the British blockade was starving the German people. Reputedly, Schimler also told Haupert that corruption in the government would prevent the United States from accomplishing anything meaningful in the war. Although this information had been presented to the Ashland District Attorney, no action had been taken. The Knights' letter concluded: "We have no purpose to do any injustice to any man, but we do feel that any treasonable and seditious acts, or utterances, demand prompt punishment. These cases must not be allowed to run on indefinitely, without anything being done. We want action on them and want it now."

The Loyal Knights of Liberty struck again a few days after their attack on Schimler. At about 9 p.m., five or six men knocked on the door of Adolph Anton. Mrs. Anton, with her babe in arms, greeted the men, who told her they worked at the dynamite plant and were looking for rooms to rent. When she refused to let them into the house, the men forced their way in, demanding to know where Mr. Anton was. Depending on the account one reads, they found him hiding in a closet or the bathroom. The Knights took him away, but not before disarming Mrs. Anton, who had grabbed a rifle in defense of her husband. Once again the victim was taken to a secluded spot, stripped, and reclothed with a liberal coat of tar and feathers. One of the Knights had the audacity or absence of mind to leave his face uncovered. The Antons recognized the man as Ephraim Gay, a house mover. They also recognized the voice of one of the masked men as that of George Buchanan, an agent for the New York Life Insurance Company. In short order both men were arrested on the charge of abducting and assaulting Adolph Anton.

The arrests did not deter the vigilantes. On the evening of May 8, William Landraint was kidnapped on his way to supper, driven from town, and treated to a coat of tar and feathers for alleged disloyalty. Landraint had worked as an income tax assessor, but he lost that position after his loyalty was questioned in a complaint by Ashland residents. He was abducted in broad daylight and given a coat of tar and feathers. Landraint was unable to identify his assailants, but the district attorney planned to interview six witnesses in hope of identifying the culprits. A month later Landraint sought police protection after receiving a threatening letter from the Knights of Liberty. In early June, another Ashland resident, Emil Kunze, showed up at the police station about midnight and asked if he could sleep in the jail. After overhearing men talk about whether to tar and feather him for being pro-German, Kunze quit his job and determined to leave town. Landraint soon left Ashland as well.

At 9 a.m. on July 2 a car drove up to the farmhouse of Martin Johnson near the town of Sweden, a few miles northeast of Drummond in Bayfield County. The visitors asked if Johnson would show them the way to a nearby fishing stream. Johnson agreed. Once they were away from the house, the men seized Johnson, took him to a secluded spot, and dressed him in a fresh coat of tar and feathers. The vigilantes had struck again.

During all of this time, Philipp had not been idle. At the end of April he sent Assistant Attorney General Winfield Gilman and detectives to Ashland to investigate the earlier tar and featherings. The Justice Department officials found it difficult to make any progress. The citizens of Ashland generally denied any knowledge of the Knights of Liberty despite the fact that the group had sent threatening letters to a number of residents. The letters began: "This is to notify you that the Knights of Liberty is organized in Ashland for the protection of American principles and to stop seditious remarks and pro-Germanism." The letter told recipients, "Your Americanism is questioned" and instructed them to fly the flag, Hooverize, buy bonds, and act like true, loyal Americans.[36]

In late July, in spite of the clear testimony from Mr. and Mrs. Anton, the municipal judge dismissed the charges against Gay and Buchanan, who had threatened the judge with tar and feathers if they were not released. After the attack on Johnson, Philipp told the Bayfield County sheriff to supply the governor's office with regular progress reports on his investigation. Philipp believed mob rule had taken hold in Chequamegon Bay region, and he blamed local law enforcement for failing to maintain law and order. He made no judgments as to the loyalty of the victims, but he reminded the mayor, "If any or all of them have been guilty of disloyal utterances they should be punished in accordance with their crime, but it should be done by the orderly process of the court, which is established by the people for that purpose, and not by a mob or by any secret organization that sets itself up as a judge of the people's conduct."[37]

Without cooperation from the people or the police, the state investigation made little progress. It was perhaps out of a profound sense of frustration that Philipp referred to Wilcox as the "tar and feather" candidate during the gubernatorial campaign of 1918. The governor held the *Ashland Press* partly responsible for the ongoing violence in Ashland. Throughout the spring and summer the *Press* provided a mouthpiece for the Knights of Liberty without comment or condemnation and was openly hostile to the governor's investigation. The owner of the *Ashland Press* was John C. Chapple, a member of the state Assembly and Wilcox's campaign manager. Neither the editor nor the candidate took a stand against the Ashland vigilantes.[38]

Philipp sought the high ground in debates about patriotism, voting,

and representative government, with one glaring exception—he questioned whether African Americans could be trusted to understand issues
of the day and vote intelligently. To deal with this "problem" he proposed
a literacy test to determine if African Americans were qualified to vote. On
several occasions he voiced the belief that Emancipation had failed and the
Fifteenth Amendment should be repealed. As a consequence, the African
American paper the *Wisconsin Weekly Blade* strongly favored Wilcox in the
fall Republican primary of 1918. The editors of the paper believed Wilcox to
be a fair and just man, and agreed with his patriotic stance on war issues.[39]

Governing in Wartime: Daniel Hoan and the Loyal Opposition

The Great War tested Daniel Hoan unlike any other mayor of a major
American city. Throughout the war Hoan remained a dedicated member of the Socialist Party, a party that clearly repudiated US involvement.
Nonetheless, his obligations as mayor of Milwaukee put him on a collision
course with his socialist comrades. Hoan was never an ideologue—he, like
Philipp, was a practical politician with a firm grasp on reality. While practical politics and a belief in the tenets of socialism informed and shaped
how Hoan carried out his municipal duties, his primary concern was administering the city. Hoan clearly recognized his obligations as mayor.
Although he was a socialist, his city council members were not. With an
element of practical opportunism foreign to many socialists, Hoan sought
policies, programs, and solutions to municipal problems the council's
nonpartisan majority would support.[40]

When Hoan took the oath of office as mayor of Milwaukee on April 18,
1916, Europe had been embroiled in war for almost two years. At first, the
war was peripheral to managing the city. Hoan functioned as any other
mayor: settling citizen complaints; worrying about sewers and street pav-
ing. When the war did affect his job, he found himself caught between the
demands of the Socialist Party and the demands of the mayor's office. By
the spring of 1916, the preparedness movement was under way, awakening
in the American people a recognition that the nation was unprepared for
war and terribly vulnerable. Preparedness parades in other large cities,
including nearby Chicago, promoted patriotism and support for mili-

Daniel Hoan served Milwaukee as city attorney from 1911 to 1916 and as mayor from 1916 to 1940. Although a socialist and an opponent of the war, Hoan was no ideologue. He was a practical politician who set his sights on ensuring Milwaukee met all of its obligations during the war. Milwaukee became one of the best-governed cities in the country during Hoan's tenure. WHI IMAGE ID 97271

tary preparations. When the Milwaukee Rotary Club planned a massive parade for July 1916, Hoan could hardly ignore it. He was in a quandary. As an article of faith, the Socialist Party and the trade unions opposed preparedness and rearmament as tools for expanding the capitalist empire and controlling the working class. Hoan's socialist comrades pressured him to reject militarism in any form, while preparedness advocates, knowing it would put the mayor in an untenable position, pressured him to give the movement his full support. If Hoan supported preparedness he risked losing trade union and socialist backing; failure to support the parade would brand Hoan as disloyal, and he would lose independent middle-class support.

Hoan accepted the pragmatic solution offered by Milton C. Potter, the chairman of the parade organizing committee and Milwaukee school superintendent. Potter suggested calling the parade "a national demonstration of single-minded American national consciousness," omitting any overt reference to "preparedness," and insisted that Hoan's participation would not commit him to any one plan or program. This superficial change would do little to hide the military preparedness focus of the demonstration, but it would give Hoan enough cover to participate. The mayor proclaimed July 15 "Patriots Day."

The *Milwaukee Journal* never referred to the march as anything other than a preparedness demonstration; but Victor Berger's socialist newspaper, the *Milwaukee Leader*, tried to live up to the fiction, if rather clumsily, in its coverage of the event. Hoan carried out his duty as mayor; although socialists elsewhere criticized his participation, local trade unionists and socialist comrades supported his pragmatic compromise.[41] However, in what was almost certainly a conscious snub, the *Milwaukee Journal* gave prominent space to Governor Philipp's participation but made no mention of Hoan's participation in its coverage of the parade. It was as if the mayor of Wisconsin's largest city had taken the day off.[42]

The American Socialist Party opposed any involvement in a capitalist war. Hoan took a more moderate position when he wrote to the Woman's Club of Wisconsin, "While I personnally [sic] believe every living soul would regret to see our country involved in a war, still if war would come, then the loyal support and assistance of every citizen will be absolutely necessary."[43]

When the United States declared war, Hoan remained consistent in his views. The Socialist Party convened an emergency meeting in St. Louis on April 7 to consider its response to the declaration. In 1914, the European socialist parties all had sided pragmatically with their governments, much to the consternation of their American comrades. The St. Louis convention remained faithful to core principles and opposed any participation in this capitalist war. Hoan was in the minority when he rejected the party's antiwar position in favor of a less confrontational approach that accepted the fact of war but positioned the party as a defender of civil liberties and opponent of conscription. Many of his comrades left the party. Although most of the disaffected socialists quietly shifted their party allegiance, some became prominent defenders of patriotic causes and hostile critics of Hoan and Berger. Hoan maintained his commitment to the socialists. Later, he explained he always stood for peace and urged "immediate negotiations looking for a just and general peace." He never approved of the war, but found the party's official position untenable. He concluded "as mayor, that there was not only no way of complying, but that it was impossible to obey some of its requirements and demands." In this act and others he took as mayor, Hoan clearly was more concerned with governing than with ideology.[44]

Shortly after the declaration of war, in a rare moment of conciliation, Bloodgood, from the Wisconsin Defense League, invited Hoan to comment on how best to organize war work in Milwaukee. Jointly they requested authority from the State Council of Defense to form the Milwaukee County Council of Defense. The socialist Hoan and the capitalist super patriot Bloodgood became co-chairs of the council; Hoan managed the council's Bureau of Food Control in keeping with his interest in programs that helped the average resident of Milwaukee. Under Hoan's leadership the bureau established public markets, fought speculation, tried to hold down prices, and facilitated the logistical system essential to ensuring the flow of food supplies to the city.[45]

During the summer of 1917, the mayor faced a problem that cut to the heart of his socialist conscience. The Selective Service Act of 1917 placed administrative responsibility in the hands of mayors in cities with populations greater than thirty thousand. Hoan was faced with administering a system he considered undeniably wrong. After conferring with Berger and gaining Berger's approval, Hoan accepted his federal responsibilities. Milwaukee became the first major city to complete draft registration.[46]

Unlike socialists who bolted the party to support the war, Hoan maintained his steadfast opposition to the war while living up to his obligations as mayor. He maintained his standing within the party by defending civil rights, by administering the city well, and by turning down or ignoring requests by prowar groups to speak or sponsor activities.[47]

Bloodgood's conciliatory attitude did not last. As chairman of the Milwaukee County Council of Defense, Bloodgood apparently concluded that Hoan was a traitor. When Hoan won the 1918 spring mayoral primary by a large margin and his reelection in the fall seemed assured, Bloodgood began making threats that were not only ridiculous but also treasonous in their own right:

I assured Mayor Hoan in the presence of many witnesses that I would have him indicted and I assured him that he would never again be mayor of Milwaukee. I am seeking his indictment on the grounds of the Socialist platform itself to which Hoan subscribed. It declares that the people did not want the war; that they do not want the war, and that it was forced on them by the ruling classes. The ruling classes can mean only one thing in America, the president and congress. That is sedition.

Bloodgood not only wanted to see the mayor arrested; he had concluded that "if the people of this county are ready, as the primary votes would indicate, to stand with the socialists and abandoned the honor of the nation and stab in the back the boys in France, then we should be treated as an enemy stronghold." Bloodgood went on to make an audacious threat: under no circumstance would Hoan take office if reelected. "The time for action has come. If the peace machinery of government is inadequate to deal with a situation like that in Milwaukee and in some other sections, there are enough of us to reinforce that machinery to wartime machinery." For all practical purposes, Bloodgood was threatening to overthrow a duly constituted government and establish martial law through vigilante action if the civil authorities would not act.

In response to Bloodgood's threats, Philipp replied, "Whoever is elected mayor of Milwaukee will be inaugurated." The governor also declared, "Peace will rule in Wisconsin. No Ku Klux Klan will rule in Wisconsin, at least not very long."[48]

In 1918 the socialists won clear pluralities in Milwaukee County, electing Hoan, two out of three state senators, and eleven out of nineteen assemblymen. For the first time, socialists were also elected from out-state Wisconsin: five to the Assembly and one to the state Senate. After the election, Percy Braman, Hoan's opponent, blamed his defeat on pro-Germans protesting the war. Hoan attributed his success to his record as mayor and considered it a rebuke to those who cried "loyalty." The *Milwaukee Sentinel* ascribed Hoan's victory to his popularity, mayoral record, and antiwar platform. Finally, the *Milwaukee Free Press* believed the socialist success was a reaction to general persecution and suppression. All four explanations of Hoan's victory had one element in common: they all attributed some part of his success to disaffected German American voters. Votes for socialist candidates in general probably reflected latent opposition to the war or a protest vote against repression and discrimination. As it turned out, the election was not only about loyalty but also a referendum about conduct of the war at home.[49]

FREE SPEECH IN WARTIME: BERGER AND THE ESPIONAGE ACT

Victor Berger was a founding member of the Socialist Party, onetime congressman from Milwaukee, and editor of the *Milwaukee Leader*. For Berger, World War I was like walking through an unmarked minefield. He tried to maintain his integrity and his faithful adherence to the antiwar position of the Socialist Party, while avoiding a violation of the Espionage Act. Unfortunately, the patriotic climate of the era made it virtually impossible for him to avoid arrest.

The Espionage Act was a perfect tool with which to control dissent. The language of the law was vague enough to allow the Justice Department to select its targets. As the most prominent socialist in Wisconsin, Berger was a natural selection. In speaking out against the war, the financing plan, the draft, and the abridgement of civil liberties, Berger exercised his First

Victor Berger was a founder of the Socialist Party of America and one of its most practical politicians. Although opposed to the war and critical of the government, Berger attempted to adhere to a careful path narrowed by the restrictions on free speech imposed by the Espionage Act. As government sanctions tightened around Berger and his newspaper, his wife, Meta Berger, played a more visible and vocal role in managing the *Leader* and advising her husband. From left to right: Doris Berger, Jack Anderson, Victor Berger, Meta Berger, and Elsa Berger.
WHI IMAGE ID 123890

Amendment rights. Unfortunately, the Espionage Act, and the actions of Congress, the Justice Department, and the Supreme Court, effectively abrogated the First Amendment during wartime. Citizens began to ask, if it is illegal to raise questions about conscription or other major war issues, how can one engage in a meaningful debate about policy?

In keeping with Socialist Party policy, Berger's political platforms, campaign literature, speeches, and editorials steadfastly presented a Marxist critique hostile to American involvement in the war. As a leader of the party and the best-known socialist in Wisconsin, Berger became the subject of one of the Bureau of Investigation's most extensive investigations and the most prominent individual in Wisconsin to be caught in the web of the Espionage Act.

When the Socialist Party met in St. Louis to determine its wartime course, Berger was alarmed at the "insane radicalism" of the party's left wing. He chose to take "an extra-ordinarily conservative attitude." In co-operation with the "old leaders" on the "constructive side" of the party, Berger clearly hoped "to steer the party" around the radicals to reach a point of coexistence with federal government and the war effort. In the end, he lacked the power to navigate the radical storm. The convention chose to remain true to the party's internationalist principles and adopted a course in opposition to the war. In a key phrase, the convention proclamation called on "the workers of all countries to refuse support to their governments in their wars." By rejecting the more pragmatic option of accepting the war, but opposing nationalism, conscription, and infringement of civil liberties, the party set a collision course with the federal government and the patriotic spirit of the time.[50]

In June of 1917, members of the Wisconsin Socialist Party began complaining to the party's State Executive Committee of intimidation and persecution at the hands of local officials and private citizens. One socialist leader was jailed for "seditious talking." The chairman of the party in Kenosha was jailed shortly before he was scheduled to speak at a rally and was released after the rally was canceled. The federal government indicted Adolph Germer, an Illinois native and national executive secretary of the Socialist Party, for distributing antiwar leaflets and a petition to repeal the conscription law. In the community of Theresa, six hundred members of the Loyalty Legion prevented socialist Emil Seidel from speaking at what they considered a pro-German meeting. In Sauk County, socialist journalist Oscar Ameringer, a colleague of Berger's, was protected from loyalist "visitors" by farmers armed with pitchforks. These were but a few of the many cases of unofficial intimidation.[51]

It was a dangerous time to be a socialist. As editor of the *Milwaukee Leader* Berger tried to accomplish the near-impossible: remain true to socialism but avoid running afoul of the Espionage Act. During the first months of US involvement, Berger's newspaper maintained its steady attack on capitalist war profiteering. In an editorial in June 1917, for example, Berger argued that capitalists had a vested interest in the war because of loans and credit extended to the Allies, particularly France and England. Should the Allied war effort fail, the *Leader* claimed, American capitalists and financiers would lose roughly $3 billion they had invested in the Allied cause. In addition, according to Berger, the war created an excellent climate for business. It drove up stock prices, produced an artificial form of prosperity based on military production, freed owners from labor troubles and provided a convenient excuse to smash the rising economic power of Germany. The war also provided the government with an excuse for solidifying power and crushing opposition. Berger was willing to push his critique to an absurd level; he asserted that the war allowed the United States to build an army large enough to annex Canada and Mexico.[52]

Berger emphasized his opposition to the war, but he made a point never to advocate resistance or interference with the war effort. In this manner he hoped to avoid a legal battle with the government. The strategy failed. In the middle of September 1917, the Post Office Department invited Berger to Washington to defend the *Leader*'s second-class mailing permit against claims that it should be revoked for violating the Espionage Act. Drawing upon his contacts, Berger scheduled meetings with Colonel Edward M. House, confidant and advisor to President Wilson, and Postmaster General Burleson, with whom Berger had served in Congress. Nothing came of the meeting with Colonel House, and Burleson made it clear that any newspaper that blamed the war on capitalism would be suppressed.

On September 22, Berger met with the third assistant postmaster general for his hearing. The meeting was perfunctory. The postal official told Berger the *Leader* had violated the Espionage Act but failed to offer any specifics. Berger denied writing anything that was pro-German or harmed the war effort and offered to observe limits if they were defined. His offer was to no avail. On October 3, 1917, the *Leader* lost its second-class mailing permit. Distribution within Milwaukee would not be a problem, but without the second-class permit, the cost of a subscription outside Milwaukee would double because of the increased mailing costs.

The *Leader* lost its appeal in the United States Supreme Court on a vote of seven to two. Justice John Clarke acknowledged the *Leader*'s articles were well written, but still considered them pro-German propaganda. The government actions cost the paper $150 a day in extra mailing fees to its statewide and national subscribers. The ban lasted three and a half years and cost the paper an estimated $180,000. During the Harding administration, Postmaster General Will Hays declared post office censorship illegal, and on May 31, 1921, two and a half years after the war ended, the *Leader* regained its second-class permit.

A combination of public pressure and covert intimidation further crippled the newspaper's financial resources. The *Milwaukee Journal* called on the US district attorney in Milwaukee to take action against Berger and encouraged cancellations from the *Leader* by declaring that anyone who subscribed to or advertised in the *Leader* was encouraging disloyalty. Berger and Ameringer had firsthand evidence of threats and intimidation against advertisers. They visited an old socialist who had recently stopped advertising in the paper. Oswald Yaeger had been a member of the party for fifty years and had donated one thousand dollars to help the *Leader* get started. After persistent questioning, Yaeger broke down sobbing, "My God, I can't help it. I can't advertise in our own paper. They told me if I didn't take my advertising out they would refuse me the flour, sugar, and coal necessary for operating my bakery. And that is all I've got in the world."

Whether the threat was from an official source or a vigilante, the baker was intimidated enough to withdraw support. On an official level, just for good measure, the post office began returning all mail sent to the *Leader* with the stamp "Mail to this address undeliverable under the Espionage Act."[53]

The next blow came on March 11, 1918. Berger ran for the US Senate seat left vacant by the untimely death of Wisconsin Senator Paul Husting in a hunting accident. The super patriots, the newspapers, the leading candidates, and the president of the United States made loyalty the litmus test for the Senate primary election. In that climate, a federal grand jury indicted Berger in February for violating the Espionage Act, but in a move almost certainly designed to disrupt his campaign, the government waited until ten days before the primary election to announce the indictment. His opponents, a variety of political aficionados, and newspaper pundits immediately urged Berger to withdraw on the grounds that he was no longer a legitimate or viable candidate. Berger responded in the *Leader* and in paid advertising. He would not leave the race.[54]

Four major candidates ran in the primary. Berger, on the Socialist ticket, and Joseph E. Davies, the Democratic candidate, ran unopposed. Because the winner of the Republican primary was likely to win the general election, the Republican race between James Thompson and Irvine Lenroot presented voters with their major choice. Early in the campaign Bob La Follette supported Thompson. Alvin Peterson, Lenroot's campaign manager, used La Follette's endorsement to brand Thompson as disloyal: "The issue is now loyalty versus disloyalty. Lenroot stands for America, Thompson for *La Follette*." Wilson joined the fray by praising Davies for his patriotism and placing the odious mantel of disloyalty on Lenroot.

Lenroot won the Republican primary; Thompson lost by only 2,414 votes, despite being tainted by his association with La Follette. Voting patterns clearly reflected discontent with the war in areas of German concentration. Shortly after the primary, Waldemar Ager, Eau Claire editor of the Norwegian temperance newspaper *Reform*, wrote to Thompson, "I think you made an astonishing fine run. Just think of the circumstances. Even your best friends could not say a word without being disloyal: Hardly to risk to speak for you. A regular terrorism seemed to prevail. Many who would have voted for you voted for Lenroot or did not vote at all. . . . The German-Am. voted mostly for Berger in our city or did not vote."

The ballot box offered German Americans and other war opponents one of the few outlets for expressing their frustration with the war. Counties that were heavily German and normally voted Democratic voted for Thompson because of the La Follette endorsement.[55]

Davies and Lenroot came out of the primary victorious and were pitted against each other and Berger in the general election. As they campaigned, Berger focused on peace while the other two candidates remained locked in a contest to demonstrate who was more loyal.[56]

Lenroot, of Superior, was first elected to Congress in 1908 after serving four terms in the Assembly. He was a clear favorite in a state where Republicans held most of the important political offices. Davies was a political operative in the Democratic Party with no legislative experience. The Wilson administration sent a variety of politicians to the state in an attempt to overcome Lenroot's popularity and Republican affiliation. The *Wisconsin State Journal* ridiculed Davies' nonexistent record and the Democratic campaign strategy: "For the past fortnight the Democratic side of the United States senate has pretty much the appearance of a holiday, so many of the members on that side of the chamber having migrated to Wisconsin to prop up the political crutches of the President's political pet, Joe Davies."

On the evening of March 26, 1918, the administration sent Vice President Thomas R. Marshall to speak on Davies' behalf. An audience of some five thousand filled the University of Wisconsin's Stock Pavilion. By the time Marshall left the stage he had successfully damaged his candidate's chances by insulting the state's ethnic populations and impugning the loyalty of Wisconsin and its Republicans. In his speech Marshall called for national unity behind the flag, President Wilson, the Democratic Party, and the English language:

> But this war is going to be worth all it costs the American people.
> It will bind us together as one people under one flag. There will be
> just one kind of American loyal to the stars and stripes and speak-
> ing the English language. I have nothing against the German lan-
> guage, but this is a land where English is spoken and I believe after
> the war no man ought to vote who is not a full-fledged American,
> speaking English.

He criticized politicians for creating the so-called hyphenated American by encouraging immigrants to "cling to the ideas and traditions of his native land" and urged Germans to either "become Americans" or "get out." In his conclusion Marshall seemed to suggest that those who voted for Berger would now switch their "disloyal" votes to Lenroot.

> The results in the primary indicated half of you are for America and
> half for the Kaiser, and all against Wilson. The Republican party in

Wisconsin now has a chance to show if it really loves its country. Will
you be a partisan in such an awful hour?

In this one speech the vice president began by insulting the German, Polish, and Scandinavian populations by attacking their linguistic and cultural
heritage and concluded by implying that it would be unpatriotic to vote
for the Republican candidate. He made party affiliation a test of loyalty.[57]

During the campaign, both Lenroot and Davies claimed to be the
true loyalty candidate, but Lenroot's record and endorsement by Philipp
made him the easy favorite. In contrast, Davies could only claim to be a
true supporter of the president. Throughout the campaign, Berger made
his position clear: "I am for peace and I want your votes only if you are also
for peace." This became the opening line for most of his speeches. The
voters had clear choices.[58]

The outcome on April 2 was equally clear. Lenroot won the election
handily with 39 percent of the vote. Davies trailed with 35 percent, and
Berger finished last with 26 percent.[59] The meaning of these results lay in
the eye of the beholder. The *Wisconsin State Journal* ran the headline: "STATE
O.K.'S WAR 5 TO 1." Although the math was wrong (the ratio was actually
3 to 1), the paper was comparing the loyalty vote (Lenroot + Davies) with
the disloyal (socialist) vote to demonstrate that the forces of patriotism had
vanquished the forces of disloyalty to vindicate the state's good name.[60]

Berger did remarkably well in spite of a variety of impediments. In
addition to his indictment under the Espionage Act, his campaign posters
were defaced, smeared with paint, or simply torn down. He was burned
in effigy and his life threatened. Businessmen refused to display his window cards, local officials arrested distributors of his campaign literature,
and newspapers refused to print his advertisements. His vote tally, just as
in the primary election a few weeks earlier, was a measure of discontent
about the war.[61]

Malicious destruction of campaign materials and interference with
campaign workers were minor annoyances compared to what the federal government was planning. The Justice Department clearly meant
to destroy Berger. Under instruction from US Attorney H. A. Sawyer and
Special Assistant to the Attorney General A. G. Goggins, the Bureau of
Investigation began to collect information on Berger in March or April of

In the senate campaign of 1918, Victor Berger faced routine harassment. This campaign poster was defaced with symbols of German militarism. The handwritten phrase "of the Russian kind" refers to the capitulation to Germany by the Bolsheviks. WHI IMAGE ID 57783

1918. The file eventually grew to more than four hundred pages of detailed surveillance reports, campaign literature, and other documentation. The federal attorneys wanted to find evidence of unpatriotic behavior and writing, misuse of the mails, and names of accomplices. They accumulated evidence from former socialists such as Algie Simons who willingly provided information, and from socialist colleagues who could be "persuaded" to supply information.

Not everyone complied. Frank Raguse, former state senator removed for unpatriotic remarks, was arrested in Sun Prairie for distributing Berger's campaign literature; in other words, he was arrested for distributing "seditious" materials. During interrogation by the US attorney in Madison, Raguse refused to answer any questions without representation. "Raguse was dismissed with a warning that his further acts would be at his own peril."

Investigators combed the pages of the *Leader* for damning editorials. American Protective League operatives were assigned the task of collecting campaign literature, especially if it included evidence of having used the US mail service. Undercover agents attended socialist meetings. At one such meeting G. T. Willett attended a campaign rally in Milwaukee.

He reported that Hoan and aldermanic candidate Paul Gauer stuck to local topics, but Berger's speech was "a harangue on the evils of war" during which he emphasized "the enormous profits made by the capitalists."[62]

As pressure mounted against Socialist Party members, the party began to modify its rhetoric. In preparation for the fall 1918 elections, the party's State Executive Committee instructed party officials and candidates: "Socialist officials universally, as well as our candidates, have and will comply with any need or request of our government in carrying on the war. In so doing they will not sacrifice an iota of their principle that they stand against war and militarism, and for an early, general, lasting and democratic peace."

This was a far cry from the "active, public opposition" of the St. Louis convention. In the *Leader*, Berger tried to de-emphasize war news and play up peace news. He encouraged readers to support Liberty Bonds, war savings drives, and the Red Cross. This shift in emphasis came, in part, out of the realization that it had become impossible to oppose the government.[63]

In the fall of 1918, still under indictment, Berger ran for the Fifth District congressional seat. On October 28, the week before the general election, he was indicted a second time for violating the Espionage Act. He and the four other socialists running for Wisconsin offices were charged with conspiracy to discourage young men from enlisting, as carried out through their writings and distributed illegally through the mail. Berger was in good company. The indictment included the socialist congressional candidates in the second, fourth, and eighth districts, the Socialist Party's state secretary, and the head of the Social-Democratic Publishing Company. The only purpose for these indictments seems to have been to influence voter behavior and harass the candidates before the election. The case never went to trial and the indictment was dismissed in January 1923.[64]

The fall election further showcased Berger's popularity in Milwaukee. He won the Fifth District congressional seat with 17,920 votes, fully 5,470 votes ahead of his nearest opponent. Six days later the war was over.[65]

FREE SPEECH IN WARTIME: LA FOLLETTE AND PROGRESSIVE WAR POLICY

For a figure like Berger, who was already in the government's crosshairs because he was a socialist, to oppose conscription was to violate the law.

In contrast, Robert M. La Follette might be ridiculed, criticized, despised, burned in effigy, and hated for many of his views, including his opposition to conscription, but as a sitting US senator from a major party, he was unlikely to be targeted for the kind of concerted surveillance and harassment suffered by Berger and other socialists.

La Follette recognized the declaration of war imposed obligations on the American people. In words similar to those used by Philipp and Esch, he told readers of *La Follette's Magazine*:

> Everyone must admit that we at least are in this war lawfully and in a constitutional manner. The obligations we, as a people, have assumed in this war have been lawfully assumed and we must lawfully accept them. We can no more repudiate our obligations to prosecute this war efficiently until it can be ended honorably than we can repudiate our obligations to pay the debts we have contracted in the prosecution of the war. Over this proposition there can be no reasonable dispute or controversy.[66]

La Follette made clear to readers that "prosecuting the war efficiently" did not require Americans to give up free speech. Two individuals could disagree on the best method for prosecuting the war. Americans must obey the law, he told readers, but had the right to criticize the war, their government, the nation's laws, and public officials. Indeed, free speech and open debate were essential for the successful conduct of the war and for promotion of a peace that would be enduring and in the best interest of the nation.[67]

In keeping with his own advice, La Follette opposed conscription and limitations on free speech because they infringed on civil liberties. He opposed issuing bonds as a means of financing the war out of the belief that this was bad fiscal policy. He believed those who profited from the war, not the common people with limited resources, should be taxed in a "pay-as-we-go" war financing program. He advocated for a declaration of war aims as a legitimate function of Congress and a necessary step toward a "just peace." He wanted Congress to state US war goals clearly so the nation would know when it was time to call an end to the carnage. Without a statement of war aims he feared that financial and industrial interests would keep the war going indefinitely. La Follette acted not out of opposition to the war, but in pursuit of progressive policies that would guide the financing and fighting of the war. Nonetheless, whenever a new bond issue came up for a final vote, he supported the measure. Repeatedly, he chose to support troops in the field despite reservations about funding mechanisms and budgets.[68]

Because he had his own progressive agenda, La Follette was at once one of the best loved and most hated men in the nation. His reputation was shaped by the legacy of his prewar actions, combined with the fact that he challenged many of the president's most important war measures related to raising and financing a massive national army. Although La Follette was often portrayed as an obstructionist, if not an outright traitor, he was in fact in pursuit of a progressive vision for the nation. He sought a world in which volunteers fought wars free of government coercion, a world in which the wealthy and the war profiteers paid their fair share. He sought a world in which the average citizen had an equal voice in government decisions, and the wealthy no longer controlled politics in their own interest. This was the same progressive vision that brought reform to Wisconsin. All too often La Follette's opponents reduced his complex reasoning to a simplistic dichotomy. On one occasion, for example, after La Follette had addressed Congress on the subject of free speech, Senator Joseph Robinson of Arkansas denounced his colleague by saying, "There is no compromise on this issue. There are only two sides to this conflict—Germanism and Americanism; the Kaiser or the President."[69]

La Follette confronted one of his greatest challenges when the Associated Press misquoted a speech he gave to the Nonpartisan League in St. Paul, Minnesota, on September 20, 1917. Ultimately, the controversy created by the news agency's error marginalized La Follette's effectiveness in the Senate and fueled the perception that he was unpatriotic.

The Nonpartisan League was founded in 1915 in North Dakota by a former socialist. Much like La Follette, the organization advocated for the wealthy to pay their fair share of war costs. La Follette stepped on the stage that evening in St. Paul at 9:36 p.m. The auditorium was packed with a standing-room-only crowd that greeted La Follette with a five-minute ovation. Governor Lynn Frazier of North Dakota introduced Senator La Follette and asked the audience to rise and sing "America," which was done "with great heartiness." As the senator prepared to speak, "the

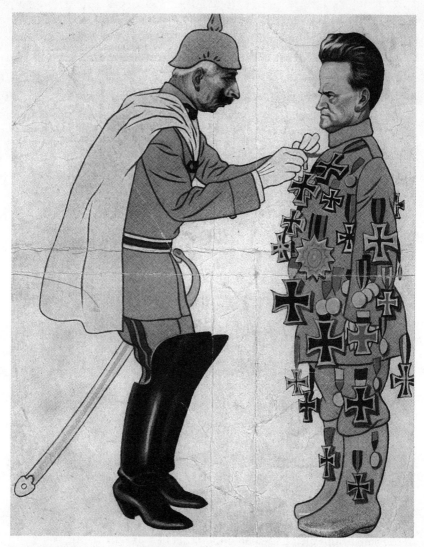

In one of the most iconic cartoons of the war, published in *Life* magazine on December 12, 1917, the Kaiser pins medals on Bob La Follette, rewarding him for his loyalty to the German cause. The senator never supported Germany. He did favor neutrality, peace, free speech, a volunteer army, and taxes on the wealthy. All of these positions challenged federal policies, and it was easier for his opponents to ridicule his ideas and brand him a traitor than to grapple with the meaning and substance of those ideas.
WHI IMAGE ID 3272

audience remained standing, applauding, cheering, shouting, waving flags, and otherwise giving vent to its feelings." Frazier stepped forward waving the flag and, rather incongruously, "the band played 'Dixie.'" The raucous audience twice gave their speaker three cheers. La Follette, with some difficulty, got the audience in their seats and quieted. Although he had a speech prepared, he spoke extemporaneously about corporate power and the failure of representative government under the control of profiteers. These were old progressive themes La Follette knew well. He heralded the growing movement of the Nonpartisan League to reestablish true representative government.

> Now, fellow citizens, we are in the midst of a war. For my own part I was not in favor of *beginning* that war.
> I don't mean to say we hadn't suffered grievances. We had—at the hands of Germany. *Serious* grievances!
> We had cause for complaint. They had interfered with the right of American citizens to travel upon the high seas—on ships loaded with munitions for Great Britain.

After interruptions for applause and banter with the audience, he picked up his theme: "I would not be understood as saying that we didn't have grievances. We did." But, he emphasized, those grievances were insufficient to warrant condemning millions of soldiers to death. The nation was legally at war by an act of Congress, and covering the costs of the war should rely on taxing profiteers, not borrowing from future generations. He finished and rushed to catch a train to his next engagement.

Unfortunately, the Associated Press quoted him as saying, "I wasn't in favor of beginning this war. We had no grievances." This statement appeared in newspapers throughout the United States the following day. The misquotation gave new fuel for the vituperative fires kindled by his opponents. Roosevelt called him "a sinister enemy of democracy" and a "shadow Hun." Senator Frank Kellogg of Minnesota delivered a blistering attack and suggested La Follette should seek a seat in the "Bundesrath."

The Senate immediately undertook an investigation that dragged on for fifteen months despite clear evidence that La Follette had been misquoted. His colleagues, however, disliked the entire tenor of the speech.

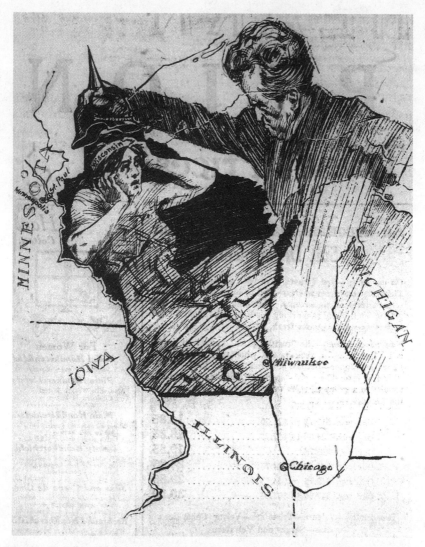

Senator La Follette had a national following of supporters and critics. The *New York Tribune* depicted him as forcing a horrified Miss Forward to support the German cause.
NEW YORK TRIBUNE, NOVEMBER 25, 1917

Throughout 1918, La Follette was preoccupied by his son Bobbie's lengthy battle with streptococcic infections and the need to defend against numerous political attacks. Finally, on December 2, 1918, a month after the armistice, he was vindicated when the Committee on Privileges and Elections voted nine to two to end the investigation.[70]

During the early days of the war, La Follette could count on a powerful friend in Madison, Richard Lloyd Jones, editor of the *Wisconsin State Journal*. La Follette and Jones shared a desire for neutrality during the first year of the war, but as Wilson gradually moved toward a belligerent position during 1916, Jones moved with him. As La Follette fought to avoid the war and then to create coherent fiscal and military policies, he found himself increasingly at odds with the paper. During 1917, Jones became an ever harsher critic of La Follette. The senator voted for fifty-five out of sixty war measures presented by the administration, but when he broke ranks in opposition to conscription, the Espionage Act, and bond financing of the war, he found himself under attack in the press, especially by the *State Journal*. William T. Evjue, progressive member of the state Assembly and business manager of the *State Journal*, became increasingly concerned by the paper's anti–La Follette bias. In the fall of 1917 Evjue quit his job with the *State Journal* and began laying plans for a new paper, *The Capital Times*, which debuted on December 13, 1917, as a voice of progressives.[71] Evjue and *The Capital Times* became one of La Follette's chief allies.

Like Berger, La Follette was considered by many people of his own time to be a disloyal opponent of the war. This view was based on the misinterpretation and misrepresentation of his wartime record. La Follette, the vehement critic with an absolute belief in himself and the righteousness of his actions, was not an easy man to like when on the other side of a verbal barrage. Even his friends found him difficult. Although never at ease or in agreement with the war, he did not consider himself an opponent of the war once America entered the conflict. His was a progressive voice speaking truth to power.

Postwar Vindication

As the war was ending in Europe, one final loyalty battle played out in Wisconsin. In preparation for the general election campaign in the fall of 1918, Philipp, Wilcox, and the Republican platform committee met in the governor's office to draft the party's platform. The supporters of Philipp and progressive James Tittemore cooperated and dominated the writing of the platform. One of the working committees presented a platform plank commending Philipp for his administration of the state during the war. Wilcox objected. He was not proud of the governor's war record and launched into a personal diatribe of criticism against Philipp. As Wilcox spoke, Philipp sat in a large chair with his head down. According to observers, when Wilcox finished, Philipp raised his head and, with unmatched anger, plainly asked, "What have *you* done for your country?"

Philipp was a large man. He rose slowly from his chair. He would be happy to compare his record with that of the senator from Eau Claire. Pacing like an enraged bear in a cage, Philipp lashed out in fury with one damning critique after another. He charged that Wilcox was using the war to advance his own career. The governor's son was in the navy and his daughter was a nurse. Wilcox was of military age for the Spanish-American War and the Great War; why had he not joined something to advance the war effort? Wilcox and his followers had spent the war harassing their neighbors to buy more bonds. Philipp alleged that Wilcox had purchased only one five-hundred-dollar bond himself. In contrast, Philipp and his family had purchased more than one hundred thousand dollars in bonds. When Philipp finished, Wilcox quietly left the room; Philipp went on to win a third term in the November election. The war ended five days later, and Philipp turned his attention to combating the Spanish flu.[72]

Philipp, Hoan, Berger, and La Follette gave voice to reason. They were not perfect men. They could be unreasonable; they could be wrong; but more important, they tried to lead with humanity and respect for people and the law. They were vehemently criticized, but the years following the war vindicated all four men. After defeating Wilcox in the primary election, Philipp served a third term as governor and is recognized today as one of Wisconsin's most successful governors. Hoan served as mayor of Milwaukee until 1940 for a total of twenty-four years, one of the longest tenures of any mayor of a major American city. Berger, while under indictment, was elected to Congress a few days before the war ended. On January 9, 1919, Berger was convicted of violating the Espionage Act and sentenced to twenty years in prison. Based on this conviction, Congress refused to seat him in 1919 and, after being elected a second time, refused to seat him again in 1920. The United States Supreme Court threw out his conviction in 1921 on a procedural technicality. The voters elected Berger to the Fifth Congressional District for a third time in 1922, and he took his rightful seat as a congressman from Wisconsin. La Follette received renewed respect once the war was over. He was reelected to the Senate in 1922 and ran for president in 1924 as a third-party candidate, garnering 16.6 percent of the vote. Bloodgood and Wilcox, hailed as patriots in their time, fundamentally misunderstood the meaning of patriotism in a democratic society and largely have been forgotten.

REFLECTIONS

The experience of Wisconsin's people during World War I suggests that fighting a major war, particularly a "total war" requiring mobilization of the entire society, is a complex and risky business. Obviously, any war places soldiers in harm's way, but a total war also places society at risk. Woodrow Wilson understood the great human cost that war imposed on the battlefield, and he tried mightily to avoid entanglement in the European conflict. He also feared the impact of war on American society. On March 19, just two weeks before he asked Congress for a declaration of war, the president told Frank Cobb of the *New York World*, "Once lead this people into war, and they'll forget there ever was such a thing as tolerance. To fight you must be brutal and ruthless, and the spirit of ruthless brutality will enter the very fiber of our national life, infecting congress, the courts, the policeman on the beat, the man in the street. . . . If there is any alternative, for God's sake let's take it!"[1]

Ultimately, Wilson could find no alternative and asked Congress to declare war on the German Empire. Experiences on the battlefield and on the home front demonstrated the wisdom of Wilson's fears. In spite of widespread ambivalence regarding the decision to go to war, Americans adapted quickly to the state of war and devoted great energy toward defeating the enemy. Herbert Hoover, Emanuel Philipp, and Magnus Swenson held great faith in the American people, and that faith was repaid sevenfold. Young men quickly filled the ranks of the Wisconsin National Guard, and many others willingly registered for the draft and, when called, went to war. Housewives became the foundation upon which Hoover built the food conservation program. Likewise, children too young to serve, and women and men too old or unfit for military service, filled the ranks of volunteer organizations, factories, and farms in patriotic support of the war effort.

The average American, regardless of personal opinion about the war, recognized the need to support the nation's cause, as demonstrated in the constituent letters to John Esch. Despite disagreements with Wilson, La Follette understood the importance of fulfilling his duty once the deci-

240

sion was made to go to war, but he also believed patriotism did not require him to abrogate his beliefs in favor of administration policies.

Some individuals and newspapers quickly developed intolerance for anyone deemed to be a "slacker" or enemy sympathizer. The war not only encouraged self-sacrifice, but it also brought out the bullies, the super patriots, the true believers who found it easier to persecute those with whom they disagreed than to understand alternate points of view. Declaring neighbors or opponents slackers, pro-German, unpatriotic, or traitorous created an unnecessary and counterproductive diversion from the real task of winning the war. This was the side of the war that produced vigilantes and a general intolerance for any point of view contrary to government policy. Leaders such as Robert M. La Follette and Victor Berger listened to their constituencies and played a critical role focusing attention on the importance of free speech and debate, even in wartime. In addition, politicians such as Emanuel Philipp and Daniel Hoan demonstrated time and again the importance of leaders who placed governing ahead of politics, recognized the value of justice and thoughtful administration, and for whom ideology created a principled point of reference and not a straightjacket.

Nations generally start wars with the assumption they will win, but war has the potential to destabilize the nations involved. World War I drained the economies of all the European belligerents and destroyed the monarchies and empires of Germany, Austria-Hungary, Russia, and the Ottomans. It also marked the beginning of the end of the colonial empires of Great Britain and France. More than eight million young men died in combat. The Great War led, at least in part, to the Armenian genocide, the Russian revolution, and the rise of Adolph Hitler.

Simple answers fail to explain the beginning of the war in 1914. Although the average person found it difficult to imagine a major war in this most civilized of times, a small number of influential military officers and political leaders still thought of war as a heroic enterprise essential for advancement of society. The major European powers had engaged in an arms race and were equipped with the most lethal weapons in history. Illogically, many military observers dismissed the efficacy of modern military technology, such as heavy artillery and machine guns, and assumed a speedy victory would result from aggressive offensives by heroic men.

Instead of focusing on a diplomatic solution, the nations of Europe responded to the crisis based on long-established military planning. They did what they had prepared to do; they mobilized their armies and went to war.

The assassination of Archduke Ferdinand and his wife provided the spark to ignite this tinderbox. Serbian nationalists, with their dreams of creating a greater Serbia by dismembering the sickly Austro-Hungarian Empire, had long worried the government in Vienna. In response to the assassination, Austrian officials decided to provoke a war by presenting Serbia with demands designed to be rejected, thereby giving them a pretext to crush Serbia. Germany had an opportunity at this point to maneuver Austria into a less belligerent stance, but chose instead to sit on the sidelines. Germany made matters worse by promising to aid the Austrians in whatever course they chose to take. When Austria subsequently invaded Serbia, the Russian government could have undertaken a diplomatic initiative to encourage Germany to restrain Austria, but instead ordered a general mobilization in defense of its Slavic neighbor—the most threatening action it could have taken.

In turn, German leaders felt compelled to mobilize against the threat of annihilation in a two-front war. They faced the seemingly overwhelming Russian army in the east and the French army in the west. The German High Command had long anticipated this scenario and carefully planned a preemptive knockout blow against the French so it could devote its full strength against the Russian juggernaut in the east. The Kaiser had second thoughts, but when told by his generals that their clockwork mobilization could not be stopped or reoriented, he capitulated. In the end, war came to Europe in 1914 because of a fundamental failure of leadership and diplomacy, and because each nation feared potential defeat much more than they feared war itself. They were better at preparing for war than for peace.

The leaders in Europe had prepared for war and for rapid mobilization. In contrast, diplomacy was slow and much more difficult to implement. While engaged in an arms race, they neglected to build equally robust diplomatic contacts and relationships that would have been useful during the summer of 1914. In addition, neither the Kaiser nor the Czar had the mental capacity to understand what was happening or the willpower to confront their generals and civilian leaders. The generals did not fear war because each side assumed victory and they lacked the imagination to predict the catastrophe they were creating.

In the United States, Wilson hoped neutrality would protect the nation and avoid involvement in the war. Even in 1917 he was still proposing peace initiatives until it became obvious these efforts would no longer be effective. Oddly, despite Wilson's extensive knowledge of American history, he failed to recognize the pitfalls of neutrality when the British controlled the seas. Despite US neutrality, Wilson also failed to rein in the banking houses and weapons manufacturers who became the facilitators of a protracted war. By 1917 Germany was becoming desperate for a way to strangle the Allied supply lines, and the German navy promised its submarine fleet would bring Great Britain to its knees before the United States could put an army in the field. It was a disastrous miscalculation.

The United States entered the war with an overwhelming vote in Congress but without any true national consensus and certainly without consensus in Wisconsin. Without an overt attack on American soil, such as Pearl Harbor a generation later, it was necessary to create a great cause for which young men could fight and die and families could sacrifice and mourn the dead and disabled. Creating that great cause did not require any cynical machinations. Wilson himself framed the issues in his request for a declaration of war. By conducting unrestricted submarine warfare, Germany was engaged in "a war against all nations." "We enter this war only where we are clearly forced into it," Wilson told Congress, "because there are no other means of defending our rights." The nation would join with others to defend against autocratic power with a simple goal: "The world must be made safe for democracy." Democratic government was not threatened by the submarines. Instead, submarine warfare came to symbolize an autocratic bully who would do anything to dominate Europe and the world. The future of humankind was at stake.[2]

Wilson delivered a measured, carefully reasoned call for war. For the most vehement advocates of war it was only natural to justify the need for war as a great crusade against an evil foe that threatened freedom. The advocates of war believed their own rhetoric that national existence and freedom were in jeopardy if the militaristic, autocratic Prussians won the war. German subjugation of Belgium seemed to confirm the barbaric nature of the Hun. Wilson made a point of distinguishing between the

German government and the German people, but many other observers were not so careful. It was easy to believe the propaganda portraying the German soldier as a rapist and baby killer because the German army routinely executed civilian hostages when they met resistance in Belgium and burned the renowned university library at Louvain. These war crimes provided the foundation for gruesome propaganda that fed the perception that the war was a matter of national survival. For many super patriots it was relatively easy to superimpose perceptions of German behavior in Belgium onto the German people of Wisconsin. In turn, it followed that a state with a large German population, a population of potential traitors, was not to be trusted.

World War I required a deep commitment from the entire society. Even without a consensus regarding the declaration of war, national unity came naturally to the American people once the war started. Most Americans seemed to accept two premises: first, that the nation was in jeopardy; and second, that patriotic duty required they support the war effort. In Wisconsin most people did their duty as a contribution toward winning the war.

The National Guard recruited up to war strength, draft registration and the draft calls went smoothly, and communities gave their soldiers unwavering support. Homemakers in Wisconsin and across the nation joined Hoover's Food Administration and became the linchpins that helped "Hooverizing" succeed at the consumer level. Bakers and restaurant associations cooperated to conserve at the retail level. The American Federation of Labor worked assiduously to avoid strikes. Hundreds of volunteers staffed the state and county Councils of Defense to facilitate the workings of the wartime economy. Farmers responded to the call to produce more food, and high school students, businessmen, county jail inmates, and women helped to plant and harvest. Women took war jobs and provided the workforce for most volunteer organizations. Local newspapers carried regular stories of the good work of average citizens supporting the war effort. Led by their congressional delegation, most Wisconsin residents openly supported the war effort even though many had opposed the declaration of war. This was patriotism at work.

The war also demonstrated how fragile civil liberties can be when the entire society is focused on what is perceived to be a life-and-death struggle. Coercion and vigilante justice reflected the dark side of home-front life. Hooverizing, fuel conservation, Liberty Bond campaigns, and charitable fund-raising helped most Americans feel a part of the war effort, but these patriotic activities were all supported by implicit or explicit threats of social ostracism, government sanction, or vigilante action if one did not attend to patriotic duty.

When critics called Wisconsin the "traitor state," Philipp, Swenson, university leaders, and other public figures defended the state by citing Wisconsin's excellent record for draft registrations, Liberty Loan drives, crop production, and food conservation. Most public figures and the general public in Wisconsin recognized the charge of treason in Wisconsin was patently absurd. Nonetheless, for the super patriots who distrusted the state's German population and viewed Berger and La Follette as living proof of traitors in their midst, German Kulture needed to be expunged from Wisconsin, the German population of the state needed to be Americanized, and traitors needed to be arrested. All too easily patriotic fervor broke free of the bonds of national unity. Just as Wilson had worried before the war, the combination of government action and super patriotic fervor created one of the greatest threats to civil liberties in American history.

Americans willingly sacrificed to win the war, but the undercurrent of coercion reflected a deep sense of uncertainty in American society. Instead of financing the war with taxes, as La Follette had advocated, the government sold low-interest bonds that everyone was expected to buy. To meet quotas local officials resorted to patriotic social pressure to encourage purchases. Occasionally that pressure took a more aggressive form as vigilantes took matters into their own hands. Being a volunteer or vigilante often originated out of the impulse to be involved and, in some small manner, to have control over their role in the war effort. By doing charitable war work or taking legal and extralegal action against perceived domestic enemies, super patriots and volunteers alike sought to gain ascendance over the forces of evil.

The war made everyone more security-conscious. The Secret Service looked for spies, the US Marshals Service hunted draft evaders, and the Bureau of Investigation dealt with cases of disloyalty. The American Protective League gave the investigation agency "eyes and ears" in virtually every community in Wisconsin. In a climate of super patriotism, any real debate over policy became almost impossible because any opposition to war policies became suspect. By the end of the war, the nation's security apparatus had become far more intrusive than at any other time in American history.

In this security-conscious, super patriotic climate, wartime controls curtailed free speech and set dangerous precedents. La Follette was battered and bruised by his opponents but survived politically because of Wisconsin's progressives and because of German Wisconsinites who were frustrated by the constant imputation of their loyalty and hostility toward German Kulture. The full force of the law came down on the Socialists, particularly Berger. The case against the *Milwaukee Leader* set a far-reaching precedent: the Supreme Court approved prior restraint of written material based on past tendencies. Even Philipp was criticized because he believed in protecting everyone's right to due process and believed in the loyalty of Wisconsin's citizens.

War inherently places a nation's future in jeopardy. The Wisconsin experience confirmed Wilson's concern that war would jeopardize American civil liberties and civic discourse. With such high stakes, the government squelched debate, stifled dissent, and became increasingly intolerant of any challenge to policy. To fight a total war, society became more regimented than ever before. When the war ended, society sprang back most of the way to its old form, but not completely. The Espionage Act of 1917 remains on the books with profound implications for free speech in our time.

The leaders of the great powers in Europe made decisions within a very narrow framework of history and grievances. They little expected the cataclysm to sweep away their old world and much of what they took for granted about power, social structure, and international relationships. In 1914, they did not intend or expect to affect the people of Wisconsin, but from the very beginning the war had economic, political, and emotional impacts in the far-off United States. American banks and industries quickly became part of the fabric of finance and industry essential to keeping the Allies on the field of battle. No matter how hard individuals tried to remain neutral, they took sides. Once the United States entered the war and began mobilizing the nation, individuals took on new roles: Young men went to war; businessmen rolled up their sleeves and joined students to plant crops and bring in the harvest; homemakers made Hooverizing a great success; farmers planted more and different crops as needed by the war effort; factory workers shifted from domestic to military production. The war united society and divided it at the same time. The average person sacrificed and adjusted as needed to meet wartime demands and felt good about contributing to the war effort. Below the surface of unity, cooperation, and support for the war effort also flowed a current of surveillance, intimidation, and suppression that was part of wartime life.

To understand the First World War and the Wisconsin experience, it is important to look at society as a whole, to tie the home front and battlefront together, to understand a variety of perspectives. The war demonstrated the great capacity of the American people for sacrifice and generosity, but also for prejudice, intolerance, and injustice. Today, as we look back across a century, it is clear the war had a profound and lasting impact on American society. The war has left us with a variety of questions: With more wisdom, could the First World War have been avoided? Is it possible to fight a total war and protect dissent at the same time? How can we make diplomacy more effective and war less likely? Perhaps the most important lesson of the Great War is the sobering reminder that when we engage in war, we undertake an enterprise over which we have little control, with potentially disastrous outcomes we cannot predict.

NOTES

Introduction

1. In this case, perception was as important as reality. Although the Taiping Rebellion and civil war (1850–1864) in southern China killed 20 million to 30 million individuals and is probably the bloodiest conflict in human history, for the Western observer with little knowledge of Asia, World War I was commonly cited as the greatest catastrophe the world had ever seen.

2. Most historians have used the phrase "super patriot" to designate the relatively small group of people who took an extremely negative view of anyone who criticized the war or the nation's political leaders. Their intolerance helped make World War I one of the most repressive eras in American history.

Chapter 1

1. This chapter relies heavily on the works of Nesbit and Buenker, both of which offer excellent overviews of the period before 1914. See Robert C. Nesbit, *Wisconsin: A History* (Madison: University of Wisconsin Press, 1973); and John D. Buenker, *The Progressive Era, 1893–1914*, vol. 4 in *The History of Wisconsin* (Madison: State Historical Society of Wisconsin, 1998).

2. Bayrd Still, *Milwaukee: The History of a City* (Madison: State Historical Society of Wisconsin, 1948), 181.

3. As quoted in Buenker, *Progressive Era*, 41–42; Nesbit, *Wisconsin*, 283.

4. Western Insurance Survey Company, "Insurance Map of the Lumber Districts of Eau Claire, Wis. October 1894" (Chicago: Western Insurance Survey Co., 1894).

5. W. A. Henry, *Northern Wisconsin: A Hand-book for the Homeseeker* (Madison: Democrat Printing Company, 1896); Wisconsin Colonization Company records, Wisconsin Historical Society, Madison.

6. Throughout this volume, the reader will encounter several individuals identified by two initials and a surname. This was common practice one

hundred years ago. For example, one routinely sees Henry C. Putnam of Eau Claire identified only as H. C. Putnam. As a matter of modern practice, wherever possible we have tried to identify the first name of the individual and include it in the text. When that is not possible, we have reverted to the use of initials.

7. Still, *Milwaukee*, 186–188.

8. Buenker, *Progressive Era*, 431–454; Nesbit, *Wisconsin*, 401–418.

9. Nesbit, *Wisconsin*, 426.

10. Paul W. Glad, *War, a New Era, and Depression, 1914–1940*, vol. 5 in *The History of Wisconsin* (Madison: State Historical Society of Wisconsin, 1990), 105; Buenker, *Progressive Era*, 344–345.

11. Robert S. Maxwell, *Emanuel L. Philipp: Wisconsin Stalwart* (Madison: State Historical Society of Wisconsin, 1959), 77–89; Nesbit, *Wisconsin*, 435–437; Buenker, *Progressive Era*, pp. 611–664.

12. US Bureau of the Census, *Thirteenth Census of the United States Taken in the Year 1910*, vol. 3, *Population* (Washington, DC: Government Printing Office, 1913), 1073–1096.

Chapter 2

1. For thorough accounts of the assassination and the beginning of the war see: Barbara W. Tuchman, *The Guns of August* (New York: Macmillan, 1962); S. L. A. Marshall, *The American Heritage History of World War I* (New York: American Heritage, 1964); Max Hastings, *Catastrophe 1914: Europe Goes to War* (New York: Alfred A. Knopf, 2013); Margaret MacMillan, *The War That Ended Peace: How Europe Abandoned Peace for the First World War* (London: Profile Books, 2013); Christopher M. Clark, *The Sleepwalkers: How Europe Went to War in 1914* (New York: Harper, 2013).

2. *Milwaukee Journal*, June 29 through August 5, 1914. These events are covered in similar fashion by every newspaper in Wisconsin.

3. Victor Berger (en route to New York) to Meta Berger, July 30, 1914, in *The Family Letters of Victor and Meta Berger, 1894–1929*, ed. Michael E. Stevens (Madison: State Historical Society of Wisconsin, 1995), 178–179.

4. Theodore Roosevelt, *America and the World War* (New York: Charles Scribner's Sons, 1915), 1.

5. *Milwaukee Journal*, August 17, 1914, 2, and August 19, 1914, 1 and 2; *Eau Claire Leader*, August 5, 1914, 1.

6. *Milwaukee Journal*, August 19, 1914, 2.

7. Ibid., 4.

8. Ibid., 7.

9. Woodrow Wilson, "American Neutrality: An appeal by the President of the United States to the Citizens of the Republic, Requesting Their Assistance in Maintaining a State of Neutrality During the Present European War," August 19, 1914, 63rd Cong., 2nd sess., S. Doc. no. 566.

10. *Superior Telegram*, August 11, 1914, 3, and August 8, 1914, 7.

11. *Eau Claire Leader*, August 5, 1914, 2.

12. *Superior Telegram*, August 4, 1914, 1, and August 6, 1914, 1. Quote is from *Superior Telegram*, August 7, 1914, 3.

13. *Manitowoc Daily Herald*, September 28, 1914, 1; *Racine Journal-News*, December 3, 1914, 3; Sophy de Schaepdrijver, "The 'German Atrocities' of 1914," *British Library*, http://www.Bl.uk/world-war-one/articles/civilian-atrocities-german-1914.

14. Herbert F. Margulies, *The Decline of the Progressive Movement in Wisconsin, 1890–1920* (Madison: State Historical Society of Wisconsin, 1968), 177, 195–196, 200; Nesbit, *Wisconsin*, 445; *Monroe Evening Times*, March 12, 1917, 2; *Milwaukee Leader*, February 9, 1917, 1.

15. *Janesville Daily Gazette*, November 6, 1914, 2 and 4, and December 4, 1914, 5; *La Crosse Tribune*, November 23, 1914, 6; *Waukesha Freeman*, November 25, 7; *Eau Claire Sunday Leader*, December 13, 1914, 3; *Wisconsin State Journal*, November 7, 1914, editorial page.

16. Victor Berger (Milwaukee) to Meta Berger, August 6, 1914, in Stevens, *Family Letters*, 179.

17. Edward J. Muzik, "Victor L. Berger, A Biography" (PhD diss., Northwestern University, 1960), 256, 269–270; Frederick I. Olson, "Milwaukee Socialists" (PhD diss., Harvard University, 1952), 335.

18. John Esch to Richard Capen (Merrillan), August 24, 1914, John J. Esch Papers, box 31, Wisconsin Historical Society, Madison, WI.

19. In general, see letters between August 21 and September 20, 1914 in Esch Papers, box 31. Specifically see: Esch to Louis A. Pamperin (Pamperin Cigar Co., La Crosse), August 29, 1914; Jos. P. Riese (La Crosse) to Esch, September 2, 1914; Jos. J. Wagner (Local #61, Cigarmakers International Union of America—La Crosse) to Esch, September 10, 1914; Esch to Carl

Kurtenacker (John Grund Brew, Co.—La Crosse), August 29, 1914; Max Rahr Jr. (V.P. of Manitowoc Malting Co.) to Esch, September 8, 1914; Harry W. Barney (Pres. of Necedah Bank) to Esch, September 21, 1914; J. Van Orden (Bank of Baraboo) to Esch, September 21, 1914; E. M. Wing (V.P. of Batavian Nat. Bank—La Crosse) to Esch, September 21, 1914; Esch to Secretary, Interstate Oil Co. (La Crosse), September 28, 1914; C. A. Goodyear (Tomah) to Esch, September 12, 1914; John C. Bum (La Crosse) to Esch, telegram, September 29, 1914. The quote is from John S. Owen (Eau Claire) to Esch, August 31, 1914. The dearth of letters that speak to the issue of American involvement would seem to indicate a lack of any real fear that the United States would become embroiled in the conflict.

20. *La Crosse Tribune*, "Peace Before a Year Passes," reprinted from the *Saturday Evening Post*, December 26, 1914, 3; September 10, 1914, 3; October 1, 1914, 6; and October 5, 1914, 5.

21. *Superior Telegram*, August 5, 1914, 2.

22. *Eau Claire Leader*, August 5, 1914, 2.

23. Thomas Bailey, *A Diplomatic History of the American People*, 8th ed. (New York: Appleton-Century-Crofts, 1969), 570–575.

24. *Congressional Record*, February 12, 1915, Senate, vol. 52, pt. 4, 3631–3634; Nancy C. Unger, *Fighting Bob La Follette: Righteous Reformer* (Chapel Hill: University of North Carolina Press, 2000), 235–236.

25. *La Crosse Tribune*, May 12, 1915, 3; May 15, 1915, 3; and March 20, 1915, 2 and 3.

26. Paul W. Glad, *War, a New Era, and Depression, 1914–1940*, vol. 5 in *The History of Wisconsin* (Madison: State Historical Society of Wisconsin, 1990); Nancy C. Unger, *Belle La Follette: Progressive Era Reformer* (New York: Routledge, 2016), 116–122; *La Crosse Tribune*, April 15, 1915, 1.

27. *La Crosse Tribune*, October 5, 7, and 8, 1915, 1.

28. Walter I. Trattner, "Julia Grace Wales and the Wisconsin Plan for Peace," *Wisconsin Magazine of History*, 44 (Spring, 1961): 203–213; Mary Jo Deegan, ed., *Women at The Hague: Jane Addams, Emily G. Balch, Alice Hamilton* (Amherst, NY: Humanity Books, 2003), 40, 93.

29. US War Department, *Annual Reports, 1914*, vol. 1 (Washington, DC: US Government Printing Office, 1915), 7–9.

30. Roosevelt, *America and the World War*, 73.

31. Margulies, *Progressive Movement*, 195; Robert D. Ward, "The Origin and Activities of the National Security League, 1914–1919," *The Mississippi Valley Historical Review* 47, no. 1 (June 1960), 51.

32. Woodrow Wilson, An Annual Message to Congress, December 8, 1914, *The Papers of Woodrow Wilson*, vol. 31, September 6–December 31, 1914 (Princeton, NJ: Princeton University Press, 1979), 423; John Milton Cooper Jr., *Woodrow Wilson: A Biography* (New York: Alfred A. Knopf, 2009), 267–268.

33. Robert S. Maxwell, *Emanuel L. Philipp: Wisconsin Stalwart* (Madison: State Historical Society of Wisconsin, 1959), 90–110.

34. Ibid., 114–116.

35. Nesbit, *Wisconsin*, 442; Belle Case La Follette and Fola La Follette, *Robert M. La Follette* (New York: The Macmillan Company, 1953), 518–519, 575–576; Lawrence J. Martin, "Opposition to Conscription in Wisconsin, 1917–18" (master's thesis, University of Wisconsin, 1952), 9. See also *La Follette's Magazine*, May 1916, 1; and Margulies, *Progressive Movement*, 174–75.

36. *La Follette's Magazine*, August 1916, 4; October 1916, 1.

37. John J. Esch to Will Ott, February 16, 1917; Esch to J. E. Beimel, February 16, 1917; Esch to Schoengarth, February 29, 1916; Esch to Lorenz, March 6, 1916; Esch to Jacob Wohld, February 25, 1916; Esch to Frear, February 24, 1916; Esch Papers, boxes 36 and 41.

38. Esch to Jacob Wohld, February 25, 1916; Esch to Charles Franke (Mauston), March 8, 1916; Esch to Congressman Frear, February 24, 1916; Esch to James A. Stone (Reedsburg), January 8, 1916; Esch Papers. The quote is from Esch to John I. Ward (Commander, M. S. Casberg Camp 411, United Spanish War Veterans Dept. of Wis.—La Crosse), December 7, 1915, Esch Papers.

39. In general, see John Esch and Henry Cooper correspondence files for April 1916 in Esch Papers. H. H. Thomas (Baraboo) to Esch, January 3, 1916; Esch to H. H. Thomas, January 6, 1916; G. W. Dudley (Cashier, La Crosse County Bank in West Salem) to Esch, April 18, 1916; Oscar W. Schoengarth (Neillsville) to Esch, February 26, 1916; Esch to Frank H. Hanson (Mauston) April 19, 1916; Esch Papers, box 36; and Henry Allen Cooper Papers, box 2, WHS.

40. *Milwaukee Leader*, July 15, 1916, 1.

41. *Milwaukee Journal*, July 16, 1916, 1–2.

42. *Wisconsin State Journal*, January 4, 1917, editorial; February 1, 1917, 12; and February 4, 1917, 1 and 14.

43. La Follette and La Follette, *La Follette*, 595 and 616; *La Follette's Magazine*, March 1917, 1–4; Thomas W. Ryley, *A Little Group of Willful Men: A Study of Congressional–Presidential Authority* (Port Washington, NY: Kennikat Press, 1975), 94–131; Unger, *Bob La Follette*, 244–247.

44. Ryley, *Willful Men*, 125; Unger, *Bob La Follette*, 245; Cooper, *Wilson*, 379.

45. Ryley, *Willful Men*, 126–131; Unger, *Bob La Follette*, 244–248; Cooper, *Wilson*, 378–380.

46. John Milton Cooper Jr., "Progressivism and American Foreign Policy: A Reconsideration," *Mid-America* 51 (October, 1969): 271.

47. *Wisconsin State Journal*, March 6, 1917, and April 3, 1917, editorial.

48. *Monroe Evening Times*, March 31, 1917, 1.

49. Margulies, *Progressive Movement*, 177, 195–196, 200; Nesbit, *Wisconsin*, 445; *Monroe Evening Times*, March 12, 1917, 2; *Milwaukee Leader*, February 9, 1917, 1.

50. Lorin Lee Cary, "The Wisconsin Loyalty Legion, 1917–1918," *Wisconsin Magazine of History*, 53 (Autumn, 1969): 340; *La Crosse Tribune*, February 1, 1917, 3; George Moore Jr. (Janesville) to Cooper, February 20, 1917; C. G. Krueger (Wausau) to Cooper, March 23, 1917; Cooper Papers, January 1 to March 31, 1917. For cited records see box 3.

51. Esch to Will Ott, February 16, 1917; Esch to J. E. Beimel, February 16, 1917; William Vollmer (Mauston) to Esch, February 18, 1917; and Alfred James (Milwaukee) to Esch, February 17, 1917, Esch Papers, box 41; John S. Owen (Eau Clair) to Esch, February 28, 1916; L. R. Balch (Madison) to Esch, March 1, 1916; G. H. Lippert (Madison) to Esch, March 2, 1916; and Telegram for five citizens of Merrillan to Esch, March 16, 1916, Esch Papers, box 36.

52. N. B. Hood (Commander of G. A. R. Post 24, Spring Green) to Esch, March 14, 1917; W. F. McGillivray (Secretary of Black River Falls Commercial Club) to Esch, March 6, 1917; Will Esch (Lodi) to Esch, March 29, 1917; Esch Papers, box 41.

53. US Congress, *Congressional Record*, 55th Cong., 1st sess., 1917, vol. 55, pt. 1, 224–225; La Follette and La Follette, *La Follette*, 585.

54. *Milwaukee Leader*, February 2, 1917, 6.

55. Nesbit, *Wisconsin*, 441.

56. *La Crosse Tribune*, March 26, 1917, 1 and 6, and March 27, 1917, 1.

57. La Follette and La Follette, *La Follette*, 596.

58. Belle Case La Follette to My dear ones, March 24, 1917, La Follette Family Correspondence, series AA, box 20, Library of Congress.

59. *Wisconsin State Journal*, April 1, 1917, 1.

60. Woodrow Wilson, Address of the President of the United States delivered at a joint session of the two Houses of Congress, April 2, 1917, 7264 S.doc.5, volume 10.

61. *Congressional Record*, 65th Congress, 1st Session, April 4, 1917, vol 55, pt. 1, 223–305.

62. Ibid., April 5, 1917, 312–315.

63. Ibid., April 6, 1917, 412–413. The Senate had only 96 seats: 82 yes, 6 no, 8 not voting; the House had 435 seats: 373 yes, 50 no, 9 not voting, 3 seats empty.

Chapter 3

1. Fred L. Holmes, *Wisconsin's War Record* (Madison, WI: Capital Historical Publishing Co., 1919), 18–24; The Adjutant General of Wisconsin, *Biennial Report for the Two Fiscal Years Ending June 30, 1918* (Madison: WI: Democrat Printing Company, State Printer, 1918); Joint War History Commission of Michigan and Wisconsin, *The 32nd Division in the World War, 1917–1919* (Madison: Wisconsin War History Commission, 1920), 27–29; R. B. Pixley, *Wisconsin in the World War* (Milwaukee: Wisconsin War History Company, 1919), 9–39.

2. *La Crosse Tribune*, January 12 and 13, 1916, 1; January 13, 1916, 10; March 10, 1916, 1 and 3; and March 15, 1916; *Eau Claire Leader*, January 9, 1916, 1; March 10, 1916, 1; and June 20–21, 1916, 1; *Wisconsin State Journal*, January 12 and 13, 1916, 1; June 22–25, 1916, 1; and July 18, 1916, 1.

3. Adj. Gen. Orlando Holway to Major D. Co McArthur, telegram, June 19, 1916; Adj. Gen. to Daniel S. McArthur, February 15, 1913, Daniel S. MacArthur Papers, Wisconsin Historical Society, Madison (hereafter cited as WHS); *La Crosse Tribune*, June 19, 1916, 1 and 3; June 20, 1916, 1; and June 22, 1916, 1 and 3; John P. Finnegan, "Preparedness in Wisconsin: The National Guard and the Mexican Border Incident," *Wisconsin Magazine of History*, 47 (Spring, 1964): 209.

4. *Oshkosh Daily Northwestern*, June 30, 1916, 1. Also see *Eau Claire Leader*, June 22, 1916, 1. Newspapers throughout the state between June 19 and June 30, especially in cities with National Guard armories, are full of news about Mexico and National Guard mobilization.

5. Emory Rogers to Mrs. Wm. A. Bruce, transcribed postcard, June 23, 1916, William R. Bruce Papers, WHS.

6. Finnegan, "Preparedness in Wisconsin," 199–213; *Grand Rapids Tribune*, June 28, 1916, 3.

7. Finnegan, "Preparedness in Wisconsin," 199–213; The Adjutant General of Wisconsin, *Biennial Report for the Two Fiscal Years Ending June 30, 1916* (Madison: WI: Democrat Printing Company, State Printer, 1916).

8. William Bruce to Dear Mother, July 13, 1916, William A. Bruce Papers, WHS. For a full account of the trip, see letters from July 10 to July 14.

9. William Bruce (postmarked Taylor, Texas) to Dear Folks, July 14, 1916, Bruce Papers, WHS.

10. W. R. Bruce (San Antonio, Texas) to Mrs. Wm. A. Bruce (Appleton), July 16 and 23, 1916; Bruce Papers, WHS; Glenn Garlock to Dear Anna, July 14, 1916, Glenn Garlock Papers, US Army Heritage & Education Center, Carlisle, PA (hereafter cited as AHEC).

11. Glenn Garlock to Dear Sweetheart, July 27, 1916, Garlock Papers, AHEC; W. R. Bruce (San Antonio, Texas) to Mrs. Wm. A. Bruce (Appleton), July 16 and 23, 1916, Bruce Papers, WHS.

12. Glenn Garlock to Dear Anna, July 14 and August 4, 1916, Garlock Papers, AHEC.

13. Finnegan, "Preparedness in Wisconsin," 210–13; Esch to W. B. Tscharner (Minneapolis), August 5, 1916, Esch Papers, WHS; *La Crosse Tribune*, October 10, 1916, 1, and October 16, 1916, 3.

14. Glenn Garlock (Camp Wilson) to My Dear Sweetheart, October 29, 1916, Garlock Papers, AHEC.

15. Glenn Garlock (Camp Wilson) to Dear Sweetheart, October 24, 1916, Garlock Papers, AHEC.

16. Finnegan, "Preparedness in Wisconsin," 210–213; Robert S. Maxwell, *Emanuel L. Philipp: Wisconsin Stalwart* (Madison: State Historical Society of Wisconsin, 1959), 118–119.

17. See Garlock letters for November 12 through 29, 1916, Garlock Papers.

18. Glenn Garlock (Camp Wilson) to Dear Anna, November 15, 1916, Garlock Papers.

19. *La Crosse Tribune*, November 20, 1916, 3, and December 15, 1916, 1, 3, and 6.

20. *Sparta Herald*, December 19, 1916, 1–2; *Monroe Evening Times*, January 13–20, 1917.

21. *La Crosse Tribune*, November 20, 1916, 3, and September 30, 1916, 4; John S. Owen (Eau Claire) to Esch, March 20, 1916, Esch Papers, WHS; Glenn Garlock (Camp Wilson) to Dear Sweetheart, November 24, 1916, Garlock Papers, AHEC.

22. "Report of the Secretary of War," *War Department Annual Reports, 1914* (Washington: Government Printing Office, 1914), 1–14; Edward M. Coffman, *The War to End All Wars: The American Military Experience in World War I* (Madison: University of Wisconsin Press, 1986), 11–19; Mark Ethan Grotelueschen, *The AEF Way of War: The American Army and Combat in World War I* (Cambridge: Cambridge University Press, 2007), 10–14.

23. Maurice Prendergast, acting editor, *Jane's Fighting Ships 1917* (London: Sampson, Low, Marston &Co., Ltd, 1917), 4.

24. *Eau Claire Leader*, March 27, 1917, 1.

25. *Green Bay Press Gazette*, April 4, 1917, 1; April 18, 1917, 4; and June 16, 1917, 1.

26. Thomas A. Britten, *American Indians in World War I: At Home and at War* (Albuquerque: University of New Mexico Press, 1997), 28–50.

27. Coffman, *War to End All Wars*, 70–71.

28. *Wisconsin Weekly Blade*, October 25, 1917, 2; and November 1, 1917, 1, 2, and 4.

29. The War Department training estimate was reported in the *Wisconsin State Journal* for May 18, 1917, 1. Material for this section came primarily from the April 6 and 7, 1917, editions of the following newspapers: *Ashland Daily Press, Eau Claire Leader, Green Bay Press Gazette, Janesville Daily Gazette, La Crosse Tribune and Leader-Press, Wisconsin State Journal (Madison), Milwaukee Journal, Milwaukee Sentinel, Oshkosh Daily Northwestern, Platteville, Racine Journal-News, Sheboygan Press, Stevens Point Journal, Superior Telegram*. Also see *Wisconsin State Journal*, May 18, 1917, 1, and *Stevens Point Journal*, April 14, 1917.

30. Joint War History Commission, *32nd Division in the World War*, 27–29; Fred L. Holmes, *Wisconsin's War Record* (Madison, WI: Capital Historical Publishing Co., 1919), 18–24; Pixley, *Wisconsin in the World War*, 9–39.

31. *La Crosse Tribune*, August 3, 1917, 1; May 5, 1918, 1; August 20, 1918, 1; and

June 5, 1917, 1. See a speech titled "Welcome to Our Returned Soldiers," October 1919, by John E. McConnell, John E. McConnell Papers, WHS.

32. *Milwaukee Journal*, March 25, 1917, 15.

33. Commanding General, 32nd Division, N. G. to Colonel T. Q. Donaldson, Inspector General, memo, December 9, 1917, on the subject Merit of training system, found in notebook titled "Diary of Major Gen. William G. Haan, Commanding General, 32nd Division," 53–59, Edward T. Lauer Papers, 32nd Division Survey files, AHEC; "Training Report: 32nd Division National Guard," December 15, 1917, Haan Diary, 60–64, Lauer Papers, 32nd Division Survey files, AHEC; Grotelueschen, *The AEF Way of War*, 10–14.

34. Glenn Garlock to Dear Anna, November 16, 1917; Glenn Garlock to Dear Wife, December 28, 1918; and Lt. Col. G. W. Garlock to Eda Landgraf, January 11, 1918, Garlock Papers, AHEC; Samuel M. Kent Diary entries for December 26, 1917, to March 10, 1918, AHEC.

35. Garlock Diary, December 7, 1917, Garlock Papers, AHEC.

36. Garlock Diary, December 11, 1917, and February 7, 1918, Garlock Papers, AHEC; Gaylord Bradley Diary, February 7, 1918, Gaylord Bradley Papers, WHS; Bruce letters to Mrs. W. A. Bruce for February 3 and 8, 1918, Bruce Papers, WHS.

37. Coffman, *The War to End All Wars*, 226–231.

38. Kent Diary, April 6–12, 1918, AHEC; Walter Zukowski, "Memoirs of Sergeant 'Zuki,'" 26–27, unpublished memoir, World War I Veterans Survey, 32nd Division, 107th Ammunition Train, Company G., File 4419, AHEC.

39. Bradley Diary, February 10–March 4, 1918, WHS.

40. Glenn Garlock to Anna, February 21, 1918, Garlock Papers, AHEC.

41. Bradley Diary, March 12 and 25, 1918, WHS; Glenn to Anna, March 13 and 29, 1918, Garlock Papers, AHEC.

42. Bradley Diary, March 9 through March 30, 1918, WHS.

43. Zukowski memoir, February 26–June 8, 1918, 29, AHEC.

44. Walter Zukowski to Dear Brother, April 18, 1918, "Somewhere in France," World War I Veterans Survey, 32nd Division, 107th Ammunition Train, Company G., File 4419, AHEC.

45. Glenn Garlock to Dear Anna, March 4, 1918, Garlock Papers, AHEC; Joint War History Commission, *32nd Division in the World War*, 34–36; John W. Barry, *The Midwest Goes to War: The 32nd Division in the Great War*

(Lanham, MD: Scarecrow Press, 2007), 30–34; Kent Diary, April 29–30, 1918, AHEC.

46. Kent Diary, June 12–30, 1918, AHEC; Barry, *The Midwest Goes to War*, 30–45; Joint War History Commission, *32nd Division in the World War*, 141. The casualties included the following: 56 killed in action or died of wounds, 25 died of other causes, 8 were missing or captured, 82 were severely wounded or gassed, 39 were injured due to other causes, for 210 permanent losses. Another 215 were slightly wounded or gassed, while 5 were undetermined as to severity, for 220 likely to return to service.

47. Kent Diary, July 30–August 4, 1918, AHEC. Also see the Bradley diary, Zukowski memoir, and Garlock letters for the same period.

48. *La Crosse Tribune and Leader Press*, August 27, 1918, 2; *Grand Rapids Tribune*, June 12, 1919, 10; *La Crosse Tribune and Leader Press*, October 20, 1918, 11.

49. Joint War History Commission, *32nd Division in the World War*, 67.

50. Ibid., 70–71; "32nd Division Historical Chart," ibid., 141.

51. Ibid., 70–71.

52. Ibid., 74.

53. Ibid., 77–85; Barry, *The Midwest Goes to War*, 73–88.

54. *Wisconsin State Journal*, September 8, 1918, 1.

55. Barry, *The Midwest Goes to War*, 118; Garlock Diary, November 11, 1918, AHEC; Joint War History Commissions, *32nd Division in the World War*.

56. Joint War History Commissions, *32nd Division in the World War*, 141; Holmes, *Wisconsin's War Record*, 19; Clark, George B., *The American Expeditionary Force in World War I: A Statistical History, 1917–1919* (Jefferson, NC: McFarland & Company, Inc., 2013), 47–56; Coffman, *War to End All Wars*, 127–128 and 177–182.

57. Garlock to Anna (presumably, first page missing), ca. late August or early September 1918, Garlock Papers, AHEC.

58. Garlock to Anna, September 1, 1918, Garlock Papers, AHEC.

Chapter 4

1. John Esch (Washington, DC) to My Dear Anna (La Crosse), April 8, 1917, Personal letters written by John J. Esch to his wife Anna, 1913–1922, John J. Esch Papers, Wisconsin Historical Society, Madison (hereafter cited as WHS).

2. H. C. Peterson, *Propaganda for War* (Norman: University of Oklahoma Press, 1939), 12–32 and 323–324.

3. George Creel, *How We Advertised America* (New York: repr., Arno Press, Inc., 1972 [1920]), 84–98; Ellen Axelrod, *Selling the Great War: The Making of American Propaganda* (New York: Macmillan, 2009); James R. Mock and Cedric Larson, *Words That Won the War: The Story of the Committee on Public Information, 1917–1919* (Princeton, NJ: Princeton University Press, 1939), 112–130; A. Scott Berg, *Wilson* (New York: G.P. Putnam's Sons, 2013), 449–456; *The Wisconsin Blue Book, 1919*, Paul F. Hunter, ed. (Madison: Democrat Printing Company, State Printer, 1919), 415–416.

4. Paul W. Glad, *War, a New Era, and Depression, 1914–1940*, vol. 5 in *The History of Wisconsin* (Madison: State Historical Society of Wisconsin, 1990), 22–24.

5. See *La Crosse Tribune*, *Wisconsin State Journal*, *Green Bay Press Gazette*, and *Eau Claire Leader* for April 6 and 7, 1917.

6. *Monroe Evening Times*, April 6, 1917, 1; March 31, 1917, 4; and April 4, 1917, 1.

7. *Janesville Daily Gazette*, April 6, 1917.

8. *Eau Claire Leader*, April 6 and 7, 1917.

9. See the folder for April 19 to April 30, 1917, in the Esch Papers, WHS, for a general view of opinions received by Congressman Esch. Twenty-three constituents wrote patriotic or prowar letters and four wrote antiwar letters during this period. For quote see: George W. Andrews (Baraboo), April 27, 1917. Also see W. H. McFetridge (Baraboo), April 19, 1917; Esch to W. H. McFetridge (Reedsburg), telegram, April 26, 1917; Philip Lehner (Princeton, Wisconsin) to Esch, April 20, 1917; Esch to Philip Lehner, April 25, 1917; and William Esch (Lodi) to John Esch, April 21, 1917, Esch Papers, box 41.

10. *La Follette's Magazine*, May 1917, 2; June 1917, 1–3; March 1918, 2; and January 1918, 11 and 16; Lawrence J. Martin, "Opposition to Conscription in Wisconsin, 1917–1918" (master's thesis, University of Wisconsin, 1952), 15; Belle Case La Follette and Fola La Follette, *Robert M. La Follette* (New York: Macmillan Company, 1953), 2:731–737, 756, 785, 789; Nancy C. Unger, *Fighting Bob La Follette: The Righteous Reformer* (Chapel Hill: University of North Carolina Press, 2000), 250–254.

11. *Monroe Evening Times*, April 6, 1917, 1.

12. *La Crosse Tribune*, April 22, 1917, 1 and 3; quoted in John Gurda, *The Making of Milwaukee* (Milwaukee, WI: Milwaukee County Historical Society, 2006), 223.

13. George B. Clark, *The American Expeditionary Force in World War I: A Statistical History, 1917–1919* (Jefferson, NC: McFarland & Company, 2013), 54–56; Edward M. Coffman, *The War to End All Wars: The American Military Experience in World War I* (Madison: University of Wisconsin Press, 1986), 212–215 and 363; David R. Woodward, *The American Army and the First World War* (New York: Cambridge University Press, 2014), 176–177 and 200–232.

14. *Green Bay Press Gazette*, May 4, 1917, 6.

15. Ibid., April 16, 1917, 3.

16. *Wisconsin State Journal*, May 18, 1917, 1, 2, 4.

17. William Clinton Mullendore, *History of the United States Food Administration, 1917–1919* (Redwood City, CA: Stanford University Press, 1941), 70–87.

18. *Green Bay Press Gazette*, May 24, 1917, 9.

19. George H. Nash, *The Life of Herbert Hoover: Humanitarian, 1914–1917* (New York: W. W. Norton & Company, 1988), 341–361; David Hinshaw, *Herbert Hoover: American Quaker* (New York: Farrar, Straus and Company, 1950), 88–105.

20. *New York Times*, April 12, 1917, 1 and 2.

21. *Green Bay Press Gazette*, July 19, 1917, 5.

22. A. H. Melville (secretary) to W. S. Gifford (director, Council of National Defense), June 28, 1917, Wisconsin State Council of Defense, general correspondence, series 1642, box 15, Deliveries folders, WHS (hereafter cited as WCD, WHS).

23. R. B. Pixley, *Wisconsin in the World War* (Milwaukee: Wisconsin War History Co., 1919), 211; *La Cross Tribune*, October 28, 1917, 1, and October 31, 1917, 6; *Oshkosh Daily Northwestern*, October 31, 1917, 3; *Sheboygan Press*, October 30, 1917, 1; Phoebe M. C. C. Ayer, Untitled report on Hoover food pledge drive, June 1, 1918, Dane County Council of Defense, Dane Series 151, box 1, WHS.

24. *La Cross Tribune*, September 1, 1917, 3.

25. Mullendore, *Food Administration*, 86–87.

26. *Green Bay Press Gazette*, January 21, 1918, 8, and February 6, 1918, 8; Mullendore, *Food Administration*, 103–120.

27. *La Crosse Leader*, September 1, 1917, 3.

28. Mullendore, *Food Administration*, 52–53; *La Crosse Tribune*, October 10, 1917, 6; December 20, 1917, 2; June 25, 1918, 6; and August 20, 1918, 6.

29. Mullendore, *Food Administration*, 318–322.

30. *Green Bay Press Gazette*, April 18, 1917, 1 and 5; April 24, 1917, 1–2; and April 28, 1917, 1–2; *Eau Claire Leader*, July 19, 1917, 3.

31. Pixley, *Wisconsin in the World War*, 357–360; Fred L. Holmes, *Wisconsin's War Record* (Madison, WI: Capital Historical Pub., 1919), 137–138. We have chosen to be conservative in our estimates of production growth. For unknown reasons, these authors do not agree on production figures for 1918. Holmes compares 1918 with 1916, which overestimates the growth in potato production because 1916 was a very poor year. Pixley compares 1918 with a five-year average, 1911–1916. By smoothing out the anomalies, this method produces a more conservative and, in our judgment, more reliable result.

32. Mullendore, *Food Administration*, 103.

33. *Eau Claire Leader*, July 19, 1917, 5. The article is a review of activity originally printed in "Forward," a weekly newsletter of the State Council of Defense.

34. *Green Bay Press Gazette*, August 10, 1917, 4, and October 17, 1917, 1.

35. *Wisconsin State Journal*, April 1, 1918, 5; February 22, 1918, 4; *Janesville Daily Gazette*, March 23, 1918, 1; *Eau Claire Leader*, March 22, 1918, 10; *Green Bay Press Gazette*, March 1, 1918, 4; March 23, 1918, 3; and April 4, 1918, 4.

36. Mullendore, *Food Administration*, 229–232; Pixley, *Wisconsin in the World War*, 99–100, 213–214.

37. *Green Bay Press Gazette*, April 1, 1918, 9; April 4, 1918, 4; May 3, 1918, 13; May 4, 1918, 4; May 9, 1918, 4; May 29, 1918, 3; and June 3, 1918, 4.

38. Pixley, *Wisconsin in the World War*, 357–360.

39. *Green Bay Press Gazette*, July 16, 1918, 1; October 23, 1917, 3; and March 25, 1918, 4; *La Crosse Tribune*, April 5, 1917, 1, and April 10, 1917, 1 and 6.

40. *Green Bay Press Gazette*, September 22, 1917, 3; and April 27, 1918, 7 and 8.

41. Quote from *Milwaukee Journal*, March 11, 1917, 9. Also see *Green Bay Press Gazette*, April 2, 1917, 5; April 12, 1917, 6; April 23, 1917, 5; April 25, 1917, 8; May 25, 1917, 9; September 22, 1917, 3; October 4, 1917, 1.

42. *Madison Capital Times*, February 9, 1918, 7; *Sheboygan Press*, February 9, 1918, 8.

43. *Green Bay Press Gazette*, October 19, 1917.

44. Coal and Transportation section, including the telegram from La Farge, based on the January 1918 correspondence of Emanuel Philipp, Emanuel Philipp Papers, box 5, WHS. Also see: *Green Bay Press Gazette*, August 18, 1917, 4; October 19, 1917, 1; and October 22, 1917, 10; Robert S. Maxwell, *Emanuel L. Philipp: Wisconsin Stalwart* (Madison: State Historical Society of Wisconsin, 1959), 145–148; Pixley; *Wisconsin in the World War*, 231; Holmes, *Wisconsin's War Record*, 149.

45. *Wisconsin State Journal*, December 12, 1917, 1; *Racine Journal-News*, December 15, 1917, 1; *Manitowoc Daily Herald*, December 19, 1917, 1; *La Crosse Telegram and Leader Press*, December 17, 1917, 1; Maxwell, *Philipp*, 145–148.

46. *Milwaukee Journal*, January 17 and 18, 1918, 1; *Wisconsin State Journal*, January 18, 1918, 1; *Green Bay Press Gazette*, January 18, 1918, 1; January 19, 1918, 1 and 8; January 21, 1918, 5; and January 22, 1918, 1 and 8.

47. *Green Bay Press Gazette*, January 28, 1918, 8, and February 19, 1918, 4.

48. *Green Bay Press Gazette*, April 28, 1917, 1, 5, and 8; April 24, 1917, 6; and April 25, 1917, 2; *Eau Claire Leader*, April 28, 1917, 6; May 2, 1917, 2; and January 31, 1918, 6; *The New North*, March 28, 1918, 7, and April 4, 1918, 1; *New York Times*, February 1, 1917, 7.

49. Henry A. Burd (executive secretary) to W. S. Gifford (director, Council of National Defense), July 17, 1917, WCD, WHS.

50. Anna Howard Shar to the State Chairmen, July 30, 1917, WCD, WHS.

51. Henry A. Burd to Council of National Defense, att. Melvin T. Copeland, December 10, 1917, WCD, WHS.

52. Quote from Henry A. Burd (assistant secretary) to C. E. Mullen, March 27, 1918, WCD, WHS. See folders on deliveries for other examples.

53. Secretary, Commercial Economy Board (Melvin Copeland) to Major Roy C. Vandercook, War Preparedness Board, September 24, 1917. Also see: Burd to Copeland, September 10, 1917; Copeland to Melville, September 24, 1917; and Burd to Copeland, December 10, 1917, folder 2, WCD, WHS.

54. US Treasury Department, *Annual Report, 1917* (Washington, DC: Government Printing Office, 1918), 1; McAdoo quoted in Charles Gilbert, *American Financing of World War I* (Westport, CT: Greenwood Publishing, 1970), 118, also see 117–144.

55. We have focused on the section of Wisconsin supervised by Frank Hixon because the survival of Hixon's correspondence provides the source material needed for an intimate look at management of the Liberty Loan campaigns. Frank P. Hixon to William B. Banks (Superior), May 14, 1917; Hixon to George C. Hixon (Chicago), May 19, 1917; Hixon to William B. Banks, May 19, 1917; Hixon to John H. Rich (Minneapolis), May 26, 1917; Hixon to Curtis Mosher (Minneapolis), May 10, 1917, and May 14, 1917; Hixon to G. W. Burton (La Crosse), May 11, 1917; Hixon and Company Papers, WHS; *La Crosse Tribune*, June 10, 1917, 1, and June 15, 1917, 1.

56. Melville to Ibach, October 24, 1917, folder 5, disloyalty—re Liberty Loan, WCD, WHS.

57. Hixon to John H. Rich (Minneapolis), May 28, 1917; N. D. Iden to Hixon (San Francisco), June 1, 1917; Hixon to E. L. Philipp, October 4, 1917; Philipp to Hixon, October 27, 1917; Hixon to E. L. Philipp, October 17 and 24, 1917; Hixon Papers, WHS.

58. Hixon to Charles A. Taylor (Barron), May 15, 1917, and Hixon to Wm. Irvine (Chippewa Falls), May 25, 1917, Hixon Papers, WHS.

59. *Green Bay Press Gazette*, September 23, 1918, 1.

60. Creel, *How We Advertised America*, 133–141; Mock and Larson, *Words That Won the War*, 101–108.

61. Creel, *How We Advertised America*, 84–98; Mock and Larson, *Words That Won the War*, 113–130.

62. *La Crosse Tribune*, April 25, 1918, 1.

63. *Green Bay Press Gazette*, May 25, 1917, 1 and 7.

64. Hixon to James T. Baker (Eau Claire), January 19, 1918; Hixon to H. P. Keith, January 31, 1918; Hixon to Walter E. Sprecher, April 2, 1918; Wm. B. Banks to J. M. McCabe (Douglas County), August 21, 1918; Geo. Bubar to Dear Sir, September 11, 1918; Hixon Papers, WHS.

65. *Green Bay Press Gazette*, October 9, 1918, 3, and October 30, 1918, 4.

66. *La Crosse Tribune*, November 15, 1917, 1; November 20, 1917, 1; November 25, 1917, 1; December 5, 1917, 1; December 15, 1917, 1; December 20, 1917, 6; October 15, 1918, 1; and October 20, 1918, 1.

67. Articles about the Red Cross seem to have appeared almost daily in newspapers of the state. These articles regularly recounted the good work the organization was doing and the need for funds. As an example see page 3 of the *Green Bay Press Gazette* for October 12, 16, and 18, 1917.

68. *Green Bay Press Gazette*, May 16, 1918, 1; May 28, 1918, 1; and August 7, 1918, 4.

69. Any individual living in the United States but born in another country and never having achieved US citizenship, was an "alien." An alien whose native land was at war with the United States was considered an "enemy alien."

70. *Green Bay Press Gazette*, June 1, 1918, 4.

71. Coffman, *War to End All Wars*, 124–128; Woodward, *American Army*, 134–171.

72. As quoted in Coffman, *War to End All Wars*, 20.

73. Coffman, *War to End All Wars*, 20–42.

74. Still, *Milwaukee*, 476–497; Gurda, *Making of Milwaukee*, 222–224.

75. *Green Bay Press Gazette*, October 24, 18, 3.

76. Coffman, *War to End All Wars*, 115–116; *Green Bay Press Gazette*, September 25, 1917, 10. Tim Colton maintains a series of detailed tables documenting ships built in US shipyards. See www.shipbuildinghistory.com.

77. Bill Jackson, "Harley-Davidson and the U.S. Military," https://www
.harley-davidson.com/content/dam/h-d/documents/communities/
veterans-military/military-history/H-D_History_H-D_And_The_Military
.pdf; "Military Metal," http://www.harley-davidson.com/content/dam/
h-d/documents/communities/veterans-military/military-history/H-D_
History_Military_Metal.pdf.

78. *Green Bay Press Gazette*, October 1, 1917, 3; September 10, 1918, 1; and October 2, 1918, 1.

79. Lars Larson, *Chequamegon Bay and Its Communities* (Whitewater, WI: L. Larson, 2005–2008), 268–328.

80. *Green Bay Press Gazette*, April 15, 1917, 5; April 25, 1917, 7; September 11, 1917, 1 and 10; September 12, 1917, 4; October 18, 1917, 1; November 15, 1917, 10.

81. *Green Bay Press Gazette*, May 23, 1918, 1 and 2; September 12, 1918, 3; July 1, 1918, 4; July 30, 1918, 2; and March 19, 1918, 12. The description of the law is from *Green Bay Press Gazette*, July 14, 1917, 10.

82. US Women's Bureau, *The New Position of Women in American Industry* (Washington: Government Printing Office, 1920), 13–35.

83. Mary P. Morgan to Louise Peters, April 16, 1918; Wisconsin Council of Defense, Women's Committee Records, series 1649, box 11, WHS.

84. Nellie Kedzie Jones to Mrs. Morgan, August 9, 1918; and Mary P. Morgan

to Mrs. Edward P. Davis, August 24, 1918, Women's Committee Records, series 1649, box 11, WHS.

85. Untitled report evaluating the State Fair Land Army course, almost certainly by Nellie Kedzie Jones, ca. late September, 1918.

86. *Green Bay Press Gazette*, October 31, 1918, 2.

87. Steven Burg, "Wisconsin and the Great Spanish Flu Epidemic of 1918," *Wisconsin Magazine of History*, 84 (Autumn 2000), 36–56. We have relied heavily on this excellent study of the flu epidemic; quotes are as quoted by Burg on pages 45–47.

Chapter 5

1. As quoted in John Milton Cooper Jr., *Woodrow Wilson: A Biography* (New York: Alfred A. Knopf, 2009), 375.

2. *Sunday State Journal*, April 8, 1917, 1.

3. As quoted in Paul W. Glad, *War, a New Era, and Depression, 1914–1940*, vol. 5 in *The History of Wisconsin* (Madison: State Historical Society of Wisconsin, 1990), 96. Also see Glad, *War and Depression*, 88–98; *Green Bay Press Gazette*, March 30, 1918; July 2, 1918, 7; and March 15, 1918, 12.

4. *Monroe Evening Times*, April 6, 1917, 1.

5. Oscar Ameringer, *If You Don't Weaken* (New York: Greenwood Press, 1969), 330–334.

6. William Esch (Lodi) to John J. Esch, April 21, 1917; William Esch to John Esch, April 20, 1917; John J. Esch Papers, box 4, Wisconsin Historical Society, Madison (hereafter cited as WHS).

7. Frank H. Blodgett (Janesville) to Henry Cooper, April 26, 1917, Henry Cooper Papers, box 3, WHS.

8. H. O. Peterson and Gilbert C. Fite, *Opponents of War, 1917–1918* (Madison: University of Wisconsin Press, 1957), 19; Ernest Meyer, *"Hey! Yellowbacks!"* (New York: The John Day Company, 1930), 12, 18. See also *Milwaukee Leader*, July 2, 1917, and July 25, 1917.

9. *Milwaukee Journal*, April 27, 1917, 2 and 4; *The Wisconsin Blue Book, 1919*, Paul F. Hunter, ed. (Madison: Democrat Printing Company, State Printer, 1919), 464.

10. These stories appeared in the *Green Bay Press Gazette*, June 9, 1917; May 30, 1917; and May 10, 1918. Similar stories can be found in most Wisconsin newspapers during the World War I period.

11. *Green Bay Press Gazette*, January 9, 1918, 8.

12. Zechariah Chafee Jr., *Freedom of Speech* (New York: Harcourt, Brace and Howe, 1920), 40–43 and 395–397; John Dean Stevens, "Suppression of Expression in Wisconsin During World War I" (PhD diss., University of Wisconsin, 1967), 78.

13. Register of Members, 1918–1919, vols. 1 and 2, American Protective League, Record Group 65, National Archives.

14. As quoted in William H. Thomas Jr., *Unsafe for Democracy: World War I and the U.S. Justice Department's Covert Campaign to Suppress Dissent* (Madison: University of Wisconsin Press, 2008), 129–130.

15. Jerry Buss, *A War of Their Own* (Oregon, WI: Badger Books, 1998). My brief retelling of the Krueger story is based on this comprehensive study of the Krueger affair and the Krueger file 248898, Bureau of Investigation Case Files, 1908–1922, RG 65, National Archives.

16. Robert S. Maxwell, *Emanuel L. Philipp, Wisconsin Stalwart* (Madison: State Historical Society of Wisconsin, 1959), 140–141; Fred L. Holmes, *Wisconsin's War Record* (Madison, WI: Capital Historical Pub., 1919), 75–80.

17. Glad, *War and Depression*, 26–29.

18. *Milwaukee Journal*, March 17, 1917, 1; March 18, 1917, part 1, p. 1, and part 2, pp. 2 and 3; *Ludington Daily News*, May 17, 1917, 7. Also see Glad, *War and Depression*, 25–26.

19. As quoted in Maxwell, *Philipp*, 133–134; Holmes, *Wisconsin's War Record*, 18–22.

20. Holmes, *Wisconsin's War Record*, 13–17; R. B. Pixley, *Wisconsin in the World War* (Milwaukee: Wisconsin War History Co., 1919), 9–13; Cooper, *Wilson*, 393–397; A. Scott Berg, *Wilson* (New York: GP Putnam's Sons, 2013), 457–460; Maxwell, *Philipp*, 132–138; *Janesville Gazette*, May 18, 1917.

21. Glad, *War and Depression*, 32–42.

22. Richard Lloyd Jones to Dear Carl, November 23, 1917; *Daily Cardinal*, November 23, 1917, 1 and 4; *Wisconsin State Journal*, undated, probably November 22, 1917, p. 1; all items located in Carl Schurz Vrooman Papers, box 10, Special File, Wisconsin Matter, 1917, Library of Congress; Merle Curti and Vernon Carstensen, *The University of Wisconsin: A History*, vol. 2 (Madison: University of Wisconsin Press, 1949), 116–117.

23. *Wisconsin State Journal*, April 7, 1918, 1–2; *New York Tribune*, April 17,

1918, 18; *Madison Capital Times*, April 26, 1918, 1 and 9; Peterson and Fite, *Opponents of War*, 107–108; Curti and Carstensen, *University of Wisconsin*, 117–121.

24. Emanuel Philipp, Untitled speech, ca. late fall 1917, Speech file, Emanuel Philipp Papers, box 18, folder 14, WHS.

25. *Chicago Herald and Examiner*, May 12, 1918, 6.

26. Maxwell, *Philipp*, 140.

27. "Address of Senator Roy P. Wilcox of Eau Claire, Wisconsin Closing the debate in favor of the adoption of the Wilcox Amendment to the Loyalty Resolution," delivered in the Wisconsin State Senate, February 25, 1918, printed and distributed by the Wisconsin Loyalty Legion, Roy Wilcox Papers, box 7, folder 3, WHS.

28. *Wisconsin State Journal*, February 25, 1918, 1, and March 6, 1918, 1; *Madison Capital Times*, March 5 and 6, 1918, 1 and 2; Maxwell, *Philipp*, 159–161.

29. Roy P. Wilcox speech, Half Moon Lake Island, Eau Claire, Wisconsin, July 4, 1917, Wilcox Papers, box 7, folder 2, WHS.

30. Maxwell, *Philipp*, 155–159; *Wisconsin State Journal*, February 24, 1918, 1 and 2; March 7, 1918, 1; and August 9, 1918, 2; *Madison Capital Times*, March 5, 1918, 1; and March 6, 1918, 1 and 2.

31. Emanuel Philipp speech, Marshall, Wisconsin, June 27, 1918; *Wisconsin State Journal*, June 28, 1918; Maxwell, *Philipp*, 169–180.

32. Opening speech of Senator Roy P. Wilcox on his campaign for governor, Menomonie, Wisconsin, July 12, 1918, Wilcox Papers, box 7, folder 2, WHS.

33. Out of 188,145 Republican votes, Philipp received 38 percent, Wilcox 37.8 percent, and Tittemore 24.1 percent; *Wisconsin Blue Book*, 1919, 93; Maxwell, *Philipp*, 176–178.

34. Emanuel Philipp speech fragment, no date, Philipp Papers, box 18, folder 14, WHS.

35. Campaign speech delivered by Emanuel Philipp in Waukesha on August 6, 1918, Philipp Papers, box 18, folder 14, WHS. "American ring" likely refers to violations of the Espionage Act; "racial lines" should be read as ethnic heritage; "minority party" would have included both the Democrats and the Socialists.

36. The best documentation of the Knights of Liberty is in a set of newspaper transcriptions created by the governor's office, Emanuel Philipp Papers, box 18, folder 14, WHS. See *Ashland Daily Press*, April 20, 1918, 1 for quoted Knights of Liberty letter. Also see, *Wisconsin State Journal*, April 27, 1918, 1.

37. The articles cited here are from the *Green Bay Press Gazette*, but similar articles would have appeared in newspapers across the state. See the *Press Gazette* for April 6, 1918, 4; April 12, 1918, 4; May 9, 1918, 2; May 16, 1918, 1; June 3, 1918, 1; June 8, 1918, 2; June 14, 1918, 8; July 3, 1918, 2; July 4, 1918, 5; and July 9, 1918, 6. Also see *Racine Daily News*, July 27, 1918, 1.

38. *Madison Capital Times*, July 26, 1918, 1 and 2, Wisconsin newspaper transcriptions, Philipp Papers, box 18, folder 14, WHS.

39. *Wisconsin Weekly Blade*, August 29, 1918, 1–2.

40. Floyd Stachowski, "The Political Career of Daniel Webster Hoan" (PhD diss., Northwestern University, 1966), 67.

41. Daniel Hoan to W. Rufus Abbott, May 19, 1916; Agnes S. Hibbard (General Secretary of the Chicago Preparedness Parade Committee) to Hoan, May 19, 1916; J. F. Hubbard (New York—Secretary of the American Defense League, Inc.) to Hoan, May 16, 1916; George R. Lunn to Hoan, June 29, 1916, including a newspaper clipping and typescript statement to the press outlining Hoan's position; M. C. Potter to Hoan, July 6, 1916; Hoan to Potter, July 8, 1916; manuscript by Osmore R. Smith explaining Hoan's participation in the National Civic Demonstration, ca. July 16 to 30, 1916; and Hoan to I. W. Irving, January 18, 1917, box 38, file 146, Daniel W. Hoan Papers, Milwaukee County Historical Society, Milwaukee, WI; Herbert F. Margulies, *The Decline of the Progressive Movement in Wisconsin, 1890–1920* (Madison: State Historical Society of Wisconsin, 1968), 197; Frederick I. Olson, "Milwaukee Socialists" (PhD diss., Harvard University, 1952), 341–342.

42. See coverage of the parade in the *Milwaukee Journal*, *Milwaukee Leader*, and *Milwaukee Sentinel* for July 10 through 18, 1916.

43. Olson, "Milwaukee Socialists," 342.

44. Ibid., 341–347; *Milwaukee Leader*, January 4, 1918, p.1.

45. Stachowski, "Hoan," 73–74.

46. *Milwaukee Leader*, April 30, 1917, 1; Olson, "Milwaukee Socialists," 345–347.

47. Olson, "Milwaukee Socialists," 347–348; *Milwaukee Leader*, August 31, 1917, 1.

48. *Madison Capital Times*, March 21, 1918, 1; *Grand Rapids Daily Leader*, March 23, 1918, 5; Stachowski, "Hoan," 79–83.

49. Edward J. Muzik, "Victor L. Berger, A Biography" (PhD diss., Northwestern University, 1960), 293; Olson, "Milwaukee Socialists," 355 and 380; Glad, *War and Depression*, 44–54.

50. Victor Berger (St. Louis) to Meta Berger, April 7, 1917, in *The Family Letters of Victor and Meta Berger: 1894–1929*, ed. Michael E. Stevens (Madison: State Historical Society of Wisconsin, 1995), 205.

51. Olson, "Milwaukee Socialists," 359; *Kenosha Evening Times*, August 6, 1917, 1, and September 9, 1917, 1; Stevens, "Suppression of Expression," 249; *Milwaukee Leader*, June 20, 1917, 6, and March 29, 1918, 2; Karen Falk, "Public Opinion in Wisconsin During World War I," *Wisconsin Magazine of History*, 25 (June 1942), 403; Olson, "Milwaukee Socialists," 359; Ameringer, *If You Don't Weaken*, 339–340.

52. *Milwaukee Leader*, May 12, 1917, 6; June 20, 1917, 6; April 28 and 30, 1917, 6.

53. *Milwaukee Journal*, August 17, 1918, 1; Muzik, "Victor Berger," 280–291; Sally M. Miller, *Victor Berger and the Promise of Constructive Socialism, 1910–1920* (Westport, CT: Greenwood Press, 1973), 191–202; Ameringer, *If You Don't Weaken*, 317.

54. *Madison Capital Times*, advertisement, March 14, 1918, 4.

55. Waldemar Ager to James Thompson, May 8, 1918, James Thompson Papers, box 1, WHS; Herbert F. Margulies, *The Decline of the Progressive Movement in Wisconsin, 1890–1920* (Madison: State Historical Society of Wisconsin, 1968), 223–230; *La Follette's Magazine*, March 1918, 2.

56. Thompson campaign platform; La Follette to Dear Friend, March 13, 1918; James Thompson to George Thompson, March 26, 1918, Thompson Papers, box 1, WHS; Henry A. Huber to Fred Huber, March 14, 1918, Henry A. Huber Papers, WHS.

57. *Wisconsin State Journal*, March 27, 1918, 1 and 4; and April 1, 1918, 12.

58. *Milwaukee Leader*, March 28, 1918, 1; Muzik, "Victor Berger," 288.

59. *Wisconsin Blue Book*, 1919, 46.

60. *Wisconsin State Journal*, April 3, 1918, 1.

61. *Milwaukee Leader*, March 30, 1918, 11; Muzik, "Victor Berger," 289; Glad, *War and Depression*, 46–50.

62. Quote from Berger file 3341, Bureau of Investigation Case Files, 1908–1922, RG 65, National Archives.

63. Olson, "Milwaukee Socialists," 363 and 378; Ameringer, *If You Don't Weaken*, 338.

64. Letters between Victor and Meta Berger and from Meta to Doris and Elsa (daughters) between March 9 and October 19, 1918, in *The Family Letters of Victor and Meta Berger, 1894–1929*, ed. Michael E. Stevens (Madison: State Historical Society of Wisconsin, 1995), 178–179, 237–245; Muzik, "Victor Berger," 289; Ameringer, *If You Don't Weaken*, 340–341; *Janesville Daily Gazette*, January 31, 1923.

65. *Wisconsin Blue Book*, 1919, 155; Muzik, "Victor Berger," 293.

66. *La Follette's Magazine*, March 1918, 2, and January 1918, 16.

67. *La Follette's Magazine*, June 1917, 1–3, and January 1918, 11; Belle Case La Follette and Fola La Follette, *Robert M. La Follette* (New York: The Macmillan Company, 1953), 785.

68. Lawrence J. Martin, "Opposition to Conscription in Wisconsin, 1917–1918" (master's thesis, University of Wisconsin, 1952), 15; *La Follette's Magazine*, May 1917, 1–2; August 1917, 1; December 1917, 1–2; February 1918, 1–2, La Follette and La Follette, *La Follette*, 731–756; Robert M. La Follette, Untitled speech/article, ca. 1917, La Follette Family Papers, Box I:B 220, Speeches and Writings, Library of Congress.

69. La Follette and La Follette, *La Follette*, 756 and 789.

70. Description of the audience, auditorium and speeches are from the "Stenographic transcript of extemporaneous speech delivered by Robert M. La Follette to the Nonpartisan League at St. Paul, Minnesota, September 20, 1917," Speeches and Writings, La Follette Family Papers, series B, box 219, Library of Congress; US, Congress, Senate, Subcommittee of the Committee on Privileges and Elections, *Hearings, On the Resolution from the Minnesota Commission of Public Safety Petitioning for Proceedings Looking to the Expulsion of Senator Robert M. La Follette, on account of a Speech delivered Before the Nonpartisan League at St. Paul Minnesota, on September 20, 1917*, 65th Cong., 1st sess., 1917, pp. 16–17 and 160; Nancy C. Unger, *Fighting Bob La Follette: Righteous Reformer* (Chapel Hill: University of North Carolina Press, 2000), 254–262.

71. William T. Evjue, *A Fighting Editor* (Madison: Wells Printing Company, 1968), 240–256.

72. Maxwell, *Philipp*, 169–180.

Reflections

1. John Milton Cooper Jr., *Woodrow Wilson: A Biography* (New York: Alfred A. Knopf, 2009), 382.

2. Wilson's War Message to Congress, April 2, 1917, https://wwi.lib.byu.edu/index.php/Wilson's_War_Message_to_Congress; Cooper, *Wilson*, 387.

Acknowledgments

Writing a book is a personal, often solitary experience; paradoxically, this would be a very short book without the help of many others, especially the librarians and archivists whose great care and attention have preserved the manuscripts, government records, books, and newspapers that form the substance from which we write history. Quite literally, if they did not keep and catalog these documents of the past, we would have meager history to write.

Our research for this book took us across the eastern United States, and we feel particularly grateful to reference archivists who made our research visits a productive pleasure. Staff at the Army Heritage and Education Center in Carlisle, Pennsylvania, provided access to the rich letters of Glenn Garlock and to a variety of other collections documenting the experiences of the 32nd Division. At the National Archives our work benefited from access to the records of the Food Administration, American Protective League, and Bureau of Investigation. Reference staff at the Library of Congress Manuscripts Division provided access to the La Follette Family Papers essential to understanding the roles played by Robert and Belle La Follette during the war. In Madison, we found the staff of the Wisconsin Veterans Museum essential to locating information that expanded our understanding of the role played by the troops of the 32nd Division and their experiences at the front.

In particular, we wish to express our deep appreciation to the librarians and archivists at the Wisconsin Historical Society. Time and again, staff went out of their way to provide assistance and to create a truly friendly and productive work environment. In particular, we appreciated Lee Grady and Simone Munson for their knowledge of the manuscript and State Archives holdings, and Nancy Mulhern and Eileen Snyder for their knowledge of federal and state government publications. Many other individuals behind the scenes made our research possible through years of dedicated, farsighted service and ongoing care. To everyone who made our work possible, we extend our heartfelt appreciation and thanks.

Our research was facilitated by the Society's commitment to providing digital access to information. Time and again, we benefited from past decisions to digitize manuscripts, images, monographs, government publications, and newspapers or to cooperate with other agencies to do so. Access to *Wisconsin Blue Books*, the *Wisconsin Magazine of History*, federal census, and many other sources in digital form helped our research in ways unheard of in the past.

Authors write books; editors clean them up. This book has benefited greatly from Carrie Kilman's expertise. Her editing invariably refined the text, made it more readable, and clarified murky passages. The final book is a much better read thanks to her skill and knowledge.

We want to specifically thank Cole Fritz, a middle school student who generously volunteered his time to help us identify military collections and whose work helped inform our decision to focus on the 32nd Division. We were impressed and encouraged by his quiet enthusiasm and interest in history.

Most of all, I want to thank my wife and co-author, Marge, who played many essential roles throughout this project. She was research assistant, analyst, editor, proofreader, and gadfly, constantly advocating for an interesting or important story and for better writing to create a more readable and interesting manuscript. Her indefatigable energy and insightful analysis was an inspiration. In more ways than I can count, she has helped create a book that illuminates the history of Wisconsin and the Great War.

Richard L. Pifer
Majorie Hannon Pifer
Madison, Wisconsin

Index

Page numbers in **bold** indicate illustrations.

About the Authors

Richard L. Pifer retired in 2015 from his position as Director of Reference and Public Services for the Library-Archives Division of the Wisconsin Historical Society. He received a PhD in American history from the University of Wisconsin–Madison. His historical research has focused on the history of the home front in Wisconsin during the First and Second World Wars. Dr. Pifer is also the author of *City at War: Milwaukee Labor During World War II.*

Marjorie Hannon Pifer worked for twenty-six years as a health care program and policy analyst for Wisconsin's Department of Health Services, until her retirement in 2015. She holds a master's degree in social work from the University of Wisconsin–Madison. Her career prepared her well for the role of historical analyst.

The Pifers live in Madison, Wisconsin, and enjoy doing research together, wilderness camping, and the company of their two children, their children's spouses, and their three grandchildren.